JOHN SAINSBURY'S
HOME WORKSHOP

JOHN SAINSBURY'S
HOME WORKSHOP

David & Charles

A DAVID & CHARLES BOOK

Text © John Sainsbury 1991, 1994

First published in Hardback as John Sainsbury's
Woodworking Shop (David & Charles) 1991.
Published in paperback as John Sainsbury's Home Workshop

A catalogue record for this book is available from
the British Library.

ISBN 0 7153 0305 8

Colour photography by Jonathon Bosley

Typeset by ABM Typographics Ltd, Hull
and printed in England by The Bath Press
for David & Charles plc
Brunel House   Newton Abbot   Devon

CONTENTS

1
THE WORKSHOP

Most of us were probably introduced to woodworking at school and thus have a clear picture of a well organised and well equipped workshop. In later life, those of us who desire to work in wood may have gained the impression that the tools required are limitless, but most work can be produced with only a minimum of equipment. We must, however, have a convenient workspace and when considering this we must ask whether the workshop is to be used for pure pleasure or if it will be producing articles for sale. If the latter is the case, then we must bear in mind the number of workers to be employed and the space each will require. Generally, however, we shall be dealing with the workshop for an individual woodworker, although we can think at the same time of possible extension or expansion should the need arise.

The foremost consideration must be its location. The workshop attached, but not directly connected, to the home is a good arrangement as it can be heated by an extension of the existing house system and water can be laid on.

If the workshop is to be a separate building, it should be constructed of timber, and corrugated iron sheeting or concrete blocks should not be used as they both encourage condensation which can be harmful to the tools and machinery. The workshop should be insulated so that noise will not annoy any neighbours, and also against heat loss.

The floor should be laid on suspended timber joists, but if it must be of concrete it should be covered with floor quality tempered hardboard or painted in a proprietary floor paint to make it comfortable to stand on. Never polish such a floor as the wood shavings will do it for you, and after a period of use the floor will need to be roughened to lessen the danger of slipping. The higher the ceiling the better as it will be helpful when long timbers are being worked, and it will also give airiness. Timber can be stored in the roof space if the design of the roof trusses allows it.

As much window light as possible should be planned, although it must be remembered that windows take away wall space which could otherwise be used for tool storage. Artificial lighting can be by means of fluorescent tubes, but tungsten lighting for the machines and directly over the bench is most desirable. Double glazing for the windows would be an added luxury, remembering that some of the windows must open to give ventilation at all times and for reasons of safety when using some glues and polishes; the provision of an extraction fan should be considered particularly if the location of the windows presents a problem.

Everything must be planned with safety in mind and, to this end, strict conditions must be laid down for the electrical circuits and equipment. Machines should each have a wall isolation switch, and cables to them should not trail along the floor. All electrical outlets should be switched, and those near the bench for use with power tools should be suspended from the ceiling, and a master switch should be placed close to the door to isolate all the equipment when the shop is vacated. Fuse ratings should be suitable for the equipment in use.

Once the actual floor size has been settled, the position of the bench must be decided upon and everything else must be placed in relation to it as the bench must have the best of the daylight. The position of one window through which long pieces of timber can be passed as they are being worked on the bench is a great help; alternatively the door position can be planned to give the same facility.

Should the basement or the attic or the spare room be the only places available, then all the forementioned points must still be borne in mind and applied as far as possible. The garage is probably the most likely area and, of course, care must be taken not only to protect the tools and other equipment, but also the car, which means that tools may have to be taken into the house and machines protected with covers, and precautions taken against rust. The point previously made about floor treatment is very relevant, as are the requirements for the heating and ventilation. The roof space may also be useful for storage.

Provision should also be made for any machine tools which will be installed immediately – or later when funds allow – since they must have a space around them so that timber can be handled safely with no danger to the operator. Often they can be stored alongside the walls if arrangements are made to provide runners or castors so that they can be pulled out for use. The position of the woodturning lathe is discussed later, and is important as moving a heavy lathe is not fun.

At this planning stage, it is worthwhile to make a floor plan: cut out a piece of card to represent each floor space needed for the various pieces of equipment and move them around until the optimum positions are found. If any piece of equipment does not carry its own lighting, then this must be borne in mind.

Some form of storage is important both to save time and for the safe keeping of tools. Tools which are in everyday use such as ordinary saws, chisels, hammers, mallet and marking-out tools can be arranged on wall racks or in clips attached to pegboard close to the bench. A floor-standing or wall-mounted cupboard is highly desirable as there are a number of tools which should be kept safely such as special planes, power tools, and accessories such as cutters, boring bits, and spare blades. Screws, nails, panel pins and similar hardware are best kept in a cupboard. Boring tools and drills should be housed in proper stands rather than in drawers where they may be in contact with other steel tools which might damage them. Special tools of every kind are best kept in their original boxes, or in boxes specially made to contain them and any related accessories; this also applies to any power tools which are only used occasionally.

The aim should be to keep the floor as free from obstructions as possible, with ample working space around all areas of work. Timber should be stored somewhere away from the workshop if possible and only brought in when required. Plywood, hardboard, and similar boards should be kept in vertical stands, and dry timber can be stored in a similar way.

Finally, if you are constructing a new workshop it may be wise to check that the local bye-laws are not contravened, and remember to get some insurance for the premises, the equipment, and yourself if your existing insurance doesn't provide adequate cover.

NOTE
SIZES SHOWN IN THE TEXT ARE THOSE QUOTED BY THE MANUFACTURER. THEY ARE EXACT, WITH APPROXIMATE EQUIVALENTS SHOWN IN BRACKETS AND NOMINATED IN IMPERIAL OR METRIC.

2
THE WORK BENCH AND HOLDING EQUIPMENT

Having discussed the working environment we must consider in detail the choice of the most important piece of equipment – the work bench. A correct decision is essential as it is an expensive piece of equipment and will, in all probability, last a lifetime. Its cost may well determine whether the bench should be made up in the workshop or if one of the proprietary brands would be the answer. But before any decision can be made, some thought must be given to the type of work for which it will be used – a wood carver, for example, needs slightly different cramping and holding facilities from the cabinet maker; at the same time the workshop itself will dictate to a certain degree the style of bench that will be most suitable.

The traditional bench has a metal vice situated at or near the left hand end of the long side and an adjustable bench stop in approximately the same position on the top. The bench top, at least, will be made of beech, although some benches found in schools and college workshops may be made entirely of this timber. Usually this design of bench has a well fixed along the back of the top to contain the tools being used at any particular time.

Unfortunately these benches fall short of perfection inasmuch as the side vice cannot be used to hold thin pieces securely for plough-planing or similar work while at the same time allowing the passage of the plane or tools; also the holding of long pieces is difficult and the irregularly shaped timbers often occurring while routing or wood carving cannot be held safely. They have another fault as in many cases the makers fail to take into account the need for several variations of height to suit the user.

Modern benches (which are frequently of European manufacture) are superior in design, one of the best features being that they invariably have a tail vice fitted at the right-hand end of the bench, either made entirely in timber or timber with a metal screw. These vices have an adjustable metal or wooden dog or dogs fitted for use in conjunction with similar dogs which can be inserted in any one of a number of holes positioned equidistantly along the bench top. Often the vice will have two dog positions parallel to each other with two sets of holes along the bench top, and this is a splendid idea since any board, of any shape, can be held securely with four dogs. Any length of timber can be held between them within the capacity of the length of the bench, even to a very thin piece which may be impossible to hold in any other way. The benches also have side vices of similar pattern but without the dogs. For ease of handling some designs have the tops located on steel pins thus allowing the removal of the top should the bench need to be moved; some designs can be folded for ease of storage, which is very necessary where space is at a premium.

LERVAD BENCHES

The most popular design is the 602 which has a solid beech top with a stow-away facility. The vice and bench top are fitted with a single row of dog positions. The centre frame has a clever construction using hinged bolts so that the top can be lifted off and the underframe folded flat in one piece in a few moments. They are made in several lengths and as with all Lervad benches the standard of finish is of the finest.

A different design is seen in the Model 610, which again can be easily dismantled. It uses two wooden vices, one at the end and another at the left-hand side. The latter has the option of holding within its

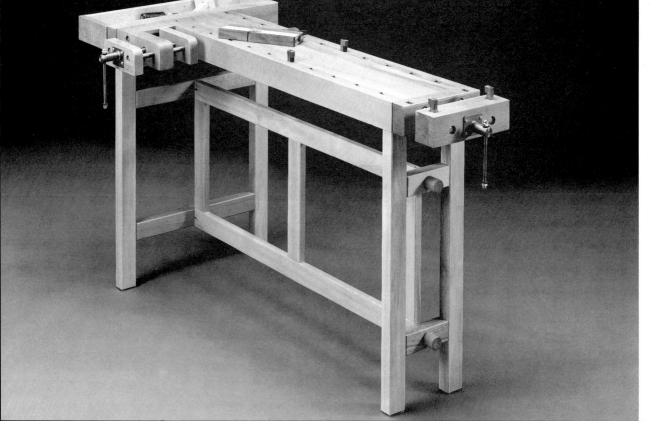

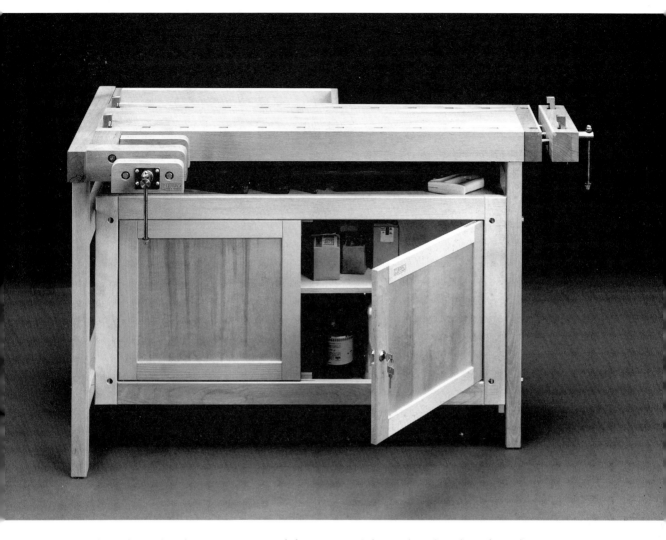

Lervad 610CU bench with cupboard storage

jaws on the outside, and with its inner jaw and the side of the bench on the inside; the inside position is ideal for holding long lengths of timber vertically without being obstructed by the vice screw as in the standard-type bench vice. Another version is the *610CU* which doesn't have the stow-away facility but is fitted with a cupboard for storage. Both the benches also have a small detachable well.

The *609* is a shorter bench and can be seen in both the right- and left-handed modes, the latter being a feature unique to Lervad.

(opposite) *Lervad 602 bench* (above) *and Lervad 610 bench with double row of bench dogs* (below)

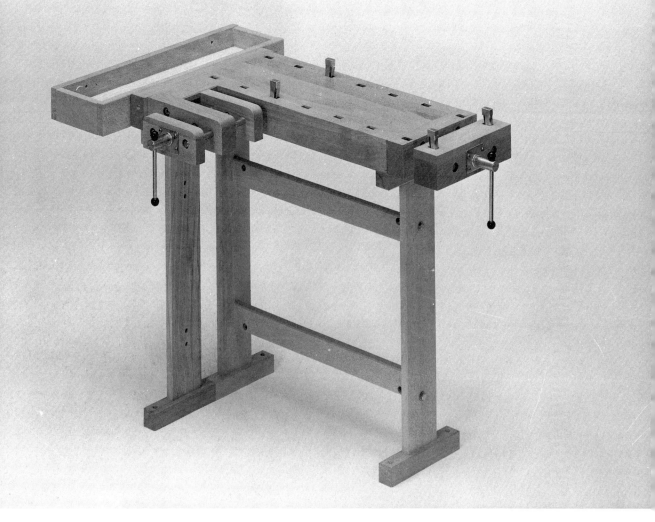

Lervad 609 short bench

SJOBERG BENCHES

Sjoberg benches are made in Sweden and have become increasingly popular. They are fitted with dogs and have both side and tail vices made of timber construction throughout; the side vice screw is fitted with a distinctive nylon pad. The bench tops are made in Swedish Birch, as are the vices.

   The *1310*, with options of size seen in the *1550* and *1910*, is available with cupboards and drawers or they can be made up to fit. The benches are of bolted construction and are easily dismantled. The *1522* is a similar bench with a solid beech laminated top.

   Certainly there is a number of options among the range of available benches and great care should be taken to choose the right one for your workshop and you. Pay particular attention to height and size in relation to your own height and the workshop dimensions; and do take into account the special requirements of the craft you intend to follow.

(opposite) *Sjoberg bench 1310* (top) *and Sjoberg bench 1522* (below)

3

MAKING YOUR OWN WORK BENCH

CHOOSING THE DESIGN

The first step is to draw a basic design, keeping in mind the workshop situation and any special requirements. The bench top can be a separate piece which can be added to a trestle or framed support, and the latter can be: (a) a free-standing structure, (b) folding for easy storage, or (c) folding and hinged to the wall. It can be constructed in timber, welded steel angle iron, round or square tube, or *Speedframe* easy assembly materials.

The top can be: (a) solid timber with a built-in well, (b) solid timber with a completely flat top, or (c) solid timber with a well and a tool rack added.

Sjoberg bench, hinged and folded

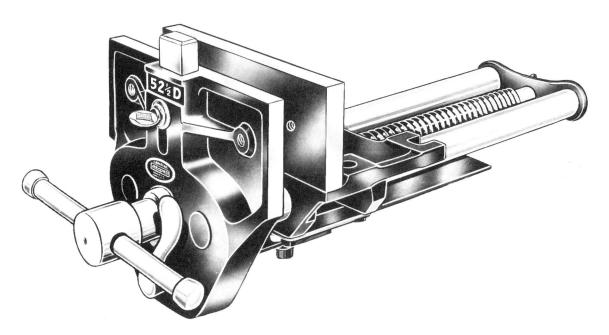

The tops must be designed with the kind of vice you want in mind, the alternatives being: (a) side and tail vices, (b) side vice only (traditional English design), or (c) tail vice only with either a single or a double row of slots for bench dogs.

The vices can be: (a) side and tail vices made from beech or a similar timber, using a metal screw or a ready-threaded wooden screw, (b) *Record*-type side vice together with *Record* dog vice, or (c) wooden vice with a double row of dogs.

Provision may need to be made for the bench to be fitted with: (a) a *Record* bench holdfast in the top and left-hand leg, (b) a carver's screw, or (c) where dogs are not being used in conjunction with the tail vice, a bench stop will need to be fitted and this can be either made or one of a proprietary brand.

THE MATERIALS

When making the first sketches of your bench you must decide on the materials to be used as they will influence the design to a large extent. Certainly it is advisable to make the bench entirely of timber, and if possible this should be beech. This wood is the ideal material as it has a very close grain, has very few knots, wears evenly, and does not easily bruise. There are however, other timbers which can be used

Record dog vice

for the top, and you should choose a closegrained one that is free from knots or hard areas which may cause uneven surface wear.

Wide boards may be hard to find, and the jointing of boards to make up the required width may be inevitable. Bearing in mind the high cost of hardwoods, the underframe may have to be made in softwood. The benches made for this book have

Wooden vice with double row of bench dogs

Bench holdfast

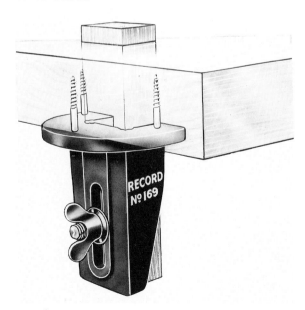

Bench stop

Carver's screw

been constructed from a variety of timbers, and the framework in some instances has been made from reclaimed timber; such timbers can be oiled, coloured or even painted to hide discoloration.

MAKING THE BENCH TOP

In the fortunate situation where the complete top can be made from one piece, it will be necessary to take precautions to ensure that the completed bench top will stay flat. To achieve this the board must be clamped at both ends.

This can be done in several ways, namely by using tongued and grooved joints, twin haunched mortices and tenons, dowels, or the more modern method of biscuit jointing.

If the top cannot be made from one piece, narrow boards can be glued together using the rubbed joint method, first preparing the timber on a jointer and finally shooting the edges straight and square using a jointer or fore plane. A stronger method is to use slot-screwing after planing the edges dead flat, straight and square; dowelling is perhaps the easiest particularly if the *Record* dowel jig is available, and both methods are described later.

A simple tongue and groove, or the alternative method of two grooves and a loose tongue can be employed if you have a router or plough plane.

A superb method is to use a router and a *Titman* finger jointing cutter. Plane the timber carefully to give long straight and square edges, carefully marking each face side and edge. The miniature finger jointing cutter has a ½in (12mm) shank, and I used it in an *Elu 177E* router set up in an *Elu 551* bench, although there are a number of similar machines and tables which could be used.

Arrange the cutter to suit the thickness of the timber, and set the fence to allow the cutter to cut at the correct depth to give a perfect mating tongue 8mm in depth. This cutter will be found suitable for jointing edges up to 1½in (38mm) thick. Place the timber carefully on the table with the face side down and the face edge against the fence; remember to set the bench clamps to allow the timber to push through without slackness. Switch on the router and push the timber through, using a pushstick if necessary. Set the cutter to give a 4mm offset by using the plunge mechanism; then take the second piece of timber, face down and face edge against the fence, and push it through the machine, which should allow the two edges to mate perfectly. The top shown has three such joints to unite four pieces of timber.

DOWEL JOINTING

Prepare the timber; place both pieces together in the vice with the edges to be jointed uppermost and the face sides outside. Set up the particular dowelling jig you intend to use for the job so that the dowels are placed centrally and equidistantly along the length of the boards. The number of dowels used will depend on the length of the boards; one every 4in (100mm) with one at 2in (50mm) from each end is about right.

Dowels of ⅜in (10mm) will be suitable for the job; bore all the holes and cut the dowels. If ordinary ungrooved dowel rod is to be cut to length, work a small groove along the length of the rod before cutting it to allow air and surplus glue to escape when the joint is assembled. After cutting the dowels to length, round off each end slightly to ease the passage of the dowel into the hole. Glue up and use sash cramps to bring the joint tightly together.

TONGUED AND GROOVED JOINTING

Perhaps the fastest and easiest way of doing this is to use the router. A panel cutter set up in the router, which can be hand-held or set up in a router table, will give a perfect cut. If two grooves are to be cut and a loose tongue of plywood used, the cutter must match exactly the thickness of the plywood used.

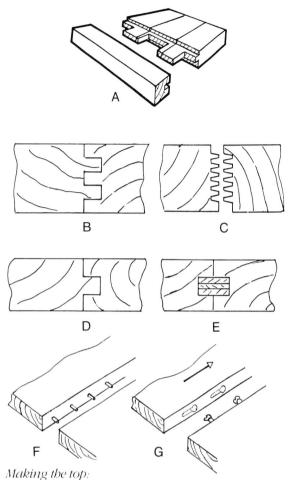

Making the top:
  A *Jointed top end clamped using the mortice and tenon*
  B *Twin tongue and groove*
  C *Finger joint*
  D *Single tongue and groove*
  E *Loose tongue of plywood*
  F *Dowelled joint*
  G *Slot-screwed joint*

The straightforward tongue and groove will require two settings to produce the tongue and another, of course, for the groove. The sizes will depend entirely on the thickness of the timber, and usually one-third is taken as a guide and the cutter matched as nearly to this as possible. Alternatively the joint can be made with a plough plane or a multi-plane, using the correct sizes of straight cutter and special tonguing cutter to match each other. Prepare the timber carefully and always work from the face side of each piece.

SLOT-SCREWING

Once again, plane the timber accurately and mark up the face sides and edges. Place both pieces edge upwards in the vice and mark out the positions for the screws with a try square at 2in (50mm) from each end and at intervals of about 6in (150mm). Use a marking gauge to mark the exact centre with a pencil line, and offset the second piece of timber by ½in (12mm), and carry the pencil lines from the first piece across the second. Mark the slot length of ½in (12mm) to the left of the screw position marks. At the gauge points on the first piece, screw in a countersunk wood screw, leaving its head protruding ½in (12mm). On the other piece bore holes at the point which coincides with the screw position, making them exactly the size of the head of the screw and to a depth of ½in (12mm). At the end of the slot lines bore a hole the exact size of the shank of the screw.

Take a chisel which has a width as near to the size of the shank as possible, and cut a slot to join up the two holes to the same depth. To assemble, place the screw head into the larger hole, hold the pieces firmly together and tap the ends so that they are flush with each other; the head of the screw bites into the base of the slot and makes a perfect joint which should not be glued.

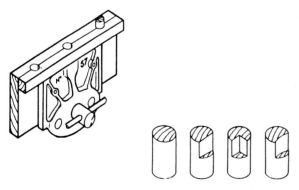

Turned bench dogs

BISCUIT JOINTING

This is a more modern method where a slot is cut to receive an elliptically shaped biscuit made in highly compressed beech that expands when glue is introduced. Designed primarily for the jointing of particle board, it will be found ideal for bench top making. The position of the cut is infinitely variable, as is the depth of the groove. Care must be taken to hold the fence tightly up against the face edge of the timber before making the cut, moving the saw blade carefully into the timber. The final assembly can be glued and cramped to make a fine invisible joint.

PANEL CONNECTORS

This method uses a knock-down fitting which has been designed to butt joint kitchen worktops edge to edge, but it can equally well be used for the bench top. The job is quite an easy one and consists of boring a 35mm hole in each piece at 35mm centres from the panel edge. A 15mm channel is cut from each hole to the outside edge to allow the fitting to be inserted. As the hexagonal nut is tightened, the pieces are drawn together to make a perfect joint.

MAKING AND FITTING BENCH DOGS

If it is intended to use a tail vice with dog positions along the bench top, the dog slots must be marked out and cut. The type of dog can be similar to the manufactured variety but can be made in the workshop from a closegrained hardwood such as beech. It is essential for the dog to drop into its slot and be flush with the bench top when not in use, but at the same time it must be prevented from dropping through the bench on to the floor; to prevent this, a step is cut at one end of each slot.

Manufactured bench dogs usually have leaf springs at their sides to hold them in position, while others have a small ballcatch inserted. These catches can be bought in any good hardware store and are easily fitted into a simple hole.

One design of dog can be turned on the lathe, with a flat at the top to butt against the timber being held. This type will necessitate the boring of a large hole to receive the main body of the dog and a smaller one bored through the bench top to take the pin. They do, however, have to be taken away from the bench and stored when not in use, which is a small disadvantage.

It is possible for a bench top to be bored to receive the circular plastic dogs fitted to the *Black and Decker Workmate*. This may well suit the woodworker who makes his own vice, and the method is ideal for holding flat boards for carving, for planing, and for holding timber when jointing; the only disadvantage is that they cannot be adjusted for height. It must be remembered that timber moves depending on the conditions under which it is stored. When bench tops are being made we must always allow for expansion or contraction wherever possible. Clamps using the tongue and groove method should only be glued at the centre, while slot-screwed joints should be left dry.

FLUSH PANEL CONSTRUCTION

Tops can also be constructed using a framework with a flush panel of thick plywood or MDF (medium density fibreboard) inserted. This type of construction is used by a number of bench manufacturers and is quite strong but a little more noisy when worked upon than those of solid construction. When

cutting mortices and carrying out work that involves hammering of any kind on this type of bench it is advisable to work over or close to one of the legs to cut down the noise and take some of the shock.

MAKING THE TRESTLE OR MAIN FRAME

Three designs are suggested and details given of their construction. All the hardware for these benches can be obtained from a number of sources, details of which are found elsewhere.

The types of timber have been described earlier in this chapter, but some general guide lines are needed as to the size of timbers to be used in each construction. Legs should not be less than 3 × 2in (75 × 50mm) in section, but very large benches may need bigger sections. The rails must be fairly wide to provide both a strong tenon and to resist movement, the latter being particularly necessary where end frames are bolted together; they need not be made up in timber of equal width to the legs themselves. The bench top can be of any thickness between 1½in and 4in (38mm and 100mm). If a framed top is being made, the flush panel of man-made board should not be less than ¾in (19mm) thick.

The construction can be made using mortice and

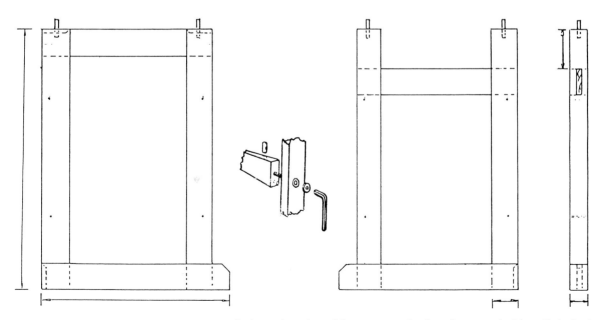

Knock-down bench-end frames morticed and tenoned, side rails bolted

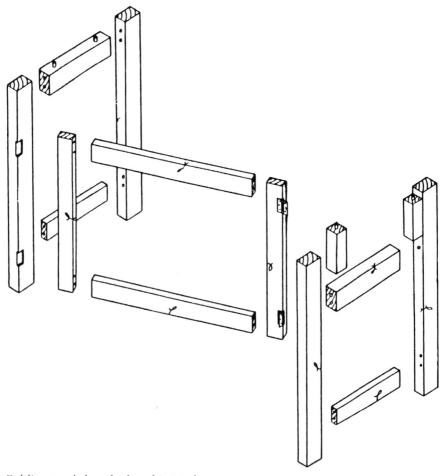

Folding trestle bench, dowel jointed

tenon joints, which will certainly provide the strongest assembly, but lighter designs could use dowel joints. Free-standing and hinged constructions can have end frames jointed with the rails attached using *Scan* screws and cross dowels. (See illustration.) Alternatively, threaded rod could be used in conjunction with separate brass heads. Where a single bolt is used, guide dowels may be inserted to prevent the rail from twisting. Pronged Tee nuts are another method which could be employed, but the idea of coarse prongs biting into timber seems to me to be a method better used for packing cases.

Tenoned joints should be glued and pinned with small dowels, and whenever bolts are used they should have a light smear of *Vaseline* over the threads to make for easier withdrawal and to prevent rust.

Provision must also be made for fitting the traditional woodworker's vice, leaving space between the legs to receive the body and providing nuts and bolts (or coachbolts) to attach it to the top. If bolts are used, these will pass through the bench top; the heads of the bolts should drop into counterbored holes so that plugs can be inserted to hide them and to protect tools from damage which might result if they were left exposed. (See pp240-2 for various methods.)

The design of bench which uses hinged end frames needs special hinges which will lock in both the open and closed position; each pair comprises one left-hand and one right-hand fitting.

OTHER REQUIREMENTS

Top finish

This needs careful thought as even if you are most fastidious the top will sooner or later become dirty or bruised. The tops of my benches have all been polished with Danish oil as this gives a very hard finish with good lasting quality. The traditional finish for beech is linseed oil but this is sticky, and there are a number of excellent modern finishes which can be considered as alternatives. Obviously the bench must be kept clean to avoid transferring dirt to the finished surfaces of workpieces. In addition I occasionally clean up the top using a cabinet scraper.

Moving the bench

Every bench has to be moved from time to time, and in making one from scratch it is as well to provide for this either by making a small drop-down frame carrying two strong castors, or by fixing two castors which just clear the floor so that should the bench be lifted at one end the castors will contact the floor and make moving easy.

Tool storage cupboards

These can always be built in when a fixed underframe construction is used; and other types can be fitted with hung cupboards. A tool rack which holds the most commonly used tools such as planes and saws can be hung under the bench.

Bench well

Many woodworkers like to have a well in the bench top in which tools in current use can be laid. Such a well can be built in, but a loss of flat working surface must be acepted. A number of manufacturers offer the well as an optional extra which can be attached by glass plate fittings, or by slot-screwing. If the well is to be removed often, it would be wise to use the second method and screw on a brass escutcheon, first cutting the slot by hand or with a router fitted with a special cutter.

The well is constructed in hardwood and jointed at the corners using dovetailed or box-combed joints, and having a plywood bottom inserted in a groove. Leave an opening at one end so that the shavings can be brushed out of the well. When made, it can be fitted either at the left-hand end or along the back edge of the top.

Tool rail

The most commonly used tools like a tenon saw, some chisels, a mallet and various screwdrivers can be housed in a rail fitting made and attached to the back edge of the bench top in the same way as the well. This can be of very simple construction, using two long battens and several distance pieces to make slots for the insertion of the tools.

Alternatively, by far the strongest and most acceptable method is to make the rail from a solid piece of hardwood. The slots which hold the tools can be cut using a morticer, a slot-milling cutter set up in a machine, a side cutting bit placed in a drill stand, or by using a panel cutter set up in the router. The resulting rack can be screwed to the back edge of the bench top or attached like a well.

Power tool panel

So many electric tools are used these days that an easily accessible supply is highly desirable, and a power tool panel can be made from a sheet of blockboard and screwed to the wall above the bench. Four 13amp sockets are provided, plus a speed reducer socket into which any of the power tools can be plugged if speed reduction is needed. Most modern power tools already have electronic speed control and must not be connected to this kind of socket. The most commonly used tools can be held in plastic brackets, while the re-chargeable screwdriver is housed in the bracket supplied with its charger. The power panel itself is connected to an isolating switch close to the bench.

Tool cupboards

These can be made up using either a frame construction with plywood panels in the sides and doors in order to give lightness for easy attachment to the bench frame, or by employing a solid cabinet construction using man-made boards. Sliding doors are best because hinged ones tend to get in the way. The cupboards should be fitted with shelves and also bracketed shelves which can be cut for tools to be held safely. The cupboard should be well organised so there is no danger of tools falling out to become damaged or cause injury. The addition of cupboards adds to the stability of the bench, and the added weight is an advantageous factor.

4

EQUIPMENT TO MAKE IN THE WORKSHOP

There are a number of pieces of equipment which you can make yourself and they can often be made from scraps of timber and man-made board. Measurements are omitted in most cases because each design can be of a size to meet your own needs and the particular work to which it can be applied. Many are well tried pieces of equipment which I have had in use for many years, and I claim no originality for them.

BENCH HOOK

This is an essential part of bench equipment. It serves to hold work safely while sawing, and it can also be used as a paring board. Proprietary designs are often too narrow; the one shown is fairly wide and the timber is supported throughout its length while the saw cuts through a slot in the upstand. It should have a strip on the underside so that it can be hooked to the edge of the bench, or held if necessary in the jaws of the vice. Attach the upstand pieces with glue and dowels; it is better not to use screws as the hook will wear over a period of time and possibly expose metal which could harm the tools.

ROUTER PLANE OR 'OLD WOMAN'S TOOTH'

Although there are several proprietary designs made in metal, you may care to make your own. The illustration shows a simple design which can be

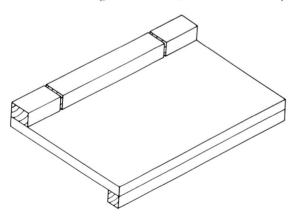

Bench hook

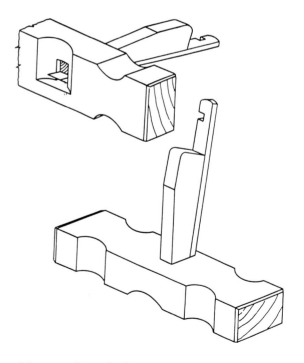

Old woman's tooth plane

made up in beech or any other closegrained hardwood. The cutter could be one from a disused plough plane, or made from a length of tool steel. Exact sizes are not specified, but the body piece could be approximately $5 \times 1\frac{1}{2} \times 1$in ($127 \times 38 \times 25$mm). Mark out the mouth and escapement carefully with a pencil and a craft knife and cut them out with a small mortice chisel. Use an in-cannel gouge to pare the relief area around the mouth of the plane vertically, and add suitable curved recesses to supply a grip as indicated. Cut a wedge from the same timber, clean up and give the finished job several coats of linseed oil.

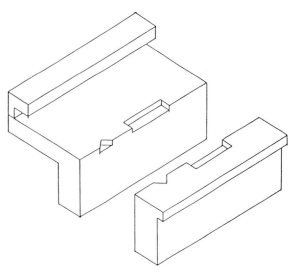

WOODWORK VICE CHEEKS

All woodwork vices should be fitted with wooden pads which are called 'cheeks' and protect the work. They are best made from a good quality hardwood, beech being particularly suitable. If the front cheek is made from fairly thick timber, the top edge can be bored to receive round dogs which can be used in conjunction with dogs inserted into holes in the bench top. Various suggestions are given for the shaping of the dogs. Use good quality dowel rods or turn them on the lathe if you have one. In the best vices the jaws toe-in slightly to ensure a good grip at the top and when preparing the cheeks remember to maintain this. For holding very small work special jaws can be made.

Special add-on jaws to hold small pieces in the woodworker's vice

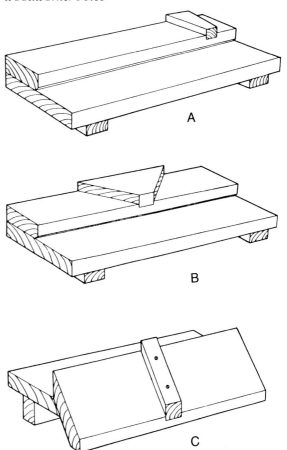

SHOOTING BOARDS

These are standard equipment in most workshops for planing and squaring the ends of boards or finishing mitred ends. They are much easier to use in planing end grain since the body of the plane is supported between two square faces. They are best made in hardwood; proprietary designs are usually made from beech. Several styles are illustrated, namely the square shooting board, the mitre shooting board and the donkey's ear which is very useful for planing mitres on the ends of narrow boards.

A Square shooting board
B Mitre shooting board
C Donkey's ear shooting board

FOLDING WEDGE VICE

Holding very thin timber strips and tiny pieces often presents a problem, and this can be solved by making a folding wedge vice. It can have a strip fixed to the underside so that it can be held in the bench vice. The wedges are best made of hardwood, but any scrap blockboard or plywood can be used for the base piece. The folding wedge can be used in a number of holding situations.

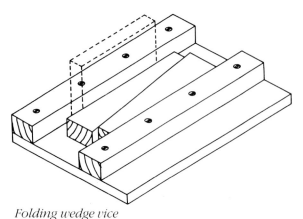

Folding wedge vice

MITRE SAWING BOARD

There are any number of devices which can be bought for sawing mitres. One design can be made in the workshop using a sheet of blockboard, or preferably hardwood should this be readily available.

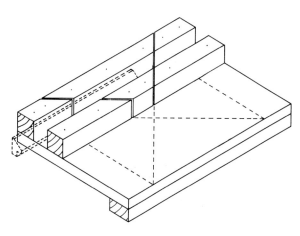

Mitre sawing board

Two upstand strips are glued and screwed to the board with a gap between to accommodate the mouldings. Folding wedges can be used if needed to hold picture frame mouldings in place but take care to avoid damage to the material. Mark out the mitres carefully and saw them using the longest tenon saw available so that both strips can be cut without error. If possible make the cuts with the saw which will be used when cutting the moulding. It is advisable to place a piece of waste wood underneath the moulding to avoid cutting the mitre board itself.

PICTURE FRAME CLAMPING DEVICE

This consists of a sheet of blockboard, the size of which will depend upon the dimensions of the picture frames being made. An upstand strip of softwood is glued and screwed along the top and left-hand edges against which the frame is located. Holes are bored at 1½in centres (38mm) to receive 12mm dowel rod. A number of lengths of dowel are cut on the sizing board and these are used in conjunction with folding wedges to cramp up the picture framing after gluing.

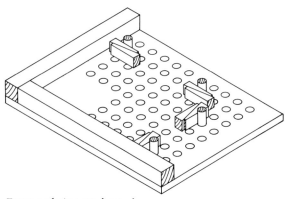

Frame gluing-up board

SIZING BOARD

This is a useful device if many pieces of the same length are to be cut. It can be made for left- or right-hand use. The upstand piece is slotted using the router or a morticer; by hand it can be done with a mortice chisel. The adjustable stop and the upstand should be made of hardwood, and if the baseboard

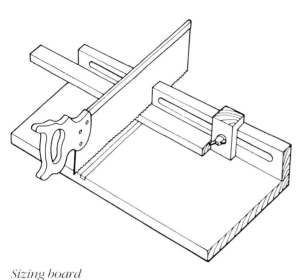

Sizing board

is made from man-made board, it must have a strip of hardwood placed in a slot which lines up with the cutting slot in the upstand. This can be replaced from time to time when the saw cuts have entered too deep.

DOWEL SAWING BOARD

Sawing dowels is not difficult – the problem arises from holding them. This little device holds the dowel in the vee, and the board itself can be held against the edge of the bench or in a vice.

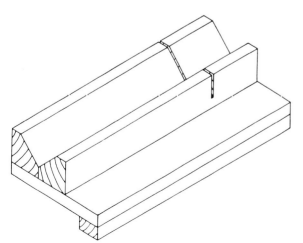

Dowel sawing board

DOWEL PLANING BOARD

Similar in construction to the sawing device, but it has an end stop against which the dowel is held for planing.

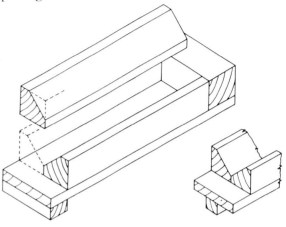

Dowel planing board

RELIEF CARVING FRAME

Holding shallow panels for carving is awkward if there is no tail vice and dog facility incorporated in the bench top. This solution consists of a sheet of man-made board with a shallow upstand all round the edge. Folding wedges are used to hold the timber firmly in place. An upstand on the underside serves to hold the frame in the vice.

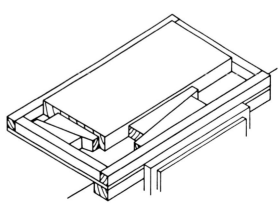

Relief carving frame

AN ABRASIVE BOARD

This is similar in construction to the carving frame. The abrasive sheet is glued in place and is useful when small pieces are to be sanded as the upstand prevents them falling off. It is also useful when sanding edges since the upstand will support the workpiece at right angles. A variation is to have a centre upstand on a larger board and have four grades of paper, one in each quarter. Abrasive boards are useful for many jobs – cleaning up the base of turnings, for example. If this work is attempted on a loose sheet, the glasspaper often moves or becomes torn, and the struggle to keep everything under control can result in the workpiece becoming out of shape. You can make a set of abrasive boards, all cut in hardboard, with one for each grade of paper in current use.

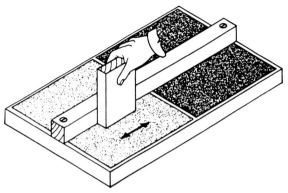

Abrasive board with centre upstand

SAWING TABLE

This is extremely useful when sawing with the coping saw or the fretsaw. Held in the vice it supports even the smallest piece, and with the teeth of the saw pointing downwards it makes for trouble-free cutting and far less breakage of blades.

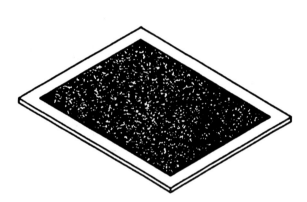

Abrasive board

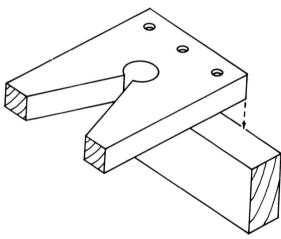

Sawing table

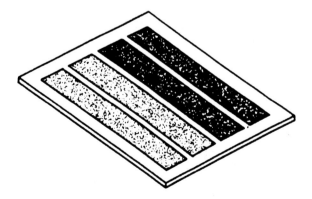

Abrasive board with various grades of abrasive paper

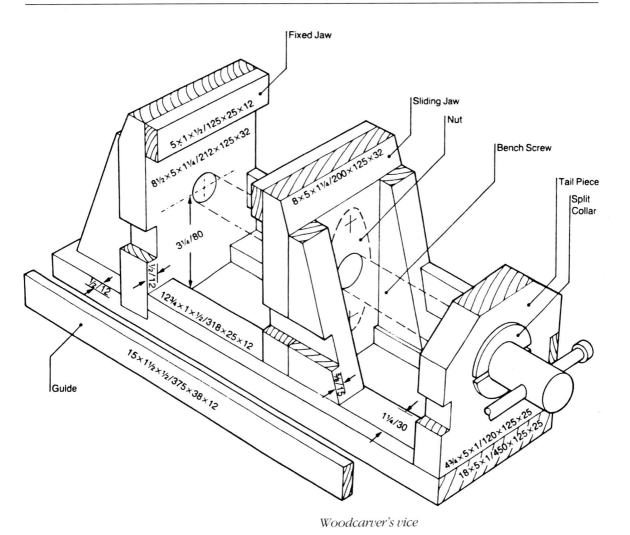

Woodcarver's vice

WOODCARVER'S VICE

The traditional vice is the *Scopas* woodcarver's chops which is made entirely in wood with its sides reinforced with steel sheet; the screw is usually steel. A number of years back while I was working for *Record Tools*, my department produced a design for one of these vices using the standard vice screw which *Record* still market. Suggestions for the chops are made here with measurements left to individual choice. Use hardwood, and be sure to leave a hole in the centre of the base through which a bolt can be passed to secure the vice through a hole bored in the bench top. The gripping faces of the jaws could have a facing of leather to protect the workpiece.

Another version is to have the front jaw extended to make a leg to reach and stand on the floor; this will take the weight of cutting and to a certain extent damp down the sound.

WOODWORK VICE

A bought bench screw, and pieces of blockboard or multi-plywood together with dowel rods to serve as guides, is illustrated here. It's the poor man's answer to the expensive vice problem, and it will be a good servant just as long as you always bear in mind the poor strength factor of the materials when compared with metal.

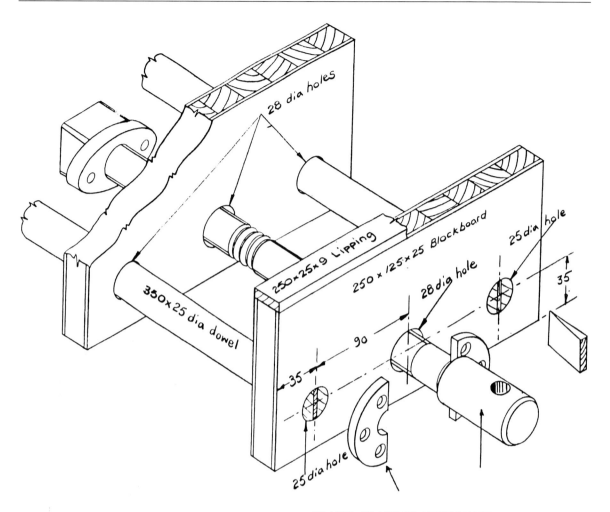

Woodwork vice

METALWORK VICE STAND

The metalworker's vice may be needed occasionally and most cabinet workshops do not have a metalworker's bench. The vice can be fixed to this small stand which in turn is gripped in the woodwork vice.

METAL FLATTING TABLE

This is similar in construction to the metal vice stand, but here the table has a sheet of steel screwed to it to serve as a flatting block. It's a useful addition even if it is only used for straightening bent nails!

PLATE GLASS FLATTING TRAY

Pupils who come to my *Introduction to Cabinet Making* course are encouraged to look very critically at their bench and block planes.

New planes should be perfectly true, but sometimes have grinding marks, and older planes may have a number of faults. Certainly most planes can be improved by flatting the soles and sides and checking that they are square with each other. This can be done using a sheet of plate glass as a surface plate and spreading a fine cutting paste of rouge and flour emery powder over it. Patience is needed, but the greater flatness and finer finish improves the performance of the planes.

Obviously a sheet of plate glass cannot be used without having it held in some way, and a shallow frame is suggested similar to that used in the wood-carver's relief carving frame but with an upstand slightly lower than the surface of the glass. A strip glued and screwed to the underside of the frame will enable it to be held securely in a bench vice.

ROUTER MAT BOARD

This consists of a sheet of multicoloured plastic foam set in a board similar to that used for the glass flatting tray; mine almost covers the smallest of my bench tops. It has splendid holding qualities and is useful for holding panels when routing.

SASH CRAMP

T-bar and bar cramps are expensive to buy, and this one is suggested for occasional use (see p157). It consists of a length of timber of at least 1in (25mm) thick and possibly 2in (51mm) wide. At one end a stout block of hardwood is bolted to the bar, down the centre of which a number of equidistant holes are bored through at intervals, and they are used to locate another stout block with a carriage bolt and wing nut. Folding wedges are used between the workpiece and the end block to exert the pressure.

VICE FOR HOLDING ROUND MATERIAL

This is designed to hold round pieces for boring on a drill press. Two arm pieces are cut with a vee in each arm to locate the work, and the two arms are hinged together with a piece of leather strapping or a metal hinge.

ADD-ON SEAT FOR A WOOD CARVER

The wood carver can often sit down to his work but a seat or chair in the workshop can be a nuisance and takes up valuable space. With a fold-away bench, indeed for any bench, a solution can be found by making a small frame into which a round seat can be dropped. The frame can be hinged to the right-hand leg of the bench and folded away when not in use. If the seat frame has a metal peg on the underside that drops into a metal socket in the frame, it will allow the seat to turn. The height of the seat can be fixed to suit the occupant, and it could be upholstered.

Metalwork vice stand

Hand vice for holding round material

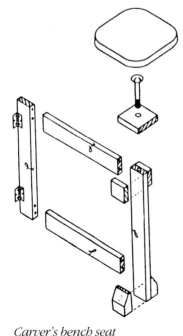

Carver's bench seat

VENEER HAMMER

Although these can be bought there is no reason why you should not make one. A nice piece of ash or other long-grained timber can be used for the handle, which should be turned down to a round section between centres on the lathe and then worked to shape and size with a skew chisel. Leave a little knob at the end to stop your hand slipping off when the hammer is pulled. The body is made from an odd piece of hardwood about 1in (25mm) in thickness. A piece of very hard timber ¼in (6mm) thick is inserted into a groove cut along the edge of the body – this will press down on the veneer to assist in laying it flat and pushing out the surplus glue. A couple of coats of Danish oil will finish the job.

ABRASIVE SPINDLES

These can be made from various sizes of dowel or turned on the lathe, and can be fitted into a power drill or mounted between centres on the lathe. The best method of gluing on the glasspaper is to use PVA adhesive and then wrap it around with string which will serve as a cramp. The one shown has a hole bored close to the edge of spindle; the glasspaper is folded so that both ends can be inserted into the slit formed by making a saw cut into the hole, and trapping the glasspaper with a dowel.

Abrasive board and spindles for use on the bench, lathe and drill

SCRATCH STOCK

This tool is needed for inlaying and working mouldings, and is simply made with two pieces of hardwood shaped to provide a stock which will run along the edge of the work. These are held together with small nuts and bolts and serve to hold the thin cutter tightly in place. Cutters are made from scraper steel or old bandsaw blades shaped to the required profile on a grinder.

An adjustable version copies the style of the marking gauge and is made from beech. The cutter is held in place by a small wedge; in this example the shape is copied from a cutting gauge made in rosewood. A screw socket is screwed into the stock, and a standard round head bolt is inserted into it. If you can undertake brazing, a small piece of steel sheet can be inserted into the screw slot.

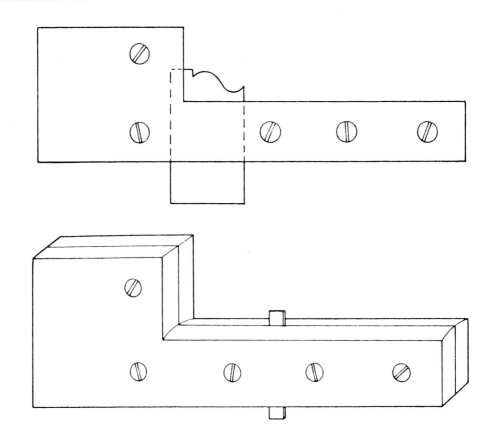

Scratch stocks and scratch stock in use

FRAME CRAMP

Four corners can be made in hardwood with a hole bored across the corners through which a length of string can be passed – a fine groove can be cut along the edges of each corner to locate it. A small strip of hardwood or dowel can be used as a tourniquet when cramping up by inserting it through a loop in the string and twisting it.

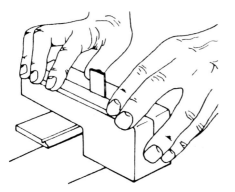

Folding bench with made vices

Knock-down bench with Record dog vice

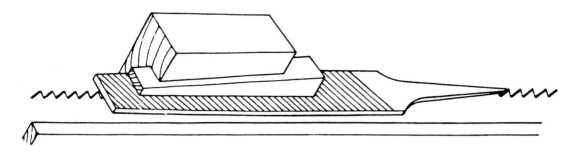

SAW TOPPING BLOCK

Saw topping block

This is to hold the flatting file for topping the teeth of the hand saws during sharpening. The file is held in place with folding wedges, and the whole device can be made from pieces of hardwood.

CHOPPING BOARD

Never use the chisel to cut directly on to a bench top, as uneven surfaces in the top can mark the wood. It is best to use a chopping board, or possibly a bench hook for the job. Choose a hardwood and not a particle board as the latter will quickly take the edges off your tools. An upstand strip is recommended on the underside so that it can be gripped in a vice. Size suggested is a minimum of 12 × 8 × ¾in thick (305 × 203 × 19mm).

WOODEN TOOL RACKS

These are best made of wood as opposed to plastic, which often is not strong enough, or metal which can damage edge tools if they are inserted carelessly. Man-made material can damage fine edges and is not strong in narrow strip form. Racks can be made easily using a morticer to cut square holes, one or other of the boring bits for cutting round holes, and the router comes into its own in cutting slots. Although wall racks are efficient, care must be taken to prevent tools from falling through and injuring someone. The illustration shows a wall rack and one for holding boring augers and drills or round-shanked machine bits.

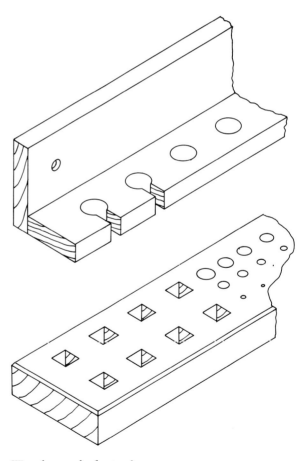

Wooden racks for tools

HOLDING BLOCKS FOR SHARPENING BORING TOOLS

It is not always possible to hold boring tools in the hand and sharpen them accurately at the same time. Small split blocks which can be squeezed in the vice will be found most useful. The one on the right of the illustration shows two blocks sliding on two steel dowels, the one on the right being split three-quarters of its length with a wide saw kerf.

SMALL WOODEN HAND VICE FOR THE DRILL PRESS

Holding small pieces of wood steady while drilling presents a problem as the steel drill press vice must be fitted with pieces of waste to protect the work and often the machine drill works very close to the steel jaws and could be damaged. This little vice uses folding wedges to hold the workpiece; should the drill overrun or run off the work it will not be damaged and your hand is at a safe distance from the cutting edge.

Holding blocks for sharpening boring tools

(right) *Small wooden hand vice for the drill press*

Spokeshave cutter holder

SPOKESHAVE CUTTER HOLDER

A spokeshave cutter is short and makes holding and sighting it difficult while sharpening. This small holder holds the cutter in a push-fit slot and its handle is shaped to fit the hand comfortably.

HOLDING DEVICE FOR ROUND WORKPIECES

Holding curved and odd-shaped pieces can present problems which can be solved by using a baseboard made from a piece of man-made board with two fixed round stops and two small eccentric cams. The cams were made from scraps of plastic fascia board. The board has an edging strip at the front underside to enable it to be held in a vice.

Holding device for odd-shaped workpieces

5

HAND TOOLS

SAWS

These are essential components of the wood-worker's kit and great care should be exercised in their selection and use. Since they are necessary for the pre-cutting and processing of timber, the function of each type of saw must be understood. A good quality saw should be chosen and will give a lifetime of use; thus a little care and perhaps spending a little extra will pay dividends.

Saws can be classified in three groups:

> Hand saws, which includes rip- and panel saws;
> Tenon saws, which are sometimes referred to as 'Back saws'. The name refers to the brass or steel back which serves to stiffen and keep the thin blade straight;
> Special saws for particular applications where normal saws cannot or should not be used.

Hand saws are selected for specific purposes. Those for cutting with the grain usually have ripsaw teeth and those for cutting across the grain have crosscut teeth.

All saw teeth are set alternately to the right and left, and in the case of a ripsaw each tooth is so sharpened as to act like a small cutting chisel which cuts a kerf to sever the timber. Crosscut teeth on the other hand, have points which cut tiny grooves causing the timber to crumble and severing it. Saw teeth are usually referred to as 'points', and they are quoted by the number per inch. Teeth are usually cut by machine, and many of the modern saws have general-purpose teeth, which are very hard and cannot be re-sharpened.

Saw makers offer a variety of handles in both wood and plastic, and some are designed badly so that they are either uncomfortable in the hand or incorrectly set. The traditional handle made in beech gives a comfortable grip but those made in plastic may tend to become greasy in the hand.

Always select a saw bearing the signature of a well-known manufacturer as this will usually be a guarantee of good quality steel and fine workmanship. The saw must be well balanced and should feel right in the hand. It should be possible to re-sharpen

Hand saw

the teeth – a point which must be borne in mind in view of the scarcity of skilled saw doctors.

Japanese saws

Close examination of Japanese saws will reveal teeth that are cut differently: the points are angled more sharply and they are sharpened to cut on the backward stroke. I have found that they give greater accuracy for the beginner and seem to cut more easily.

Saw aftercare

Immediately after buying, the saw should be fitted with a protective device for the teeth. Almost always they are protected with plastic guards, but many users prefer to make a grooved cut in a strip of hardwood to cover the teeth, holding it in place with cord or a band cut from an old car inner tube. Saws should be hung on the walls or in a cupboard and protected with a thin film of oil when not in use, but remember to wipe the saw before using it otherwise the oil may be transferred to the timber and make an ineradicable mark. The old-time craftsman would keep his saws in a purpose-designed case which he would make himself. When saws are put away for any length of time they should be protected by being wrapped in rust-inhibiting paper. A *Teflon*-coated saw should not corrode and the *Teflon* improves its performance by enabling it to run more easily.

TENON SAWS

There are several types in this group, all of the same basic construction but serving different purposes. The blades are thin, fairly short by hand-tool standards, and rectangular in shape, with very fine pointed teeth. A strip of brass or steel is folded over the back of the saw to add rigidity and strength; brass is usually regarded as the better choice. The handles are usually similar to those of larger saws although the smaller handles tend to be of an open design. Tenon saws are for making accurate cuts and joints, working throughout on the bench top or in the vice; because of the back they cannot be used for long or deep cuts.

Dovetail saws

The smallest of the group is the Dovetail saw which is usually 8in (200mm) in length with as many as 26 points to 1in (25mm). The blade is extremely thin and this makes it ideal for accurate cutting of

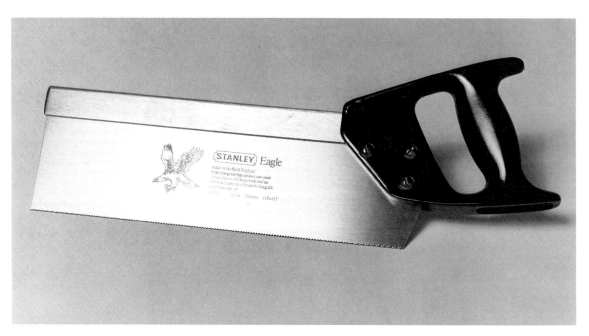

Tenon saw

Dovetail saw

dovetail joints; the fact that there is no set on the teeth also helps to give a fine saw cut. Usually the handle is the open design which is a necessary feature for the woodworker with large hands.

Tenon saws

These are usually between 10in and 14in (250 to 355mm) in length and up to 20 points to 1in (25mm). They are used to cut tenons and other joints, and the longer ones are handy for making wider cuts across the grain.

There is another version of the dovetail saw that is making a reappearance; it is usually referred to as a 'gent's backsaw' (a throwback to the Victorian days when companies like *Marples* and others made tools for enthusiastic amateurs and called them 'gentlemen's'). Usually up to 10in (250mm) in length they have a turned handle which can be difficult to hold. One manufacturer makes the saw with a cranked handle which can be offset either to the right or left.

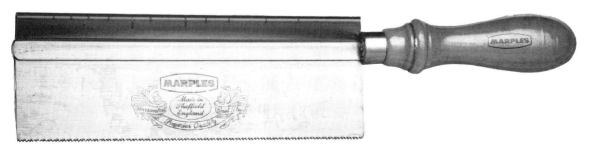

Gent's backsaw

CHOOSING THE HAND SAW

Saws from well respected saw makers generally have blades which are taper ground, which means that the saw blade is tapered in thickness from the handle to the toe, but with the same thickness immediately behind the teeth. This prevents any binding of the saw in the kerf and also permits a smaller set to be applied to the teeth.

The ripsaw

This is the longest of the hand saws, frequently being between 28 and 30in (710 and 760mm) long with between 3½ and 5 points to the inch (25mm). Some older pattern saws have smaller teeth at the toe, and smaller versions sometimes have an extra point or two. The ripsaw is used for cutting planked timber lengthwise.

The crosscut saw

This type of saw varies in length between 22 and 26in (560 and 660mm) and between 5 and 7 points per inch (25mm).

The panel saw

From 20 to 24in (510 to 610mm) long, this usually has seven or more points per inch (25mm). It is used for thin timber or plywood.

Certainly there may be variations between manufacturers, but the foregoing will serve as a guide. Reputable saws will have handles secured by brass screws; this is very important as handles may work loose in use or there may be variations in temperature and humidity causing the timber to shrink or swell and the handle to work loose.

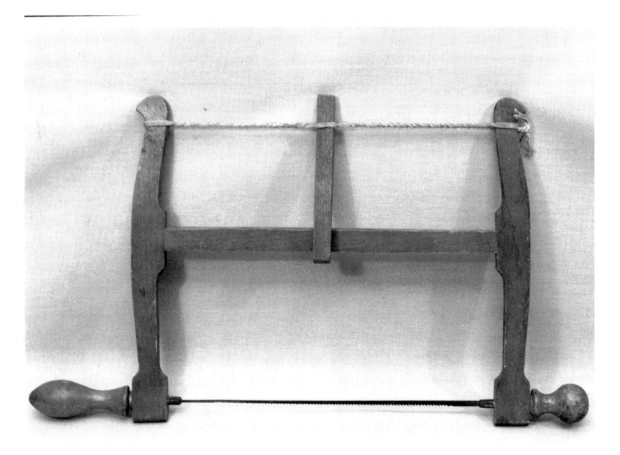

Bow-saw

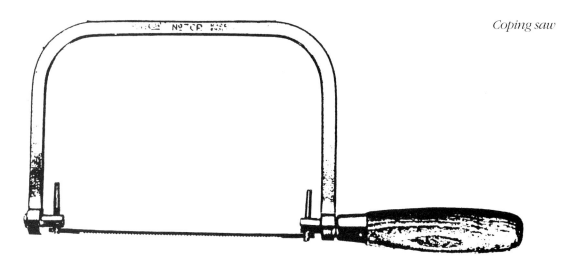

Coping saw

SPECIAL SAWS

When curved cuts have to be made by hand several saws are available, all designed with the size and type of work in mind.

Frame- or bow-saw

For larger work the frame- or the bow-saw can be used. They have very thin narrow blades held in place with removable and renewable pins that are located in the lower ends of the two frame arms through brass ferrules attached to the handles. The handles can be turned to position the blade in the direction in which the saw is to move. The frame arms are held apart by a stretcher or beam with tiny stub tenons located in mortices. Tension is applied on the saw blade by using a wooden toggle working in a strong cord wrapped around and connecting the ends of the frame arms.

Blades can be between 8 and 28in (203 and 710mm) long, and have 9 points to the inch (25mm). The total depth of cut is controlled by the distance between the blade and the beam.

Larger versions of those mentioned above are used in Europe and they often have wider blades so that they can replace hand saws in many instances.

Coping saw

This is a smaller and very popular saw. It has a fine steel frame and the blade, which is 6in (152mm) long, has a small cross pin at each end which serves to locate it in a slotted spigot at one end of the frame,

while at the other it is again positioned through the frame and into a turned handle.

The blade can be turned into the direction of the cut by twisting the handle and lining up the other spigot to match at the same time. I have always preferred to have the saw teeth pointing towards the handle so that the saw cuts on the back stroke; this not only makes for easier cutting but also reduces the number of blade breakages. When cutting thin material and smaller work, a fretwork saw table with a vee throat set up in the vice will help to hold the work down, and the teeth set towards the handle will also make for easier cutting.

The throat-depth of the frame permits cutting up to $4\frac{1}{2}$in (112mm) from the edge of the workpiece. The blade is easily fitted, and it is possible to cut an enclosed curve after threading the blade through a

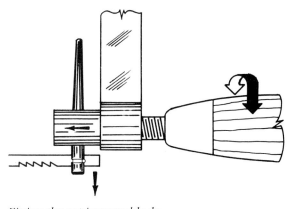

Fitting the coping saw blade

Keyhole saw

hole bored in the waste. The saw is not only useful for cutting small curves but will also help to remove the waste when cutting dovetails; it also has a number of uses for the wood carver.

Keyhole saw

This is used to cut keyholes and similar enclosed holes; it is sometimes referred to as a 'padsaw'. It has a tapered saw blade which locates in a slot cut through a round handle; the ferrule of this handle is fitted with a small knurled screw which can be tightened to fix and set the blade at any length between 5 and 15in (125 and 380mm), depending on the overall length of the blade. Teeth are usually 8 to 10 points per inch (25mm). Some keyhole saw handles will also accept hacksaw blades.

Nest of saws

A useful set of tapered blades of different sizes which fit into a slotted handle, and thus offers a number of alternative uses, particularly for those who only do occasional DIY work. A keyhole saw blade is often included in the set.

Fretsaw

For extremely fine work in thin sheets of wood, metal, or plastic this saw has no rival. Several sizes of frame are available offering depths of throat up to 20in (510mm) from the edge of the board or panel. The blades are a standard length of 6in (150mm), and are held in place with small clamps which also apply tension through the frame. Blades are available for sawing wood, metal and plastics.

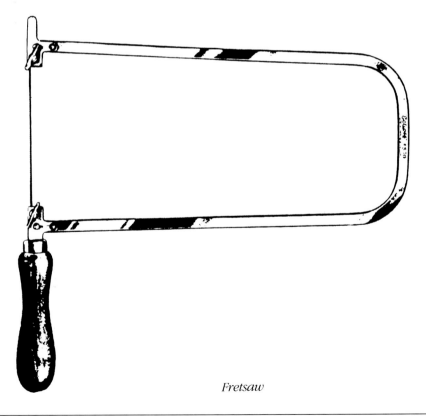

Fretsaw

Special all purpose saw

Eclipse 66 saw

A recent introduction which has a steel blade with notches cut in the end. These can be fitted into lugs on the handle so that the blade can be presented to the work at one of several angles. The saw is useful for cutting wood, plastics, rubber and other materials; it has a *Teflon* coated low friction blade with very little set on the teeth and works extremely well.

Flooring saw

For the woodworker needing to gain access under floorboards, this saw is the answer. The blade is 13in (330mm) long with 7 points to the inch (25mm). The top edge of the blade is angled at the front to allow the saw to be used vertically close to a wall. The edge of the blade carrying the teeth is slightly curved to facilitate the cutting of the tongue in a tongue and grooved board without having to pre-bore to get the saw started.

Log saws

Sometimes a log becomes available which may be suitable for turned or carved work. Usually the easiest way to convert it is to transport it to a saw mill, but these are scarce nowadays and recourse may need to be made to one of the number of log saws available.

The two-man crosscut saw is perhaps the best answer. These are usually equipped with large teeth which are gulleted to ease the removal of the waste from the kerf. The teeth are often referred to as 'lightning', and the blade itself is curved to keep the teeth in constant contact with the timber.

The one-man crosscut is similar in the design of the blade to the two-man, but has only one enclosed handle and a movable handle which can be fixed in any position along the top of the blade to give extra grip and weight. The saw can also be used by two men if the movable handle is fixed to the end of the blade.

There are a number of more modern log saws which have tubular metal frames which will accept blades between 24 and 30in (610 and 760mm) long. They are held in place with small screws, with the tension coming either from the frame itself or being exerted by a small lever. Some of these saws have teeth which cut in both directions and all the teeth have gullets to expel the sawdust.

Flooring saw

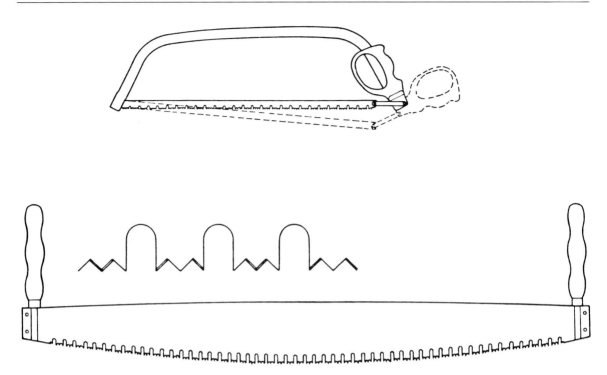

Log saw and two-man crosscut saw

PLANES

Planes have been in use for more than 2,000 years, and it is difficult to imagine being able to work without them as they are used not only to prepare timber before making joints in cabinet work, but also in cleaning up the work prior to polishing or finishing.

Many planes of this century and the latter part of the last are of metal construction throughout, although there are still several manufacturers who market some beautiful examples of the wooden plane. The inventive genius of many men went into the early metal planes of the *Stanley Company* of the USA; and the *Norris* and *Spiers* Planes were wonderful examples of the planemaker's craft. Today we see near-perfection in those made by *T. R. Ellin* and the *Calvert Stevens* plane from *Record-Marples*.

Planes can be divided into two principal groups – bench planes which are mainly used for bringing timber to size and at the same time planing it flat and true; and special planes for making different types of cuts.

To appreciate the value of the plane, a clear under-

standing of its cutting action is necessary. The cutting iron (also called the 'cutter'), is the most important part and this is made of a very high quality steel designed to give a long-lasting cutting edge. It must be set squarely in the body of the plane and be adjustable so that the cutting edge protrudes only by the thickness of a hair below the sole of the plane. The angle at which the cutting iron is ground and sharpened is extremely important, as is the angle at which the whole of the cutting mechanism is set in the plane body, and the best results can only be obtained if these conditions are met. The basic requirements of any plane are that the timber shall be left flat, straight, smooth and with its edges square with one another.

Bench planes are fitted with a cutting iron which has a cap, or back, iron bolted to it on its flat face. The action of planing is simply that the cutting iron cuts and lifts the shaving; the amount of lift depends on the distance between the cutting edge and the front of the mouth; the shaving strikes the cap iron which

Setting the cutting unit

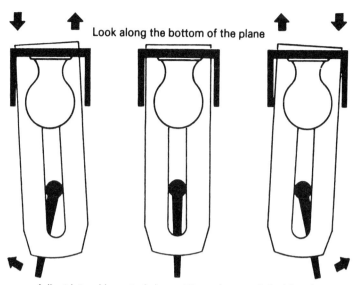

Look along the bottom of the plane

Adjust lateral lever to bring cutting edge parallel with sole.

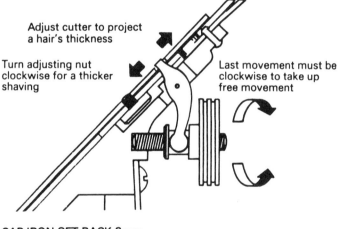

Adjust cutter to project
a hair's thickness

Turn adjusting nut
clockwise for a thicker
shaving

Last movement must be
clockwise to take up
free movement

CAP IRON SET BACK 2mm
For coarse work and soft woods

CAP IRON SET ALMOST LEVEL
For finishing and difficult grained hardwoods

SETTING DISTANCE
● Cap iron and mouth set WIDE for coarse work and easy grain
● For finishing and difficult grained wood – fine cap iron
   setting & narrow mouth, giving thin shavings

Calvert Stevens plane

Cut-away plane to show the action of the cap iron

turns, breaks, and rolls it out of the escapement of the plane. The closer the cap iron is to the edge, the sooner the shaving breaks. Tearing of the shaving ahead of the cutter is limited by the closeness of the mouth.

Most metal planes give adjustment of the mouth through repositioning the frog; really fine adjustments can be made so that the coarsest of timbers can be planed with success. For roughing work the mouth can be opened wide so that the plane will work like the old-fashioned wooden roughing plane which only had a single cutting iron. Should the mouth become choked with shavings it may indicate a loosely set cap iron, or one which is of poor shape and is not bedding properly against the flat surface of the cutting iron. Choking can also occur if the cap iron is too closely set, or the mouth too narrow.

Most planes can be set finely enough to plane end

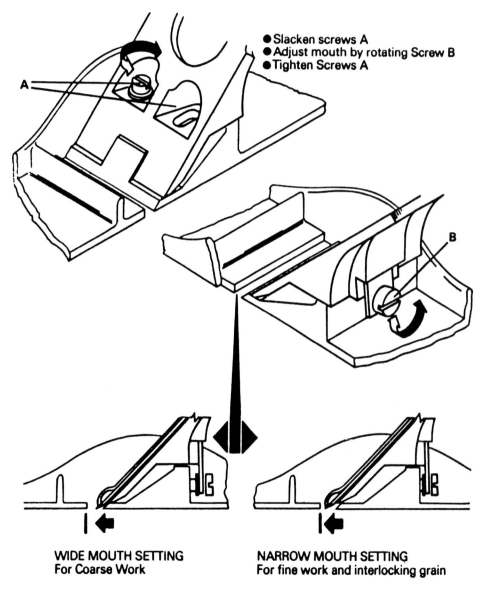

● Slacken screws A
● Adjust mouth by rotating Screw B
● Tighten Screws A

A

B

WIDE MOUTH SETTING
For Coarse Work

NARROW MOUTH SETTING
For fine work and interlocking grain

Adjusting the mouth

grain, but there are planes which are designed for special jobs which will also do this one, namely block planes, shoulder planes and plough planes. In block and shoulder planes the cutting iron is set at a lower angle, with the ground bevel of the cutting iron uppermost; thus the bevel itself serves as the cap iron and rolls the shaving over. When the cutting iron is set in this way, it tends to have a slicing action which is the best type of cut for end grain. The mouth is quite narrow, and the best designs have adjustable mouths as they cannot be fitted with frog adjustments.

The adjustment of the cutting mechanism in wooden planes is a matter of setting by eye and tapping the cutting iron with a hammer to obtain the correct projection. Metal planes are usually fitted with levers or adjusting screws to give lateral and fore-and-aft adjustment. Wooden planes without mechanical adjustment are still made, but illustrated is one which can be adjusted in a similar fashion to, and as accurately as, a conventional metal plane.

Bench planes are also available with corrugated soles which allow air to pass between the sole and the timber, thus breaking any suction which might occur on very finely planed surfaces. This is a valuable feature which is not always properly explained nor understood.

Many planes that are made in wood are built from best red beech which wears evenly and stays sound for a lifetime of use, particularly if the timber is carefully chosen with the medullary rays running vertically up from the sole. European smoothing planes have a horn-type handle at the front with the body shaped to receive the hand at the rear. Other bench planes are the same design as their predecessors, usually with a metal striking button at the front and a wooden wedge fitting in front of the cutting iron. A more refined group has full adjustment of the cutting iron plus a metal lever cap which is a substitute for the wedge-holding system. Such planes are available in sizes which compare with the metal planes, and they fulfil the same functions.

Some wooden planes are fitted with soles of lignum vitae, a timber which retains its flatness and resistance to wear for many years, and because of its oil content their polished soles give performances equal to those of any metal planes. An attractive timber, Goncalo Alves, has been used for some of the smaller planes – this timber has some of the qualities of lignum.

BENCH PLANES

Jack plane

This is the most used of the bench planes, and the smoothing plane the most used and abused plane of this group.

The jack plane is ideal for wood preparation. It is 14in (355mm) in length, with a 2in (50mm) wide cutting iron which is often made from tungsten vanadium steel, in modern examples the handles being of beech. A larger version of the same length has a 2⅜in (60mm) wide cutting iron. These planes are milled and ground to close tolerances and produce a satin-smooth surface if the cutting iron is sharpened and stropped properly.

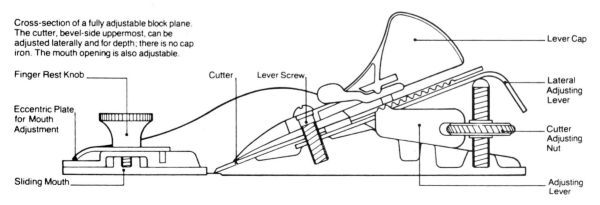

Cross-section of a fully adjustable block plane. The cutter, bevel-side uppermost, can be adjusted laterally and for depth; there is no cap iron. The mouth opening is also adjustable.

Finger Rest Knob

Eccentric Plate for Mouth Adjustment

Sliding Mouth

Cutter   Lever Screw

Lever Cap

Lateral Adjusting Lever

Cutter Adjusting Nut

Adjusting Lever

Block plane showing the low cutting angle

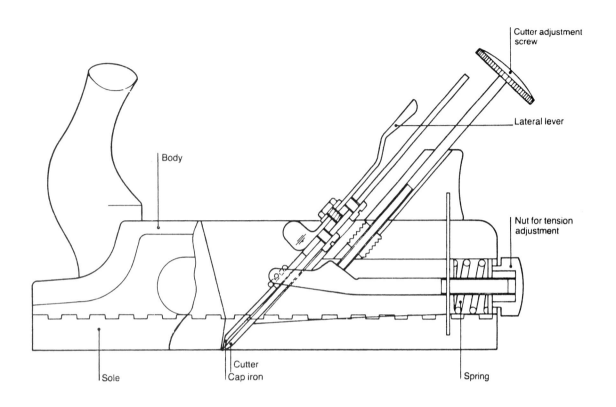

Cutter adjustment screw

Lateral lever

Body

Nut for tension adjustment

Sole

Cutter
Cap iron

Spring

Wooden plane showing the adjustment

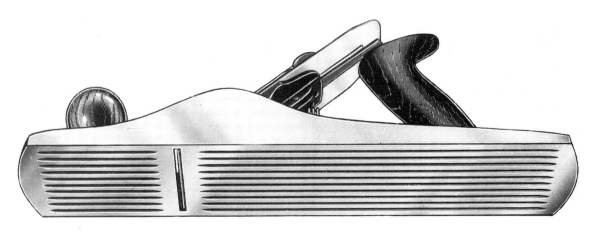

Plane with corrugated sole

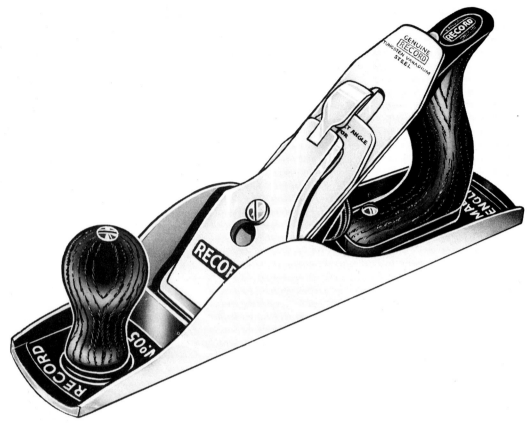

Record 05 jack plane

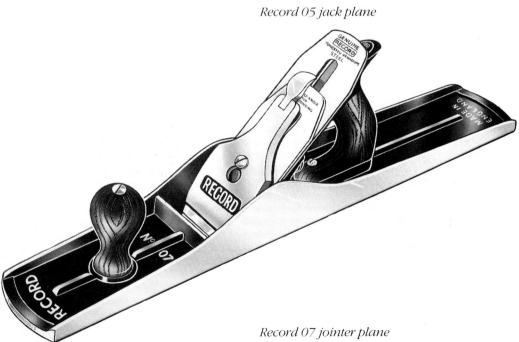

Record 07 jointer plane

Try plane

This is for planing long edges for rub-jointing and other work where precision is required. They are made in two lengths of 18in and 24in (455 and 610mm). My favourite plane of this kind is a *Record 08*, being 24in (610mm) in length and having a 2⅝in (66mm) cutting iron.

Fore plane

The shorter of the two jointer planes is often called a 'fore' plane. The longer planes usually have reinforced soles to counter distortion and to ensure lengthwise accuracy in planing.

Smoothing planes

These are available in three lengths, namely 9½, 9¾ and 10¼in (240, 248 and 260mm), with cutting irons 1¾, 2 and 2⅜in (45, 50 and 60mm) wide. They are used for cleaning up finished work when thin shavings need to be removed.

Block planes

These are small planes that range between 6 and 8in (150 and 200mm) in length and have a low angle setting for the cutting iron. The type of adjusting mechanism varies according to the price you pay.

The *09½ Record* plane has all the adjusting facilities of a bench plane, plus an unusual feature where the forward portion of the sole can be moved to allow mouth adjustment. Another design has two positions for the cutting iron so that the plane can be used with it in the forward position to act as a bull-nose plane.

A more modern version is a plane which has a Vee-shaped underbody; one side houses the cutting iron and the other acts as a fence. This plane is for edge trimming; the cutting iron is held in a similar fashion to that used in the side rebate plane but is angled slightly forward to give a perfect slicing cut. It will trim edges up to ⅞in (21mm) thick both with and across the grain and perfectly square; it can be used on man-made board.

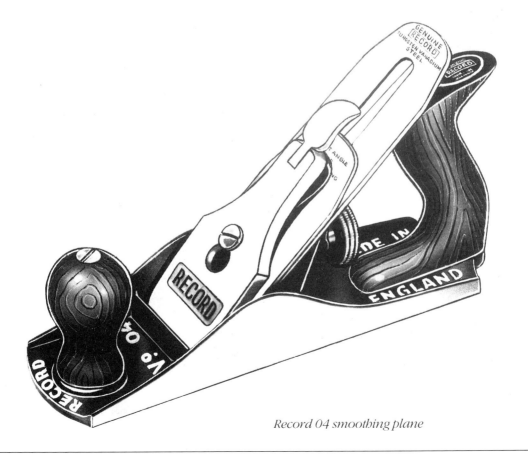

Record 04 smoothing plane

Record 9¹/₂ block plane

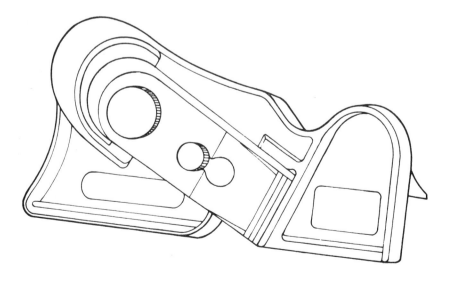

Edge trimming plane

Rebate and fillister planes

One of the best of these is the bench rebate plane of which the *Record 010* is a fine example. This plane is exactly like a jack plane but its cutting iron extends the full width of the sole and is fully adjustable. It is fine for trimming rebates which have been first cut on a saw-table, or making adjustments to plough- or router-cut rebates, or on special work such as fielded panels.

The *Record 778* is a rebate and fillister plane which has two positions for the cutting iron so that it can be used to cut closely into a stopped rebate. The cutting iron is fully adjustable in the rear position, and is $1\frac{1}{2}$in (38mm) wide. The plane is fitted with a spur which is housed in the right-hand side, and this can be set up to cut a kerf across the grain ahead of the cutting iron. The fence can be set across the sole of the plane to limit the width of cut, and it can also be transferred to the left-hand side when cutting fillisters. When the fence is removed it becomes a square plane, and this is an added advantage when cuts are to be made beyond the limits of the fence with the plane working against a planted-on strip which serves as a guide. Another version of this plane has a single arm fence.

The side rebate plane is needed whenever a rebate or groove has been cut and needs to be enlarged. It has two cutting irons, one for working on the left-hand side and the other at the right, and is a far better way of trimming away errors than resorting to the chisel. There is no adjustment and the cutters have to be set by eye. The noses can be removed to allow the plane to be used as a side-chisel plane to work tight into the corners.

Record 010 bench plane in use trimming a rebate

778 rebate and fillister plane in use

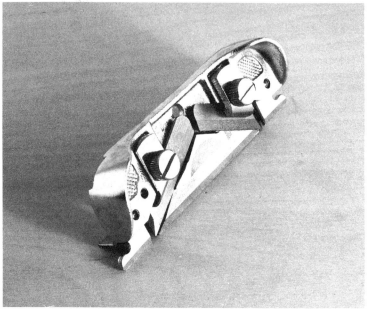

Stanley 79 side rebate plane

Plough planes

These are used to work grooves and rebates, and for making special cuts like tongues and grooves and decorative beads. The *Record Multi-purpose 050C* plane was originally designed as two separate planes: the *044* plough and rebate, and the *050* combination.

The design of the plane has undergone rationalisation and a wide range of cutting irons is available; they are optional extras which give a multiplicity of cuts, and you can now make your own choice of cutters to suit your particular needs. The fence can be set in any position and at either side; spurs are provided for kerfing across the grain, and the cutting iron is fully adjustable. The plane is fitted with a unique depth stop, and a similar arrangement is used to house the bead stop. It is a most comfortable plane to use and there is plenty of room for the hands.

The *Multiplane* is made only by *Clico* of Sheffield and carries the name *Clifton*. It is similar to the earlier *Record* which was originally designed around the *Stanley 55*, and is an expensive plane which can be used to make all the cuts possible with the *Record 050C* and many others. Excellent fine adjustments are possible; long and short fence arms are supplied which can be fitted in two positions in the fence to permit it to be passed across the cutter to limit the width of cut. A special slitting cutter can be fitted at the rear on the right-hand side; two fully adjustable depth stops are also fitted, one on the body and the other on the sliding section. Special bases can also be fitted which slide over the fence arms and convert the plane to cut hollows and rounds.

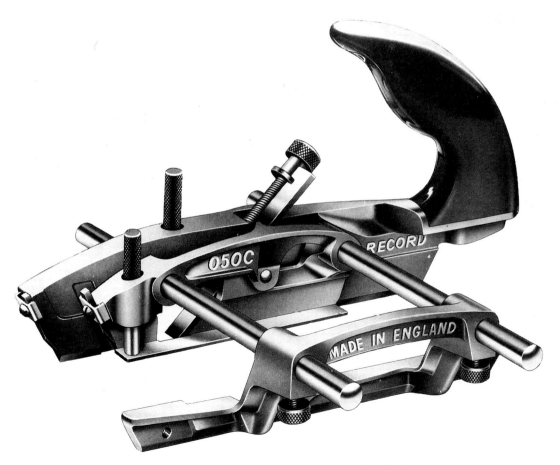

Record 050 plough plane

405 multiplane – cutting a bead

Shoulder plane

This is one of the finest planes for trimming end rebates and other cuts in end grain, which is available in several cutter widths. The *Record 073*, unlike the others, has full fore-and-aft cutting-iron adjustment as well as an adjustable mouth. The cutting iron is set at a low angle, and in use it has the bevel uppermost. The sole and sides of the plane are very accurately machined and square with each other, with the cutting iron just clearing the sides to permit cutting exactly into the corner of the cut. It is indispensable when trimming secret-mitred lap dovetails and similar joints.

Another plane bearing the *Clifton* name is a revived *Record* design – the *Three-in-One*, or *311*, as it was once named. It is a fully equipped shoulder plane with forward and backward adjustment of the cutting iron which, again, is set at a low angle and used with the bevel uppermost. The long nose can be removed and a short one substituted to convert it to a bull-nose plane; and the mouth can be adjusted by using the thin shims provided. Used without either of the noses the plane becomes a perfect chisel-plane, ideal for finishing cuts where other planes cannot reach and giving the perfection of cut almost impossible with a hand-held chisel.

077 bull-nose plane

This is purpose-made to work into corners and stops, and is similar in design to the *Three-in-One* plane. It has mouth adjustment by use of shims, a low cutting angle for the cutting iron which is also adjustable forwards and backwards. Once again, the sides and sole are very accurately machined, with the cutting iron just clearing the sides for perfect corner cutting. It can also be converted to a chisel-plane by removing the nose.

Record 073 shoulder plane

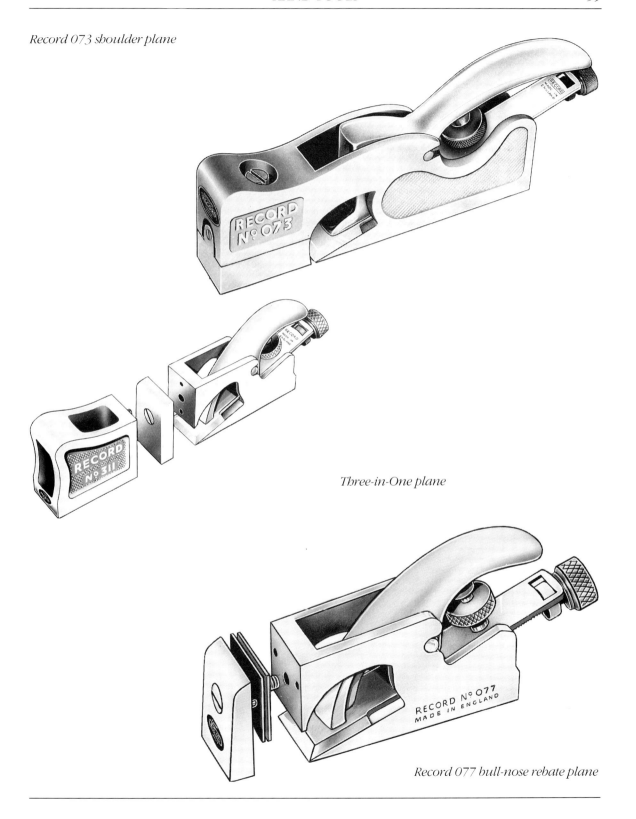

Three-in-One plane

Record 077 bull-nose rebate plane

Router plane

This is designed to work on surfaces below the surrounding face of the work, and as a result it can be used for clearing groundwork in wood carving and for trimming the bottoms of housings, as well as for through and stopped grooves. Its ability to cut grooves around a curve is a unique feature.

The plane is held by two handles; the cutter is fully adjustable for depth and has two positions; the centre one for general work and the forward one for bull-nose or closer cutting. The fence is positioned in shallow grooves in the underside of the sole and can be set in either right-or left-hand positions; it can be used on both straight and curved work. The depth stop sits freely in its housing, the final depth being set by positioning a shoe at the top of the stop. When the plane is used on a narrow edge, the mouth can be closed by reversing the depth stop with the shoe in place to close across the mouth; this will prevent the plane from tilting over and the cutter digging in as the plane is pushed forward.

The Vee-shaped smoothing cutter gives the best cut, but there are two others, ¼ and ½in (6 and 12mm) widths, which both have a chisel shape. A smaller version of the plane has a ¼in (6mm) cutter which can be turned in its housing to give normal or bull-nose working.

Planes for musical instrument makers

These are needed to carry out the very precise work done by musical instrument makers. It was, and sometimes still is, the practice of the craftsman to make his own, and some fine examples appear in auction salerooms from time to time.

These planes were made to fit the hand, and were able to cut the finest shavings in a small area; the timber used was beech or box. At the present time both finger and palm planes are available, and are

Stanley 71 router plane, showing three cutters

Router plane with mouth closed and round fence
fitted, cutting a groove

Sainsbury palm plane

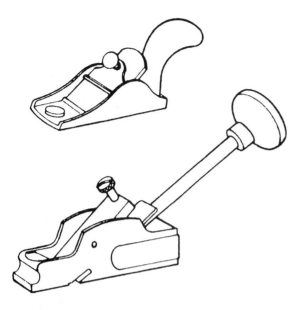

Palm planes

made in various shapes and a variety of metals. The illustration shows a palm plane which is similar in construction to the block plane but has a small handle. Another design has a long rod fitted with a round knob to fit into the palm of the hand.

Circular plane

Early designs of circular planes were made of wood and the soles were of fixed radius; thus a pair of matching planes with concave and convex soles was needed. The modern plane dispenses with the necessity for this since the sole is flexible and can be set to suit both concave and convex shapes. The *Record 020C* uses a standard bench plane cutting iron and has exactly the same adjustment. Setting the sole is easily carried out by loosening the locking screw on the adjusting nut and turning the latter until the sole of the plane is in contact with the work and taking up the correct curvature. Then the locking screw can be tightened and the setting of the cutting iron adjusted. The plane body is shaped to fit the hand quite comfortably.

Record 020C circular plane

(opposite)
Convex cutting (above)
and concave cutting (below)

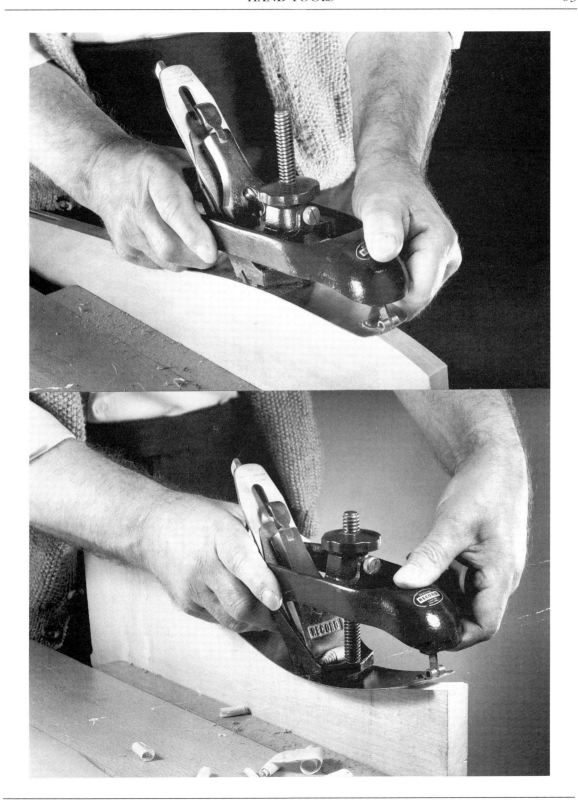

Spokeshave

Using the spokeshave

Spokeshave

This is a cutting tool which, once the technique of using it is mastered, is a pleasure and a joy to use. Although wooden designs are still available, modern versions are made in malleable iron; avoid cast-iron ones that break easily. They are made with either a curved or a flat sole, and in each case the cutter can be finely adjusted. The curved sole model can be used for finishing concave or convex curves which have been cut with the bow- or bandsaw, while the flat sole design is extremely useful for cutting chamfers, even stopped ones. Only a hair thickness of cutter should be seen along the sole; the index fingers are placed in the little housings shaped to receive them, and, with the front edge of the spokeshave held down, cutting is poetry in motion.

Drawknives

These are sometimes called 'drawing' knives and were the predecessors of spokeshaves; unlike them, drawknives are drawn towards the operator. They were and in some instances still are, the tools of the cooper and wheelwright for all their shaping and chamfering work. It can be used for roughing out with the bevel uppermost; by reversing the bevel to face downwards, very fine controlled cutting can be carried out.

The drawknife is also widely used by chairmakers and occasionally by woodcarvers and cabinet makers for some of their curved work.

A variation of the drawknife is the 'inshave', which is designed with a sharply curved blade that is particularly useful in the shaping of Windsor chair seats and similar in-curved work.

Scrapers

The cabinet maker's scraper is used for the general smoothing of wood, particularly crossgrained timber, or for the cleaning up of finished work prior to polishing. It can also be used by the furniture restorer and the french polisher for removing old polish and restoring surfaces before re-polishing.

The scraper is virtually the only tool which can be used where veneers are being restored as, because of the thinness of the veneers, a plane cannot be used: it is really an essential tool due to the expanding use of man-made boards which have veneered surfaces.

The standard scraper is made from thin sheet steel which can be flexed by the fingers to present a slightly curved cutting edge to the work. The edge itself has a tiny burr which is applied with a small ticketer or burnisher. This burr bites into the upper surface of the timber when the scraper is angled away from the operator, and fine shavings are removed as the tool is pushed along the work. Various shapes of scraper are available to deal with a range of moulding profiles.

The double-handled cabinet scraper is one of the most indispensable tools in my kit. Here is a tool which sets up the correct angle; the curvature of the cutter can be set easily with a built-in adjusting screw, and the two handles make it an easy tool to

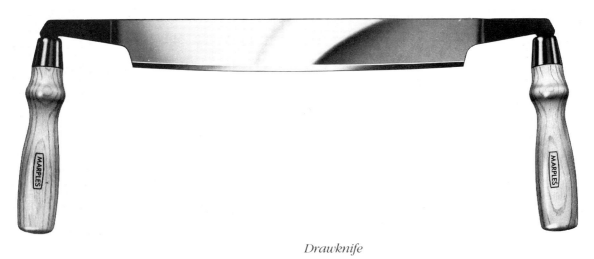

Drawknife

control. The scraper blade has an angled edge on both sides and is sharpened in a similar way to the standard tool. To set the blade, place the body flat on the bench, push the blade in so that it touches the bench top, tighten the holding screws, and then turn the centre screw to apply the curvature.

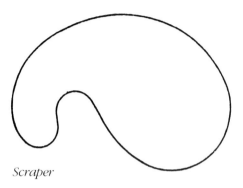

Scraper

Adzes

These were probably the ancestors of today's planes, certainly they are great tools to use although they can be difficult to master at first. Most of the old beams seen in many ancient buildings were planed with this tool.

The carpenter's adze is made in forged steel with a rectangular poll into which the hickory shaft is fitted; the shaft has a well designed curve which allows optimum presentation of the cutting edge to the work. The shaping of the poll allows the head to be held firmly when in use, but also allows it to be withdrawn.

Usually weighing about 5lb (2kg) it is a tool which has to be treated with respect and used properly. A smaller version is used by wood sculptors – here, the blade is about 2in (50mm) across and the handle is much shorter.

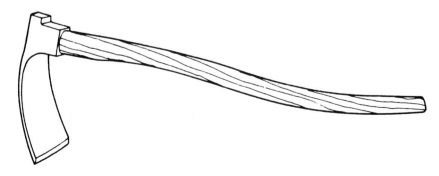

Adze

CHISELS

There are many types of chisels, all designed for specific jobs; undoubtedly they are the most popular and most abused cutting tools. Chisels can be used in either hand; when extra weight is needed, their handles can be struck with a wooden mallet.

When selecting a chisel, take care that it is the correct tool for the job, that it comes from a reputable manufacturer (which will serve as a guarantee), that the steel is good quality, and most important that it has a handle which fits your hand to give a firm and comfortable grip without being tiring. Too often in the past handles did not fulfil their true function as many were too big and were dangerous – the old design of mortice chisel with an oval and tapered handle was an example.

Many plastic handles are available, some of which become extremely slippery and give a poor grip, especially in a warm hand. *Marples Bluechip* chisels are worth looking for. Hold the chisel in both hands to check the balance as the handle should not be too light, and also look to see that the blade is correctly fixed in the handle.

Examine the blade for flatness and for accurately ground bevels: badly ground chisels, particularly on the flat side, can take a long time to bring to a state where the cutting edge appears as a perfect black hairline. In the case of a bevelled-edge chisel check that the long bevels are ground to a thin edge so that the chisel can be used to make the cuts required in the corner of a stopped dovetail.

The mortice chisel should have a blade which conforms exactly to the specified width. Examine the wooden handle to check for splits or other flaws; the timber, which may be ash, beech, or boxwood, must be closegrained and also be free from knots, although knots in boxwood add to its strength. Ash is

Black and Decker Workmate

Power tool board

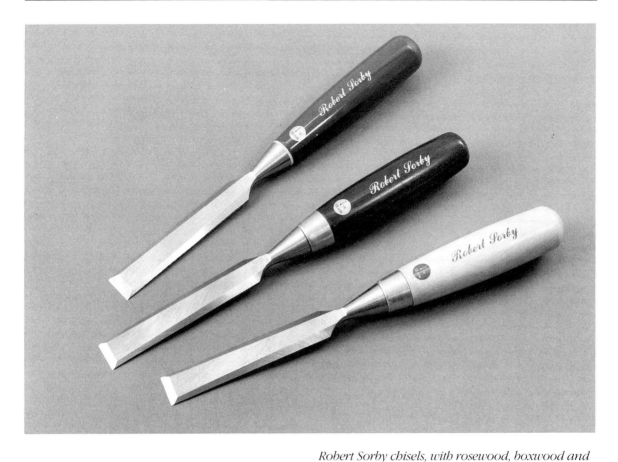

Robert Sorby chisels, with rosewood, boxwood and plastic handles

widely used for handles and is fairly open-grained but it makes up for this by its elasticity. The handle must be fixed really firmly as often the chisel has to be wrenched from side to side to remove it from the workpiece. Boxwood (*Buxus sempervirens*) a very slow-growing timber indigenous to Europe, was often used for chisel handles in the old days; it does not grow to any great size and most of the handles were made from branches.

Cellulose acetate butyrate is the hardest and toughest plastic used for handles, followed by cellulose acetate and polypropylene; all are described as split-proof but in very cold weather they may not prove to be so.

Bench hook

TYPES OF CHISELS

Firmer chisels

These are general purpose tools although in recent years there has been a change to bevelled-edge chisels, probably because of the cost involved in having two sets.

A firmer chisel has a fairly thick blade and is designed for heavy work, while the bevelled-edge chisel, with its long edges finely ground, is the chisel for working dovetails. All fine cutting can be carried out with it; vertical and horizontal chiselling in the straight and on curves, dovetailing, chamfering (both with and across the grain), stopped, through and dovetailed housings.

Mortice chisels

Neither the firmer nor the bevelled-edge chisel

Firmer chisel

Marples Blue Chip bevelled-edge chisel

should be used for cutting deep slots such as mortices; a mortice chisel should be used for them.

The *London* pattern chisel is designed for this task – it has an accurate-to-size blade which has been thickened and given a solid bolster for strength. Its handle is made with a leather washer between it and the bolster to take the shock of blows from a mallet, and a similar design is made with a plastic handle. These chisels have a reach of approximately 6½in (165mm) and as they are always exactly the width specified you can set your mortice gauge to the chisel and not to the rule. A registered chisel, which closely resembles a mortice chisel, has a thicker blade, a steel ferrule, and a steel hoop at the striking end of the handle.

A special mortice chisel similar to the London pattern but with a curved swan neck shape on the blade is used for hollowing out the recesses for mortice locks and similar jobs.

Paring chisels

The long thin paring chisel has no equal when it comes to cutting housings across the grain or for any task where a long reach is needed. The blade is thin and finely bevelled on its long edges to work into corners; indeed, it is the best chisel which can be used to cut dovetailed housings. The handles are usually of the carver shape and made in boxwood. It is also available with a cranked neck which keeps the hand clear from the work top and allows the chisel to work flat on the workpiece. When choosing this type of chisel be sure that it is flat across and throughout its length; although a slight upturning of the blade may be apparent, this helps in cutting a perfectly flat surface.

Pocket chisel

This is the exact opposite of the long thin variety. The butt or pocket chisel is a shorter version of the bevelled-edge chisel and gets its name from its main use which is the cutting of recesses or housings to receive butt hinges.

Drawer lock chisel

This has a similar function; it is made of square section bar and is cranked to an angle of 90° to form blades at both ends. One blade is at right angles to, and the other in line with, the main body which

London pattern mortice chisel

Registered pattern chisel

Long thin paring chisel

enables the tool to be used inside the restricted area of a drawer.

Gouges

These are chisels of curved section. They are classified as in-cannel and out-cannel, the former having its bevel ground on the inside, and the latter, on the outside. The in-cannel is used primarily for the vertical and horizontal paring of concave curves, and the out-cannel for general curved work, including carving. Suppliers' catalogues show the curves and sizes. The in-cannel patterns are also available with a long cranked blade; handles are usually in boxwood.

Corner chisel

Formerly called a bruzz this was a standard tool of the wheelwright who found it particularly useful to clean out the mortices which receive the spokes of the wheel as the bevel is applied on the inside. It is fine for taking out the round corners left by the router cutter in morticing and other work.

Out-cannel gouge

Cranked in-cannel gouge

Corner chisel or 'bruzz'

KNIVES

These are needed for a variety of tasks, including amongst others marking out and cutting veneers. The marking knife is often ground on one side only to suit either the left- or right-handed worker, or ground on both sides. The former is better as the cut made by the knife is a vertical one and is ideal for positioning a cutting tool, such as a saw, to cut accurately to the mark.

There are a number of craft knives with an assortment of blades to suit many tasks and the chapter on wood carving describes some curved ones.

BORING TOOLS

These are needed to make holes in timber for a variety of purposes; dowels, screws, nails, and bolts – all need holes to receive them. Boring bits can also be used to cut holes in work turned on the lathe, to remove the waste when cutting some joints, or to clear away the ground in low-relief wood carving. The type of boring tool to be used depends on the purpose for which the hole is to be used, and the tool itself determines the method used to turn it.

Auger twist bits

These are the boring tools most commonly in use and have shanks which end in tangs that fit into a carpenter's or joiner's brace. They are made in several styles to suit particular jobs, and normally have leads (or points) with screw threads to draw or wind the bit into the wood, spurs or wings to scribe the periphery of the hole, and cutters or lifters to lift and remove the waste. Each bit has a spiral flute which serves to guide the waste out of the hole.

The most popular one is the solid centre or Irwin pattern which has a single twist, two spurs and a strong screwed lead or point. It is available in many sizes, including metric.

The Jenning's pattern is the bit most popular with cabinet makers over the years and it has a double twist which helps to give the bit support in the hole and to keep it square; it cuts a near perfect hole. The Scotch nose bit was designed for hard or rough work, particularly in hardwoods. Similar to the Jenning's in its twist, it has no spurs; the side wings

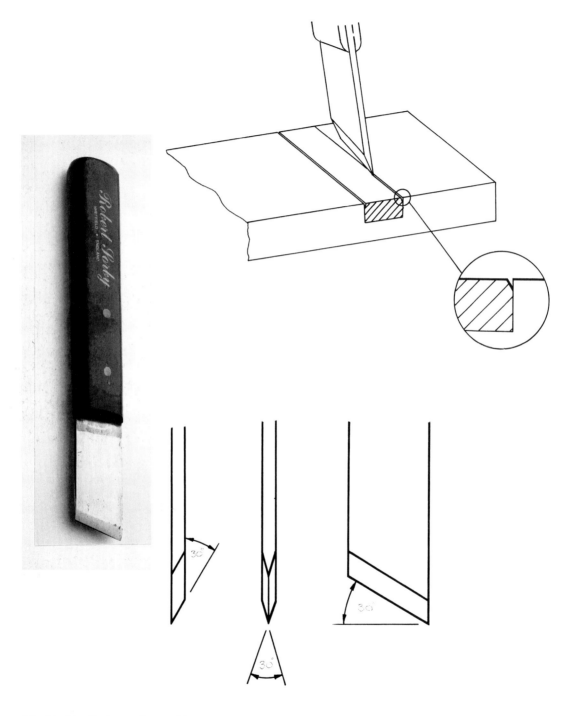

Marking knife; its angles and in use

Stanley knife with snap-off blades

Solid centre auger bit

Jennings pattern auger bit

combine with the cutters to scribe the periphery and cut the waste. Its thread has a coarser pitch to lessen the chance of breakage in very hard timbers.

The expansive bit is most useful and although quite expensive it does save buying a great number of those previously mentioned, which may only be used occasionally. There are several patterns; they normally come in two sizes, each having two cutters. Extra cutters can be bought to bring the range of size options up to 6in (150mm). The bit consists of a solid body with a finely cut screw point; the cutter slides in the body and is held in place with a spring and screw, and at the end of the cutter is a spur. The cutter can be set at $^1/_{32}$in (0.8mm) divisions against a datum line scribed on the body. Great care must be exercised when using the bit – never set it beyond the maximum diameter stated by the maker otherwise it may be damaged. It cuts best in softwood, and care must be taken in hardwoods; also, never use it to bore deep holes. One American design has the size set by a small pinion which runs in a rack on the underside of the cutter, the size registering against datum lines.

(above) *Scotch nose pattern auger bit*

(right) *Expansive bit*

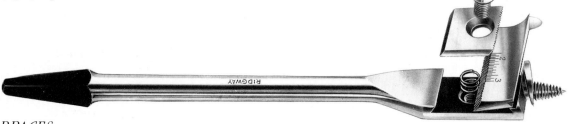

BRACES

Auger bits have a squared tang which fits into the brace. These are either plain braces, or designs fitted with a ratchet so they can be used where it is impossible to rotate the brace through 360°. Another style is the corner brace which can be used in severely restricted corners. The principal feature of a brace is the sweep of its handle, averaging 10in (250mm). A good one will have a steel frame with a head (or nave) running in ballbearings; both head and handle are usually made from good quality hardwood, although plastic ones are often available. Jaws can also be fitted to hold wood drills.

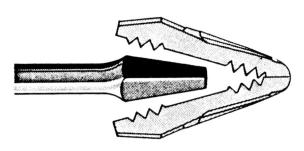

Brace jaws

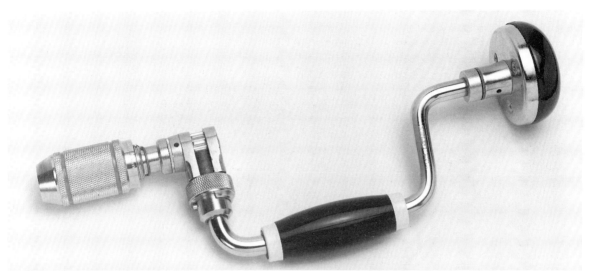

(above) *Stanley ratchet brace*   (below) *Brace in use*

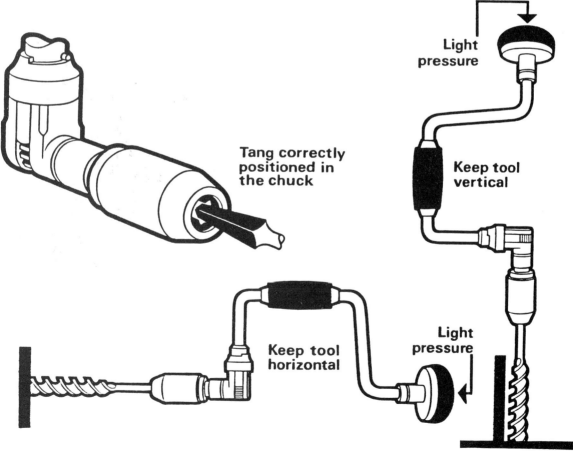

Tang correctly
positioned in
the chuck

Light
pressure

Keep tool
vertical

Keep tool
horizontal

Light
pressure

HAND DRILL

This has a chuck size of ¼ or ³/₁₆in (6 or 8mm), and has three jaws designed to hold engineering twist drills known as Morse or Jobber's drills. It is most useful for boring small holes and where the electric drill may not be available or convenient to use.

DRILLS AND BITS FOR POWER DRILLS

Probably the best and cheapest bit designed with the electric drill in mind is the spade type, also known as a 'flat bit'. Its action is unique in that it scribes and scrapes the hole without the accepted lifter and spur of the auger bit. It has a long brad point which allows the user to cut holes at an angle (a difficult task ever since the solid nose auger bit disappeared from the market). It has flats on the shank for gripping in the jaws of the chuck, and it can be sharpened very easily. It will bore holes in hard and soft wood, end grain, knots, stringy and wet timber, as well as Perspex and other plastics. It can be fitted with an extension shank which is really useful when cutting in restricted areas; and it can also be used with or without the extension on a wood turning lathe. Sizes range from ¼ to 1½in (6 to 38mm).

Always run the bit at fast speeds; don't push too hard when cutting into end grain since the bit may run off-centre. Always allow the bit to stop in the hole before withdrawing it; take care when boring a hole completely through to position a piece of waste wood to avoid breakout.

Jobber's drills

These are also known as Morse or engineer's drills. They do not have a point, and care must be used to avoid running off-centre; also clogging and burning of the drill can sometimes occur as the flute is not cut wide enough to pass the shavings through easily.

A better tool to use is the wood drill, which has adequate shaving clearance and is available in sizes up to ½in (12mm). An even better drill is the lip and spur drill which has a simple brad point and two spurs to scribe the periphery of the hole. It has a round shank and is usually available in high-speed steel in sizes up to ½in (12mm). It centres very accurately, bores a clean hole, and passes the shavings through without problems.

Forstner bits

A Forstner (or a sawtooth machine bit) should be used whenever flat bottom holes are needed, or where holes have to be cut overlapping the edge of the work, or overlapping each other. The Forstner has a small brad point and runs on its knife edge periphery; it has two cutters or lifters and it has long been the favourite tool for this kind of work. The

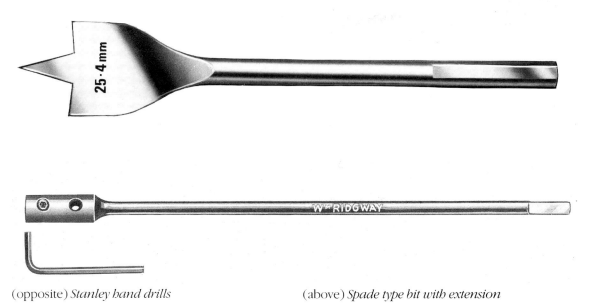

(opposite) *Stanley hand drills*   (above) *Spade type bit with extension*

(above) *Wood drill*　　　　　　　　　　(below) *Lip and spur bit*

(above) *Forstner and* (below) *saw-tooth cutters*

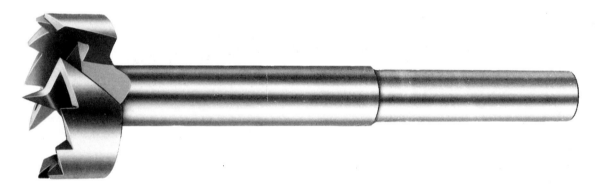

sawtooth cutter substitutes ripsaw-like teeth for the knife edge of the Forstner, but in all other respects works in the same way. Both types are available with a ½in (12mm) shank diameter and in sizes up to 3½in (90mm).

The sawtooth bit has become extremely popular with the woodturner for boring deep holes in end grain and is suitable for soft or hardwoods which may be in any condition. The design used in the USA has only one lifter, with one-quarter of the periphery cut away to clear the shavings.

Countersinks
These are needed to recess screw heads below the surface of the work. There are two kinds – the rosehead, which has a conical end and is the most used, and the snail countersink. Both are available in several sizes and made in both carbon and high-speed steel. Avoid the head becoming clogged, otherwise the bit may burn.

A combination bit can also be useful; it not only bores a hole for the shank of the screw, but also countersinks. Extended cutting will also counter-bore the hole so that bolt heads may be covered with a wood plug.

The *Wolfcraft* screw starter is a tool designed for boring and countersinking holes for countersunk screws. It is not unlike the old-fashioned gimlet in

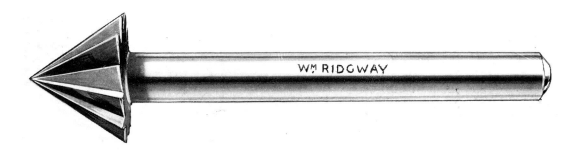

(above) *Countersink*   (below) *Wolfcraft screw starter*

Wolfcraft hand countersink

Plug cutters

design, but is fitted with an adjustable countersink for different depths of holes. There are two sizes for up to 4.5mm holes.

A hand countersink can save a great deal of time. The *Wolfcraft* design can be used on wood, metal, or plastics for the countersinking and de-burring of holes, and has a head ¾in (19mm) in diameter with a plastic handle which fits comfortably in the hand.

Rotary rasps for wood are popular and come in a number of different shapes and sizes. The shanks are approximately ¼in (6.35mm) in diameter and they can be used in an electric drill for the shaping, tapering, enlarging, and de-burring of holes, as well as for a variety of odd jobs around the workshop.

PLUG CUTTERS

Whenever a screw or bolt head will be unsightly it can be covered with a plug cut from the same timber as that being used in the construction. The hole must first be counterbored to pass the head of the screw

and a plug of matching size can then be cut and glued into the hole.

Plug cutters are obtainable in several different types and in a variety of sizes up to 2in (50mm). The tubular design cuts a perfect cylindrical plug; its single cutter scribes, cuts, and lifts the shavings – in fact, it cuts a circular groove and ejects the plug through an opening in the side of the tube.

Another tubular type, much simpler in construction and cheaper to buy, cuts a thin, slightly tapered plug which must be removed by hand. The wing-style cutter has four small lifters around its periphery and ejects the plug.

All plug cutters must be used in a drill press or drill set up in a stand. Since they have no brad or screw point to run on, the tool must be eased in at the point of entry, and the timber held firmly with the hands kept well away from the revolving cutter. Thin timber will often split, where the bit breaks through, and this can be a little alarming; be careful always to have a piece of waste wood underneath when, or if, this happens to avoid damage to the cutting edges.

A bit which isn't a cutting tool at all must be included in this section as it is used in the carpenter's brace. This is the screwdriver bit which can be obtained in several sizes and has a square tapered shank to fit the chuck jaws of the brace.

MARKING-OUT TOOLS

Obviously, all measurements and details of joints must be transferred accurately to the timber, and the choice and correct use of good marking-out tools is therefore of paramount importance to avoid disastrous consequences.

Folding rules
In the UK the traditional rule is the four-fold, which is available with imperial or metric markings, or both: the zig-zag type is most commonly used in the USA. The UK rule will be marked in millimetres and centimetres and often inches and feet as well, while the USA are still using imperial measurements in feet, inches, and sub-divisions. Good folding rules were and still are almost invariably made in close-grain boxwood, but other substitutes are presently in use, including plastics.

The two-fold steel rule is also in common use and is usually marked up in metric or inches with millimetres or sixteenth of an inch sub-divisions.

Flexible tapes
The most widely used measuring device is the tape of flexible steel running in a steel case. Many types have a hard plastic face on to which the measurements are etched; plain steel ones need a little lubrication from time to time. All such tapes are very hard wearing and long lasting and can be obtained in lengths up to 3 metres (118 inches). They are also ideal for measuring round jobs or for ascertaining the girth of a log.

Callipers
For taking and transferring measurements from round or straight stock, callipers should be used, and they are a very necessary tool for the wood-turner. There are two principal types – those which have a centre hinge pin, and those which have

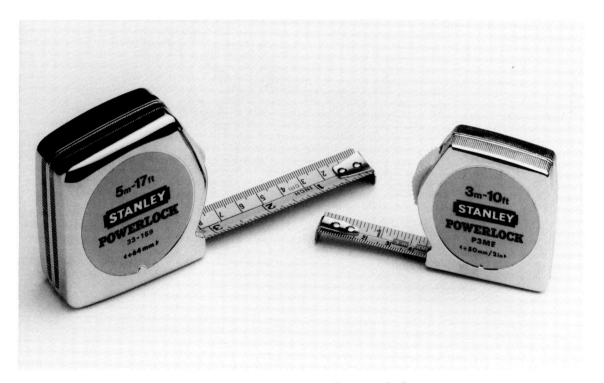

Stanley Powerlock tape

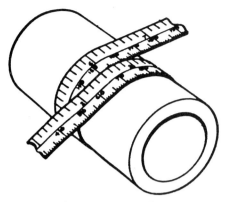

Tape used to measure girth

spring-divided legs; the latter are better as they can be fixed by a screw, while the former can easily be upset with the slightest pressure. Designs are available with legs to measure both inside and outside dimensions, and also a combination type with outside and inside measuring legs at opposite ends is popular among woodturners. Several sizes can be obtained.

Measurements can also be taken and transferred by another kind of calliper gauge made in boxwood and brass, where a brass slide moves in the body and measurements are easily taken. They are available in a number of sizes.

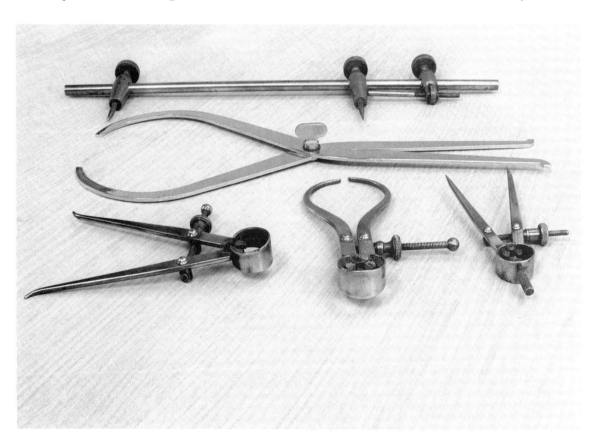

Callipers, dividers and trammel

Mitre sawing board

Shooting a mitre

Picture frame clamping board

Sizing board

SQUARES

These are a vital part of the tool kit and must be of the best quality as it is almost impossible to think of any woodworking activity which doesn't require the use of the square at some time. The tool kit should contain a 6in and 12in (150 and 300mm) square; a wooden stock, preferably of rosewood, is first choice, but I have a *Stanley* all steel 12in (300mm) which I have used for many years. The best quality wooden stocks are faced with brass to prevent wear and there are a number of designs which have measurements along the blade. *Marples* make a very accurate square with a blade which extends the length of the stock, ensuring a perfect right angle throughout its life. Another design of stock has a secondary cut at 45° at its blade end so that it can also be used to mark at 45°.

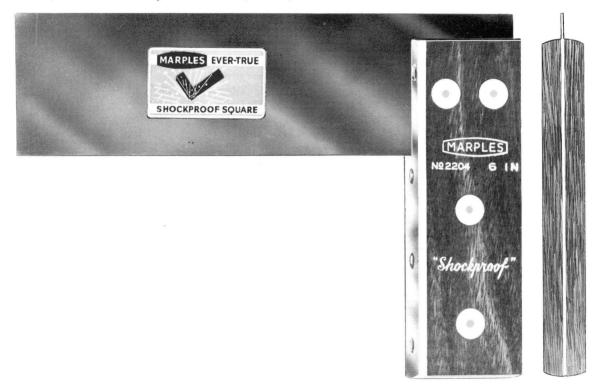

Trysquare

Mitre square

This is a misnomer since its blade is set at an angle of 45°; again, it is a precise tool built like the trysquare, with a hardwood stock and steel blade.

Combination square

This is a variation with both square and 45° options available on a single stock. The rule is set out with both metric and imperial measures and can be set at any position through the stock. On some designs the stocks are fitted with a little vial so that the stock can be used as a spirit level, and on others the stock houses a small steel scriber.

The *Wolfcraft* general purpose square is made entirely of metal and can be used to scribe at 90°, 45° and any other angle by using the protractor.

The *Combinal* is a multi-function tool made in aluminium and consists of a 760 × 50mm (30 × 2in) blade to which a stock can be added. It can be used as a marking-out square or it can be set at angle graduations of 15°. It can be fixed to the bench and used as a guide for the router, jigsaw or circular saw, and can also be used as a straight rule or as an angle measuring gauge.

Testing the trysquare and 45° angle

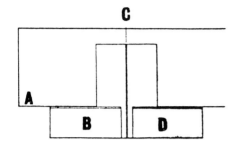

Checking the square for accuracy using a 90° corner.

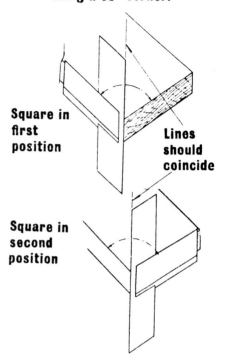

Square in
first
position

Lines
should
coincide

Square in
second
position

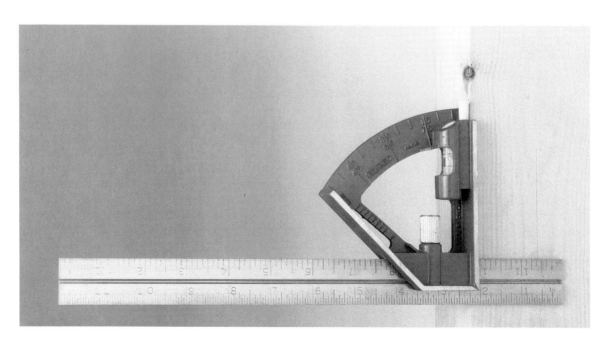

Stanley combination square

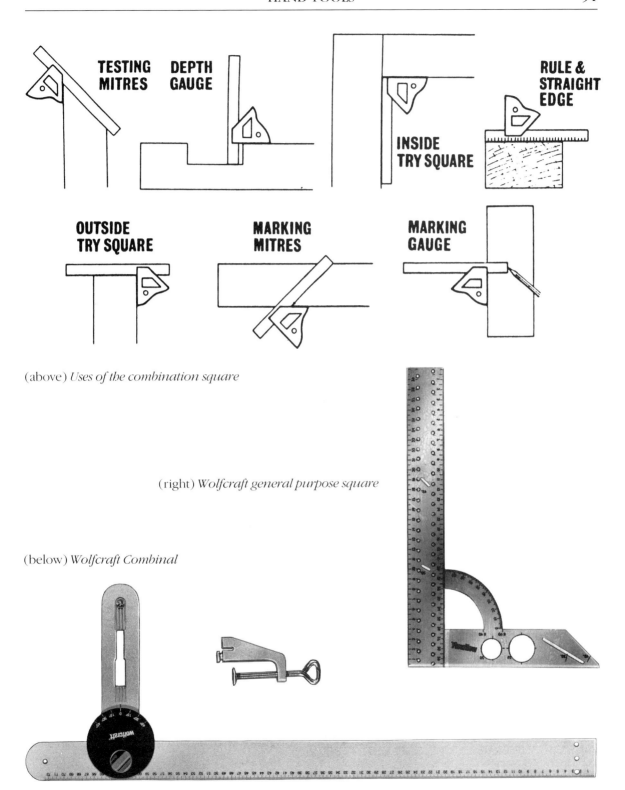

TESTING MITRES

DEPTH GAUGE

INSIDE TRY SQUARE

RULE & STRAIGHT EDGE

OUTSIDE TRY SQUARE

MARKING MITRES

MARKING GAUGE

(above) *Uses of the combination square*

(right) *Wolfcraft general purpose square*

(below) *Wolfcraft Combinal*

Sliding bevel

Needed to mark out angled lines and also to mark
out dovetailed joints. To use it, set up an angle on the
edge of the bench, place the bevel against the edge
of the bench, align the blade (which slides into any
position), then tighten down on the screw – sometimes this is a half wing nut.

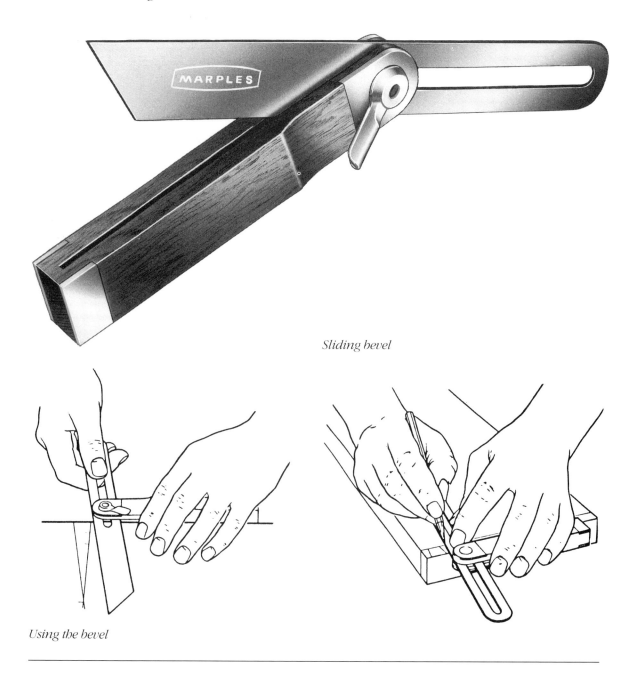

Sliding bevel

Using the bevel

Angle divider

A very useful tool to have, particularly when angles of varying degrees have to be marked out or transferred.

Centre square

This comes into its own in the hands of the wood-turner and is a great time-saver.

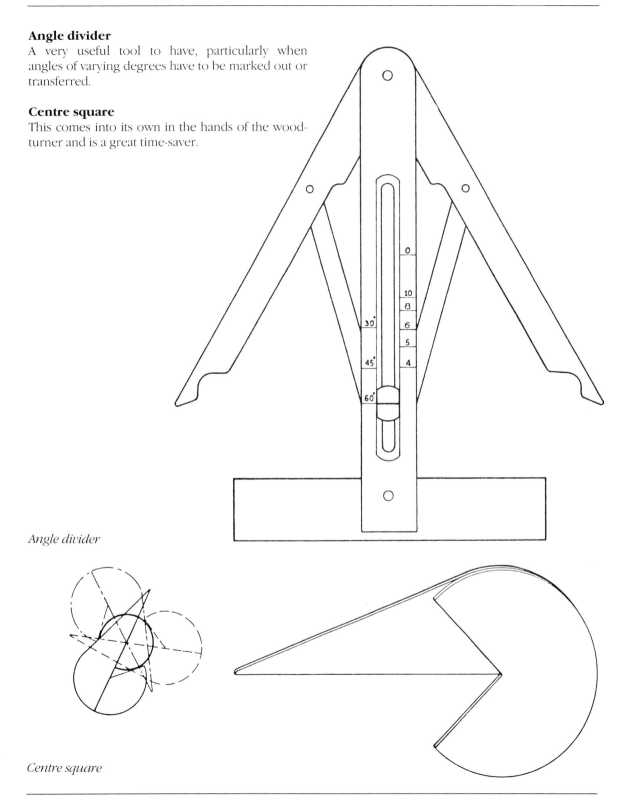

Angle divider

Centre square

Mitre template

Another useful tool which combines a square and a 45° square is the mitre template. These are usually 6in (150mm) long and are ideal for marking out small work.

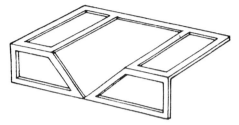

Mitre template

Marking out

All pencil marking out should be done with a finely sharpened, not too soft, pencil. The rule in marking out is that all lines which have to be cut across the grain must be marked with a knife to get the sharpest line, and all lines with the grain which are to be cut must be marked with a marking or mortice gauge. There are also occasions when lines across the grain are marked with a cutting gauge.

Marking gauges

These are the primary marking tools for lines with the grain. The usual pattern consists of a hardwood stock, often faced with brass to prevent wear, through which a stem passes. This stem has a spur fixed at one end and the stock can be fixed in any position along its length by turning a thumbscrew. Some gauges have measurements along the stem which start at the point of the spur; with this type, care must be taken to centre the point if it should have to be filed as a result of being damaged.

Cutting gauge

If a great deal of cutting is to be done across the grain, the cutting gauge can be used. In this, the spur is replaced by a little cutter held in place with a small brass wedge. They can be shaped to any of the shapes illustrated and can be made from scraps of hacksaw blade. The tool is useful for inlaying and veneering, and it can also be fitted with a cutter

Marking gauge

Marking gauge with ruled stem

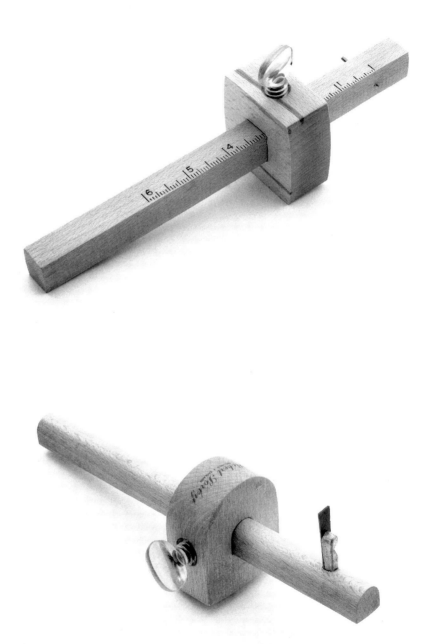

Cutting gauge

and used as a scratch stock when inlaying bandings and stringings.

Ulmia, a German firm, makes a marking gauge that has four stems with measurements along each one. With this gauge it is possible to mark out mortice and tenon and other joints requiring two lines at one setting. There is another gauge with twin beams.

Mortice gauge
The traditional way of marking out mortice and tenon joints is to use a mortice gauge; the one shown is made in rosewood throughout. The stock can be set at any position along the stem, which carries a fixed spur close to one end with another spur set in a slide. This slide can be moved by turning a thumbscrew at the end of the stem to set the spurs at the required width of mortice. A cheaper version is made in beech and has a simple slide.

Trammel gauge
Where there is a need to gauge large panels and wide pieces of timber, a combination trammel and panel gauge is available. The trammel heads can be located at any position along the stems and the tool can also be used to mark out circular work, which is

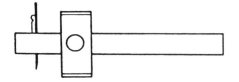

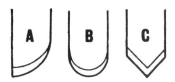

When marking out a groove the cutter is reversed.

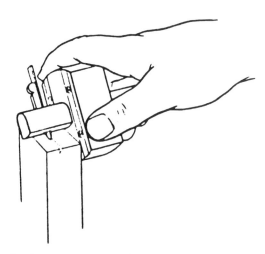

Cutting gauge cutter shapes and gauge in use

Mortice gauge

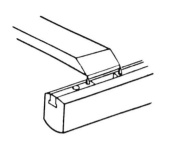

Set the spurs to chisel width when marking a mortice.

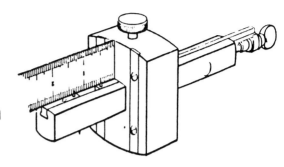

Hold stock firmly against the wood. Trail the spurs pushing the gauge away from the body.

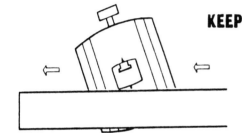

KEEP THE SPURS SHARP

This type can be reversed and used as a marking gauge

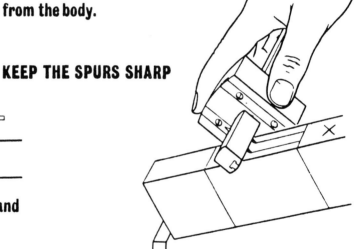

Setting and using the mortice gauge

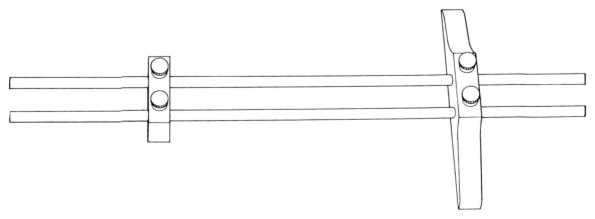

Trammel and panel gauge

Kunz trammel heads

a useful feature. Trammel heads can be bought separately and fitted to a beam made in the workshop from a strip of hardwood nicely planed and polished.

Butt gauge

A purpose-designed tool used in the marking out of the housings on doors for butt hinges. The spurs are located on slides, and once the gauge is set up the complete job of marking out for one or any number of doors can be carried out without further settings. It can also be used for marking up for the locks. A centre punch as used by a metalworker will be found useful to start the holes where boring is to take place or marking up screw positions through the hinges. One with a fine point is well worth having. Remember to keep the stock of the gauge tightly against the face of the timber and push the gauge away from you, trailing the spur; that is, you should be able to see the spur as the tool is pushed away. A light touch is all that is required as heavy gauge lines are not necessary.

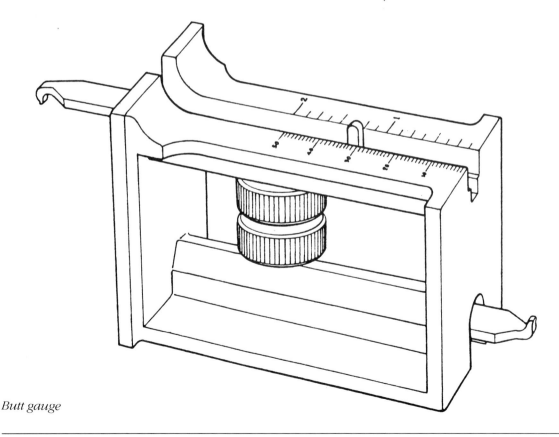

Butt gauge

SCREWDRIVERS

These are much-abused tools and are used for all sorts of unrelated jobs. Unfortunately, choosing a screwdriver is made a complex matter by the proliferation of styles and sizes available. In the old days all the handles were wooden and there was a limit to the variations and sizes which could be turned out by the manufacturers. With the introduction of plastics of various kinds the scene might well be described as daunting!

The choice must largely be determined by trying the screwdriver in the hand. The tool should seat comfortably, but don't be deceived as some are so comfortable, they are impossible to turn. Driving screws can be most painful if you are using the wrong size, as well as the wrong shape of screwdriver. The blade of the screwdriver must also be chosen to fit the recess or slot exactly. The best blades are made from chrome-vanadium steel, and it is best to buy from well known manufacturers as a guarantee of good quality. There are several screwdriver patterns, including the standard fixed blade, the ratchet, and the spiral ratchet. The favourite wooden-handled screwdriver in many workshops is the cabinet pattern, which is styled to fit the hand, and is made with the handle in ash, boxwood, or beech. The blade is flattened close to the ferrule so that a spanner can be used to apply extra torsion if necessary. Blades are from 3 to 10in (75 to 250mm) in length and are designed for slotted screws. A screwdriver designed for close work is the crutch type; its handle is a flat oval in shape and made from beech; the blade is 2in (50mm) long.

Screwdrivers are often struck with the hammer, and there is a pattern made with the steel passing through the handle to prevent breakage.

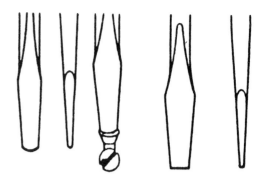

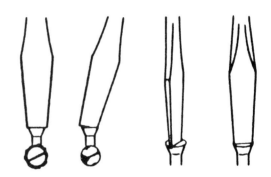

The screwdriver point must fit the slot

Cabinet screwdriver

Cruciform-pointed screwdrivers
Most of these have either *Philips* or *Pozidriv* points with plastic handles and they usually come in blade lengths from 3 to 8in (75 to 200mm), and also a 'chubby' size. They must be examined carefully to ensure an exact fit with the screw heads, and it is advisable to choose one carrying a well known name as the metal must have the correct hardness to ensure long lasting performance.

Some patterns have loose blades which can be inserted and locked into their handles so that either a cruciform or a slotted point is exposed.

Ratchet screwdrivers
These have three-way actions with the option of a fixed blade, and driving and withdrawing positions. Some patterns have a selection of pointed and slotted blades which can be interchanged; they are usually contained in a hollow plastic handle.

A useful screwdriver to have around is the offset for getting into awkward places – it can do 'round the corner' jobs in fact!

Bradawls
One way to make a start for a screw is by cutting a small hole with the bradawl. This usually has a small round blade sharpened like a chisel but with two bevels; the handles can be plastic or wood. The tool is inserted with the chisel-like blade across the grain to prevent splitting; then twisted through 90° several times to push it into the wood. Bradawls are usually classified as small, medium or large.

Gimlets
These have largely fallen into disuse, but will be found useful as a substitute for the bradawl. It has a small screwpoint and a fluted twist through which the waste emerges.

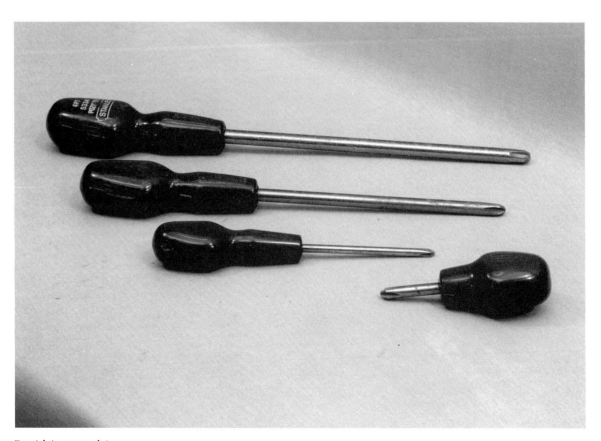

Pozidriv screwdrivers

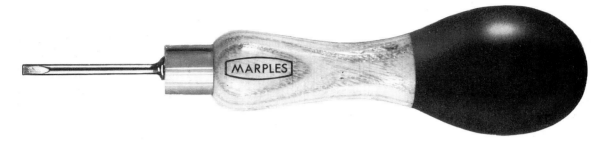

Bradawl

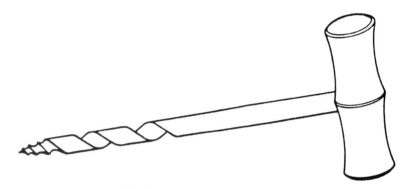

Gimlet

HAMMERS

There is certainly a multiplicity of hammers, and some understanding of their various purposes is necessary. Many hammers are badly made and often from the wrong materials.

The shafts are sometimes ash or hickory for strength and resilience, but many are now made of steel or plastic. A good wooden handle has its shaft end oil-shrunk to ensure a good fit and is wedged with a tiny wrought iron wedge.

Warrington pattern

This is probably the most popular and it has its drop-forged head carefully ground at the poll end with a flat peen for starting nails. It is available in six sizes: no. 00 6oz (170g); no. 0 8oz (227g); no. 1 10oz (283g); no. 2 12oz (340g); no. 3 14oz (397g); no. 4 16oz (454g).

Pin hammer

This is a light pattern with a head shaped similarly to the Warrington. It weighs $3\frac{1}{2}$oz (98g) and has a slim handle, and is used for driving pins, small nails, tiny brads, and glazier's sprigs.

Claw hammer

Generally made with a steel handle, also available with a wooden shaft. The latter is called the adze eye, which takes its name from the square eye of the carpenter's adze. There are two different shapes of claw; the straighter one is used for lifting nailed boards and opening packing cases; the quicker curve makes for easy removal of nails. The good claw hammer when stood on its head will balance with the shaft making an angle of 45° with the bench. The claw must be quite sharp and be forged to grip the nail; the best test you can give it is to drive a 4in (100mm) round wire nail through a 2in (50mm) plank. Then grip the pointed end with the claw and draw the nail through the plank, head last.

Steel-shafted hammers have some form of plastic or rubber coating on the handle.

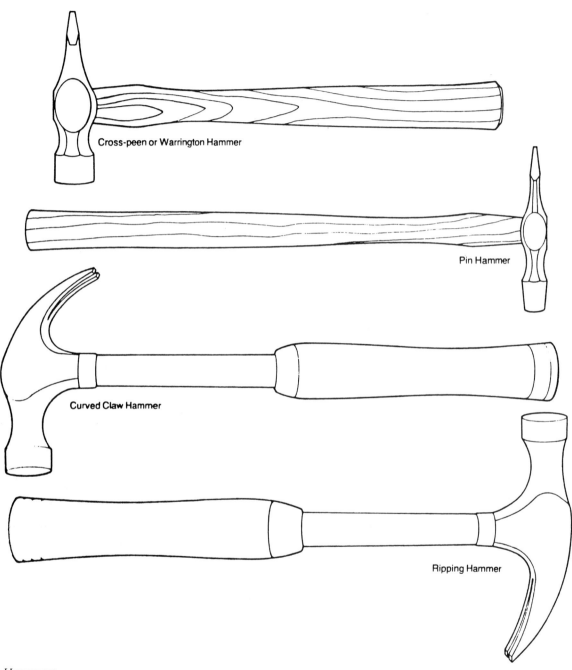

Cross-peen or Warrington Hammer

Pin Hammer

Curved Claw Hammer

Ripping Hammer

Hammers

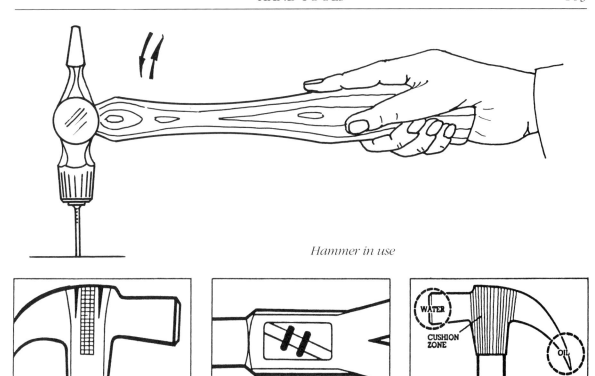

Hammer in use

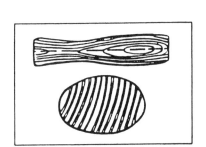

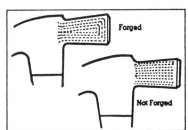

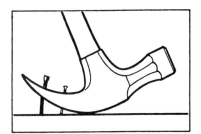

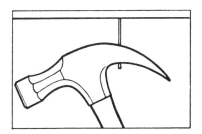

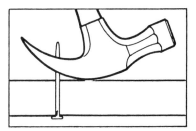

Stanley claw hammer in use

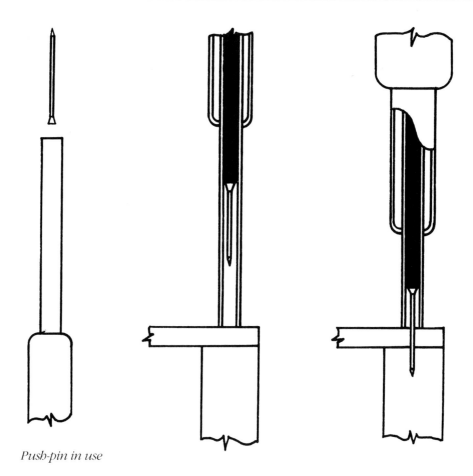

Push-pin in use

Push-pin

This is a useful tool which can be used to sub-stitute for the hammer. It has a barrel with a magnetised spring-loaded plunger and when a panel pin is dropped inside, the magnet holds it. A push on the handle drives it into the timber; the barrel supports the pin and prevents it from bend-ing. A very useful tool where a great number of pins have to be inserted.

Nail punches

Particularly useful for punching panel pins and small-headed nails below the surface of the wood. They are available in sizes to suit the size of nail head and are identified by numbers 1 to 6. The point is usually cupped to prevent the punch slipping off the nail.

Pincers

The best tool for withdrawing nails or pins. They are available in several sizes, measured from the tip of the arms to the centre pivot. The end of one arm is usually bifurcated to act as a tack lifter. Always place a waste block under the pincers when withdrawing a nail to prevent leverage marks on the finished work.

Mallets

These are best made in beech and fitted with an ash or hickory handle. The handle is wedge-shaped to lock firmly into the head. The most popular size has a 4in (100mm) head, but other sizes can be obtained.

Dowel planing board

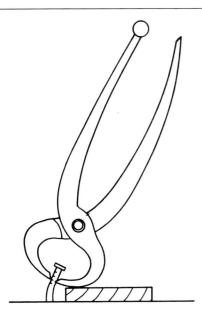

(left) *Withdrawing a pin with the pincers*

Mitre saws

Wooden mitre boxes have been popular for many years and are used particularly in the making of picture and other frames. Unfortunately after a period of use inaccuracies can creep in as a result of wear on the kerfs which guide the saw.

There are a number of excellent mitre-sawing devices made in metal, of which the *Nobex* range is typical. A number of different sizes are available with deep and shallow reach saws; the saw slides in a rigid frame and can be set at any angle and safely locked. The devices are designed to be screwed directly to the bench or to a board which can be held either in the vice or between bench dogs on the bench top. A length stop, a cramp, and a support for long workpieces are fitted.

(above) *Carpenter's mallet*

(opposite) *Dowel sawing board*   (above) *Nobex mitre saw*

Black and Decker Quattro drill

THE DIAGRAM BELOW DISPLAYS THE LIQUID CRYSTAL DISPLAY SCREEN AND PUSH BUTTON CONTROL PAD.

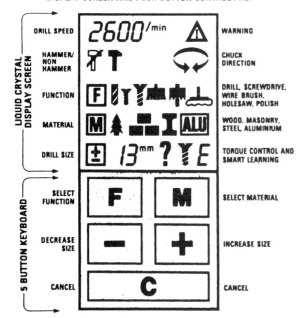

Black and Decker Quattro drill display panel

6
POWER TOOLS

The most widely used power tool in the home or woodworker's workshop is without doubt the electric drill, and soon after its introduction came several attachments to make it a multi-functional tool – circular saw, jigsaw, and planing attachments were the most popular. Manufacturers were quick to see the possibilities, and a wide variety of single purpose tools is now available at very reasonable cost.

The range and capacities of the many attachments make it possible to set up a workshop without the need for the heavier space-taking machines described in Chapter 7. Electric hand tools are dangerous if badly designed or carelessly used and should only be purchased from reputable suppliers. Most use a 220–240volt system, although some are now available using 110 volts, which is standard in the USA and some other countries. Such tools can, of course, be used but they need a transformer. Most tools are double-insulated which avoids the use of an earth wire.

When buying power tools it is advisable to buy an extension lead, preferably one supplied by the tool maker; it will be heavy duty quality and give longer life than the cheaper kinds. At the same time buy a cable reel which will store the cable safely and cut down wear and tear. Always run all of the cable completely off the reel when in use as this will eliminate any possibility of heat build-up.

Power tools constantly have so many new additional features that considerable care has to be exercised in their selection. Drills can have single or two speeds, or an infinitely variable range of speeds which can often be selected on a dial; many have torque control which allows the turning power provided by the drill to be adjusted or reduced, as when using the screwdriving function. Some operate as a single-speed drill, with forward and reverse motions, or they can be converted to give a hammer action for masonry work; many can be converted to act as screwdrivers without difficulty. The chucks can have 1/4, 5/16, 3/8, and 1/2in capacities (6, 8, 10, and 12mm). Routers not only have a range of collet capacities but can also have single or variable speeds either by operating the switch itself, or by dialling. Some power tools are equipped with a 'soft start' feature which eliminates torque and the resulting jerk when the tool is first switched on. Many cordless tools are now in use offering a long period of use before re-charging and this is particularly useful when driving screws.

Almost every power tool can be assembled to a table or stand to convert it to a bench- or floor-standing machine. This is a point which should always be kept in mind when making a decision, particularly if larger machines cannot be accommodated; and, of course the cash saving can be considerable.

THE ELECTRIC DRILL

This is the workhorse of power tools and drills of very high quality are included in the *Black and Decker Quattro* range. All have hammer actions which makes the drilling of masonry and concrete easy at the touch of a switch. Variable speed can be selected in some models, and the turn of a dial in the trigger caters for different drill sizes as well as materials of varying hardness and texture. All these drills have torque control which allows the turning power to be adjusted.

The *Quattro Digital* has automatic speed selection, soft start, reversing, electronic torque control, and a liquid crystal display panel which makes it just about the ultimate in drills. All have 1/2in (12mm) capacity chucks with 550 or 650 watts output, and speeds varying from machine to machine between 0 and 3,000rpm. All models in the range have a front handle, a screwdriver bit, and a depth stop.

The *Bosch* range of drills is an excellent example of ergonomic design as they fit beautifully into the hand, giving complete comfort during prolonged spells of drilling. Each handle is slim, easy to adjust, and has a ridge to prevent the hand from slipping. The recessed grip on the drill spindle lightens work requiring a high degree of pressure, and the switch is easy to reach. Most are equipped with infinitely adjustable electronic control for accurate and sensitive drilling. The top speed available is 3,000rpm on the *GBM 6E* model; forward and reverse is standard on the *GBM 10 RE*, and the fact that screwdriver bits can be directly inserted into the drill spindle is a useful feature. This drill has a belt-holding clip so that the user has both hands free, and the drill is always close to hand.

Cordless tools

These are now well accepted by woodworkers and most power tool manufacturers offer a range, and the cordless drill and cordless screwdriver are certainly often used for a number of jobs both in and out of doors.

Panasonic probably have the most superior range of drills and drivers yet seen; charging times vary from manufacturer to manufacturer and *Panasonic* have come up with the 15 minute 'coffee break' charge, which is unique. The *EY 6200BC* cordless drill and screwdriver offers speeds at no-load of 350 and 1,300rpm. It has a ½in (12mm) chuck capacity, and the handle is comfortable and also houses the battery pack. The charger is equipped with a lamp display that indicates the status of five charging functions at a glance. The drill can be used after recharging for only three minutes, and this is a useful feature to have in an emergency. This model also has a versatile support handle which is fitted at the forward end of the body, and it can be used for drilling in metal or wood, and with hole saws fitted; in its driving mode it can cope with screws for steel and wood.

Bosch have the *GBM 12* which has a twelve-volt

Bosch GBM 10RE Professional drill

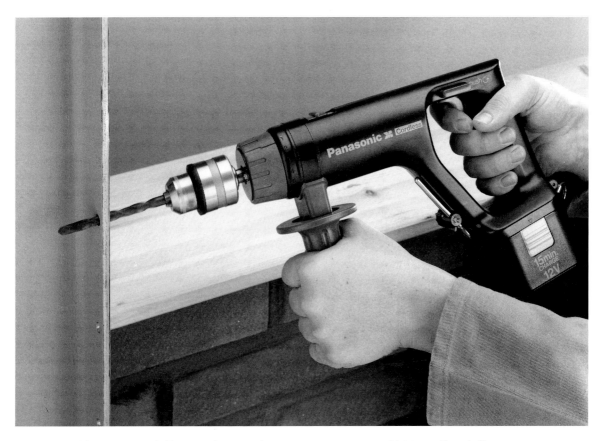

Panasonic EY6200 cordless drill

battery enabling more drilling and screwdriving from one charge. Re-charging takes one hour and the charger is automatically switched off by temperature and charge-time monitors if overloading threatens. The electronic control ensures steady starting up as well as smooth speed control and sensitive operation correct for the material being worked on. The speed and torque in forward as well as reverse rotation can be well matched to the particular job by means of the mechanical dual-speed gearing. Screwdriver bits and the chuck key are conveniently stored in the drill casing. Speeds of 500 and 1,000rpm enable holes up to ³⁄₈in (10mm) to be drilled in metal and ⁵⁄₈in (15mm) in wood. The drill weighs about 3¹⁄₂lb (1.5kg).

CIRCULAR SAWS

I struggled for a long time with a circular saw attachment fixed to a *Wolf* drill then changed to a *Black*

and Decker 7¹⁄₄in (185mm) blade saw which I have used for many years. Portable circular saw design has made vast strides since those days and a look at the *Festo* range of circular saws illustrates a number of tools with the flexibility to tackle work in a great number of materials.

The *ATF 55E* is typical, it has a 240 volt universal motor with a power consumption of 1,200 watts and speeds of 2,000 to 4,600rpm. The saw blade is 160mm (6¹⁄₄in) in diameter with a cutting depth up to 51mm (2in), and the facility to cut bevels between 0° and 45°; the blade has a protective cover and riving knife. The saw has controlled smooth start-up which protects the motor, the gears, and the bearings. Its idling speed is also controlled, and makes much less noise than normal. Since the power consumption is controlled, the cutting speed is constant, but the cutting speeds can be set to suit various materials. A visual LED display indicates whether

Bosch GBM 12 VE cordless drill

the saw is being used correctly or is overloaded, and an electrically controlled overload cut-out and a thermal overload control prevents damage to the motor. The saw is fitted with a dust extraction connection and has good safety cover which allows the saw to be seen through a visor panel.

All the saws in the range can be used with the *FS* guide rail, which is available in several lengths and gives greater precision in cutting, plus cleanly cut edges and a scratch-free workpiece, together with low friction while moving the saw. A high quality tungsten-carbide-tipped blade is supplied and a fitted spindle stop makes for easy changing. Other saws are available with different depths of cut.

JIGSAWS (also called 'sabre saws')

There are a number of options available in most jigsaws, and one of the most desirable is the 'change-direction' blade. The *Black and Decker 538SE* has electronic speed control giving strokes between 800 and 3,200 per minute. The correct speed for the material can be dialled into the unit, and the motor speed is then electronically adjusted to suit the task in hand. High speeds are provided for timber and man-made materials, while lower speeds are suitable for cutting plastics and tiles. The 'change-direction' or scrolling facility is particularly useful whenever curves or tight angles have to be cut, and this means that the blade can be locked quickly to point forwards, backwards or sideways, or continuously steered during cutting to form even the most complex shapes without problems.

The *Bosch PST 65* pendulum jigsaw is electronically controlled with speeds between 500 and 3,000rpm, and the thumb wheel for setting the speed is integrated into the switch. The electronic control offers not only precision sawing and precise operation to selected settings, but also smooth 'acceleration' if necessary. The saw blade can be easily and quickly changed without the need for a screwdriver or other tool, and the bayonet closure ensures the secure positioning of the blade without any chance of the blade becoming loose or changing position while in use.

A three-stage pendulum action of the saw blade ensures minimum wear and tear on the blade and reduces operator effort. The saw is fitted with a dust extraction facility. Depth of cut in wood is possible up to 65mm (2½in); in plastic 20mm (¾in); in aluminium 15mm (⁹⁄₁₆in), and in steel 6mm (¼in).

The *Festo* pendulum jigsaw is an elegant and professional-looking tool with infinitely adjustable electronic control for a wide variety of materials. It can be used with the previously mentioned *FS* guide rail system which guarantees very precise cutting. The stroke length is 25mm (1in), with a depth of cut up to 54mm (2¼in); bevel adjustment up to 45° is possible at both sides. The saw blade rests in a three-stage guide, and runs in a lifting guide mechanism which gives stability and precise cutting, while the pendulum guide roller also provides a rear support for the blade. A splinter guard is also provided which gives clean-cut edges while the adjustable pendulum stroke gives versatility. A plastic base runner is fitted to prevent scratching the workpiece, and the saw table is fitted with an extractor duct. Other worthwhile features are that the body provides a comfortable two-hand hold; a chip guard allows an unimpeded view of the cutting action, and the saw can be fitted to a work module which converts it to a saw table.

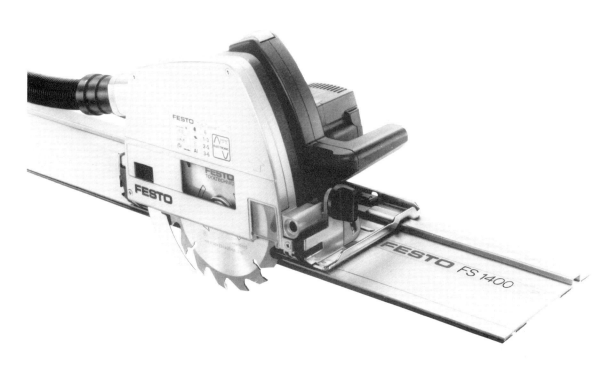

Festo FS1400 circular saw, with FS guide

Black and Decker 538 electronic jigsaw

(right) *Bosch pendulum jigsaw PST 65*

(below) *Festo pendulum jigsaw HL85E*

PLANERS

The portable power planer is no substitute for its bigger brother the bench planer, but it cannot be bettered for planing a job in situ like a sticking door, or for roughing down sawn timber away from the workshop – it is certainly useful for work 'on site', particularly if it can be used in the inverted position to convert it to a small bench planer.

An example with almost every feature is the *Festo HL 850E* (the whisper-quiet). It has a width of 82mm (3¼in) with a maximum cutting depth of 3.5mm (¼in), and an unlimited rebate depth due to the unique fact that the front edge of the planer head is fully exposed, permitting 'into-the-corner-cutting' as with the bench rebate plane. The electronic control

gives a run-up speed of 10,000rpm. A very simple chip thickness adjustment is made using a mechanism built into the support handle. Great stability is provided by a rigid planing base and a bearing housing in die-cast aluminium. The planer head has only one cutter which eliminates the need to adjust the cutter diameter, while the *Spir-o-cut* cutter produces a quieter action through the 'pulling' cut of the blade. The spindle is fitted with a lock button which allows quick and safe cutter change and there is a safety rest which prevents the cutter head from contacting the workpiece surface.

The planer has a fence which can be used for curved and straight work, and the whole machine can be attached to a fitting so that it can be inverted to convert it to a bench planer. A dust extraction point

Festo power planer

is also provided which is accessible from both sides, and the handles are well shaped and positioned to give firm control. There are no problems in use, but the workpiece must be held securely, and checked to see that it is free from nails and screws.

MISCELLANEOUS TOOLS

All-purpose saw

This saw is made by *Bosch* and is a modern innovation which has an orbital blade motion. It is fitted with a cut-out feature which stops the blade immediately the power is turned off, and it is also fitted with a safety catch. The saw cuts fast, with little physical effort being required. In addition, the orbital action prevents a build-up of rust on the blade which could result in overheating. It is fitted with a 550 watt motor, which permits cutting timber up to 150mm (6in) in thickness, and 12mm (½in) in steel and aluminium alloys.

Bosch all-purpose saw

Chop saw

This is a saw of increasing popularity and it is ideal for the picture framer and for work around the home demanding angled cuts. The fully guarded blade is 8¼in (210mm) in diameter, giving a 2³/₁₆in (55mm) depth of cut. It requires a 1,050 watt input, and runs at 4,000rpm.

Orbital sanders

These have been with us for over forty years, and although the electronics and sizes have changed, they are still the same useful tools for general sanding work.

Festo have a number of sizes to suit specific jobs, with one- and two-hand-held models which are useful in a number of trades other than woodworking. Speedy material removal to delicate finishing with dust extraction facility is common to these machines.

The *RS1* model is fitted with a 240 volt universal

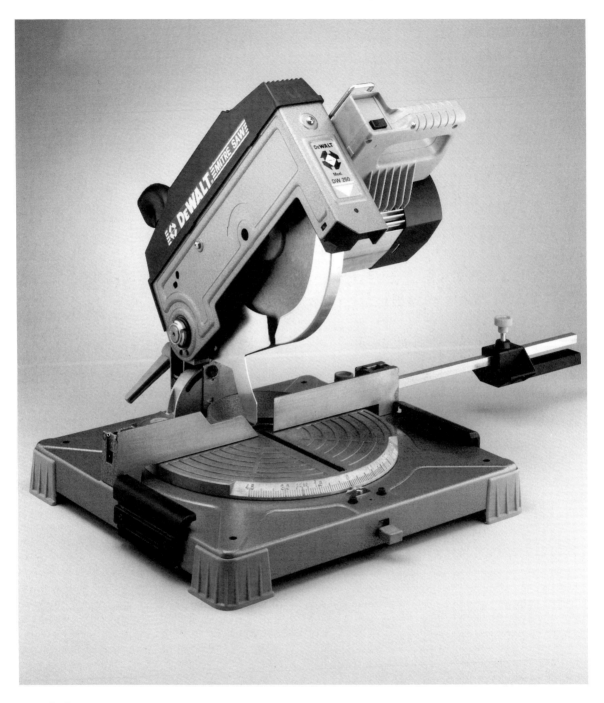

Dewalt chop saw

Festo orbital sander

motor and a power consumption of 550 watts. The motor speed is 6,000rpm giving 12,000 × 5mm strokes per minute. The standard sanding base is 115 × 225mm (4½ × 9in) and is interchangeable. The tool handles well, and has a handle at the front which can be swivelled to steer the machine in any direction, while the rear handle contains the switch and locking button. There is a clamping device that tensions the paper to give longer life by eliminating the sagging which often causes the paper to tear. *Festo* also have an ingenious method of instant fixing of the paper which they call 'Stickfix'. The sander is fitted with turbo dust extraction and has a simple connector for attaching the extraction hose. The *RS4E* is a one-hand sander with a base size of 80 × 130mm (3⅛ × 5⅛in) and its electronic control gives speeds between 4,000 and 10,000rpm with 8,000 to 20,000 strokes per minute. Another in the range has an extended base which allows sanding on both sides – this is a useful feature for sanding hard-to-reach places and also grooves and joints.

Angle grinders

This is not a woodworker's tool, but, with the introduction of wood-cutting discs like the *Arbortech*, it will have increasing use in the woodshop. The *Black and Decker SR800E* Plus has 600 watts input with a speed of 10,000rpm. It accepts a 4½in (115mm) disc and is fitted with an electronic safety clutch. A spindle lock makes disc changing easy. A side handle makes for good control and the switch is conveniently placed under the right-hand body grip. The machine is adequately guarded and should never be used without the guard, unless ordinary sanding discs are in use on timber. The development of different kinds of cutting discs will widen the field of work possible with this machine.

Black and Decker SR 800E Plus angle grinder,
fitted with Arbortech cutter

Belt sander

Some woodworkers prefer the straight cutting action of a belt sander, but care must always be taken to hold the machine down flat otherwise the edges of the belt may score the work; also, take care when working on edges and curves to avoid tearing the belts. There are several sizes of machine to suit different widths of belt.

The *Bosch PBS 60* is an example of a machine accepting a belt width of 60mm (2⅜in), and it has an input wattage of 550 with a no-load speed of 280m (920ft) per minute. Other features include integral dust extraction and removable handles to permit working into corners and near edges. The system of belt tensioning is effective and the tool handles well. A range of models is available to suit most applications.

Rotary sander and polisher

A tool which must become popular although it is not well known at the present time is the *Festo Rotex*. This machine combines both rotary and eccentric motion for removing material at a high rate, but for fine sanding the rotary motion can be switched off; it also has an electronic speed control which provides different sanding speeds to suit the work. It can be fitted with hard or soft sanding pads, a 25 piece polishing set is available; and it employs the 'Stickfix' method of attaching the sanding discs.

Drill stands

Most small workshops will not have the bench or the floor space to accommodate a drill press. The drill stand will be found to be an excellent substitute and need not be fixed to a bench.

The basic requirement is that it will hold the electric drill securely; all modern stands have the 'Euro-norm' fitting on the drill housing, but where there are problems of fitting, collars are often available. A good quality solid steel column is desirable with adequate springing to return the drill to its topmost position. An effective guard should be supplied with the stand, and the table should be slotted to attach a drill press vice; the stand must also have a depth stop fitted.

The *Wolfcraft Heavy Duty* stand is a typical example. The one illustrated has a machining table fitted.

Drill and mill attachment

This is an excellent workshop aid which can convert your electric drill into a router. If you already have a router with a removable body, it can be fitted to the drill and mill, enabling the router to be used at any

Bosch belt sander

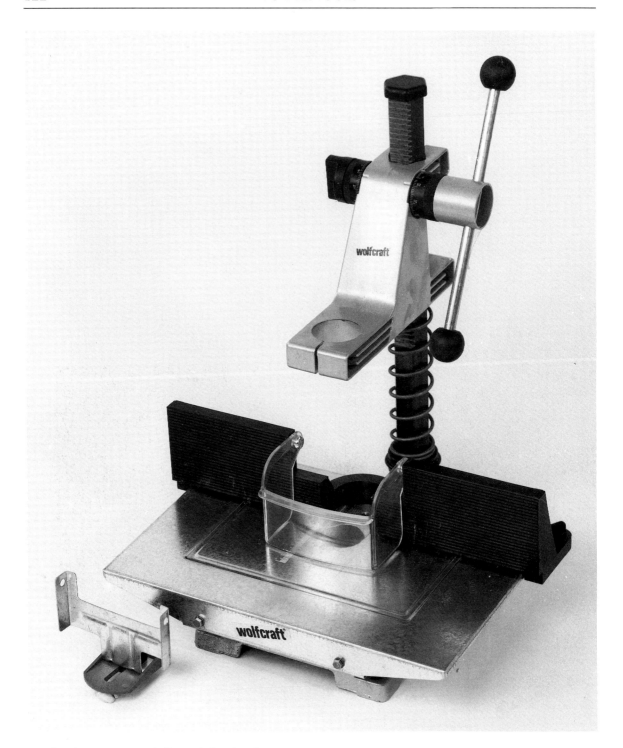

Wolfcraft Heavy Duty drill stand, fitted with a machining table

(opposite) *Wolfcraft drill and mill attachment*

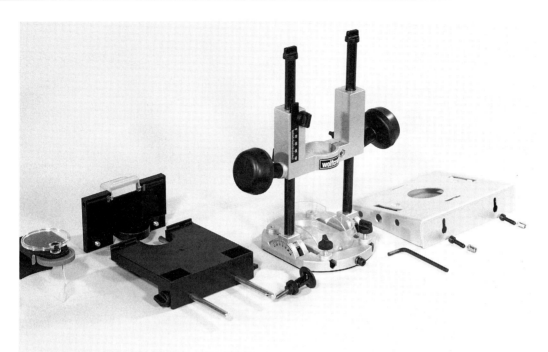

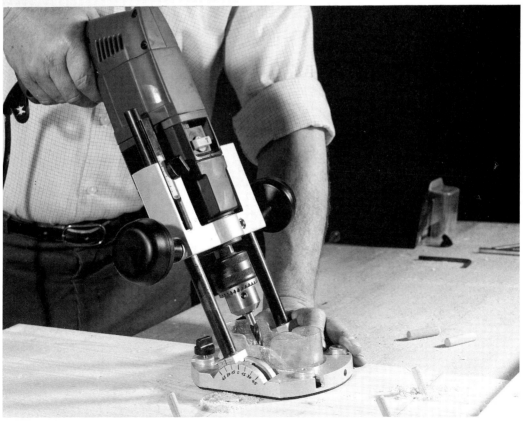

Wolfcraft bench sander attachment

angle to increase its versatility. It can be used to drill holes at any angle up to 45°, and I have found it extremely useful when drilling holes in the wall to receive plugs, particularly at an angle or above the head. A small table can be fitted to the side of the woodwork bench converting the router or drill into a milling device for cutting curves with the curved milling guide, and it also has a guide for circle cutting.

Bench sander

Another attachment which can save space and money is the bench sander to which an electric drill can be attached. The *Wolfcraft* model can be attached to the edge of any bench or table. Its table can be tilted to 45°, and it has a small adjustable fence enabling square and angled work to be carried out. If you intend to set up your own grinding and sharpening corner, you can consider one of these which, when fitted with the paper of the correct grit size, will give excellent grinding and sharpening facilities. The disc is 178mm (7in) in diameter.

Benches for storing power tools

One of these may be useful for the small workshop and for the woodworker who may only need to set up a power tool in the bench mode occasionally.

The *Wolfcraft Pioneer 6170* combines the function of a small workbench and power tool table with the added feature that it can be folded quickly and easily for storage. The overall height is 830mm (32⅝in), and the overall width is 850mm (33⅜in). The shaper and sawing table measures 400 × 500mm (15¾ × 19⅝in) while the worktop measures 450 × 500mm (17¾ × 19⅝in). The steel underframe is fitted with a tool tray and wheels for easy transportation; a vice with wooden jaw is also supplied and the top is bored with three rows of holes which can be used for cramping up with bench dogs. The top can be swivelled for easy tool mounting, and a fence together with a transparent guard, a switch clamp, and a pushstick are supplied as standard. It will accept a drill, jigsaw, circular saw or router, and a number of *Wolfcraft* attachments can also be fitted.

7

FLOOR-STANDING AND STATIC MACHINES

These can be very expensive investments, and consequently buying one must be considered very carefully. The main considerations are the work load which can be undertaken, the working space needed, and the overall cost in relation to the volume of work the machine is to be given. The cost of buying planed and prepared timber can be considerable, and the saving of this cost, together with the saving of time must also be prime considerations, particularly in a small production workshop.

They divide into two groups, namely bench-mounted or floor-mounted machines, and almost every type is available for the home workshop, or those designed for production work. Several multi-purpose machines are popular, especially where space is at a premium and a convenient and permanent position in the workshop can be allotted to it.

When preparing to buy a machine, the following points need to be considered:

Its position on either the floor or the bench.

Whether or not it can be brought through the door of the shop.

Space must be sufficient to allow timber to be passed through the machine and to leave it at the opposite end. In small workshops this means having an opening window or a door placed conveniently.

Good space around the machine so that you can move safely.

The position of the isolating switch must be decided upon, and the method of conducting the power to the machine must be safe – trailing cable can be dangerous cable!

Solid floors present no problem, but suspended floors will need to be checked to ensure they will carry the weight of the machine.

Special arrangements may be necessary where the machine has to be pushed against a wall.

Adequate lighting is essential not only for setting up the machine but for general safety while using it.

The amount of waste created by machines is considerable and wherever possible an extraction system, either as a permanent or a portable feature (which can be moved around the shop) should be considered. Shavings tend to polish the floor and make it slippery and this can be dangerous.

CIRCULAR SAW

The most widely used machine is the circular saw and probably it will be the first machine you will install. Whether it be floor or bench mounted, the main features will be the same. The saw must be able to make angled cuts, and cut accurately across the grain at 90° and other angles. It must have a good flat table, be adequately guarded, and the fences must be at right angles to the table and to the sawblade wherever they are positioned.

The *Startrite Tilt Arbor* sawbench is a typical pattern, having a robust 22 × 23in (560 × 585mm) steel table with two accurately ground mitre gauge slideways. A steel bar which is securely bolted to the front edge provides the slide support for a rip fence which can be quickly and firmly fixed in any position. This fence also has a fine screw adjustment and a divided scale for extremely accurate setting.

The saw arbor is in high tensile steel and mounted in 'sealed-for-life' bearings while the drive is by means of a short centre dual vee-belt from the motor. The mounting of the drive mechanism is adjustable and entirely independent of the base. Two fast-acting handwheels provide rapid height and angle settings with a positive stop at 90° . The

Startrite Tilt Arbor sawbench

rise-and-fall and tilt motions are locked simultaneously with a single handknob. A heavy-duty welded steel cabinet includes a sawdust chute, a removable cowl, bolting-down holes, and provision for the attachment of extraction tubing.

The safety guard and riving knife both conform to British standards and the knife always aligns correctly with the sawblade. The scales are easily read, and there is ready access to the saw through a large insert in the table alongside the blade.

A push-button starter with thermal overload and no-volt release protection is fitted, and the machine is driven by a 1¼hp motor, giving a peripheral blade speed of 6,750ft (2,059m) per minute.

The 9in (230mm) diameter saw gives 3½in (90mm) of saw projection at 90°, and 2⅛in (55mm) at 45°. The table capacity is 14⅛in (358mm) from the rip fence to the right of the saw, and 8½in (215mm) to the left. A full range of sawblades and other accessories is available.

Many tables can be fitted with an extension piece for large workpieces, and some of the larger ones have roller-mounted sliding tables. The *145* and others can also be fitted with a roll-off table to support the timber as it passes through the machine.

THE PLANER

Although planing timber by hand will always be with us since we demand a very high standard of sizing and finishing, an increasing number of high quality machines and tungsten-carbide-tipped knives ensures a very high degree of perfection and helps to eliminate the hard work.

The jointer is the term sometimes applied to the planing machine, underlining one of its principal uses which is the shooting of edges for board jointing. The planer/thicknesser is now the accepted machine for timber preparation and a wide selection is available.

In this regard a number of factors need to be considered, such as the capacity relative to the thickness of cut, and also the width of the cutter, and the thickness of material which the machine will accept. High revolutions of the spindle are required if the knives are to do their work and this factor must be checked together with the cutter block, which should conform to industrial safety standards.

Machines must be capable of feeding the material through when thicknessing, and this can be by either belt or chain drive, or a separate motor can be fitted for the purpose. The hinged tables which convert the machine to thicknessing operations must be fitted with a safety lock. Controls must be accessible and the scales for setting up easily seen; while the chutes must be well designed to carry away the waste without the working parts becoming choked.

Startrite Planer and Thicknesser PT260
This is a typical example of a low-cost machine, but it has most of the features required. It is well made and attractively finished, having cast-iron tables which are accurately machined and ribbed for strength. Two knives are located in a steel planer block which runs in 'sealed-for-life' bearings. Deflector plates

protect the infeed and outfeed rollers from being clogged with shavings.

The machine is fully guarded, having a cutter block bridge guard, a rear fence guard, a thicknessing guard, and a chip deflector. The planer fence tilts to 45°. The table has a surface capacity of 10¼in (260mm), with a total table length of 39⅜in (1m). Its outfeed table is 10⅜in (265mm) wide and the infeed 13½in (342mm). There are two knives and the cutterblock speed is 6,000rpm, while the thicknessing depth is 7in (180mm) and the width 10¼in (263mm). It is fitted with a push-button starter with overload and no-volt protection.

Rebates can be cut to a depth of ⁹⁄₁₆in (14mm) and there is a special holding device which can be fitted for safety. A lever action on the feed table allows quick and easy setting to the depth required. The thicknessing table can be raised or lowered by means of a handwheel on the right-hand side, which can be locked against an easily read scale calibrated in imperial and metric.

THE BANDSAW

There are many designs available and the choice should be made carefully as a machine not having the correct features can really be a source of great trouble. A floor-mounted model is probably the best choice, and a number of them can be adapted to stand on a bench. The capacity of the throat and the depth of cut are important, and the maximum width of blade which can be used considered having in mind the material which will be sawn. The actual construction must be robust, and the machine should have large wheels which are totally enclosed with hinged doors. A tracking and tensioning device for the blade, with top and bottom guides, is an obvious necessity.

Startrite Bandsaw 301
This machine is a good example of a machine for general small workshop use, and has a medium capacity at reasonable cost.

It has a rip fence, a mitre gauge, a circle-cutting attachment and a depth stop for tenoning. The motor is direct drive, and its cutting speed is suitable for

Startrite Planer and Thicknesser PT260

timber, plastics, laminates, and man-made boards. It has a throat capacity of 11¾in (295mm) and a full 6in (152mm) under the saw guides. The guides comprise simple blocks with large working faces and tungsten-carbide thrust pads to reduce maintenance; they can be adjusted for blades up to ⅝in (16mm) wide. The table tilts to 45°, and used in conjunction with the mitre guide, accurate compound angles can be cut. A simple circle-cutting attachment is also fitted. A fence, which locates on a steel bar fixed to the front of the table, presents the timber squarely and attached to it is a stop bar for use when tenoning.

Maximum protection is assured with steel guards over the wheels both above and below the table; interchangeable wheels are a feature and they are mounted in 'sealed-for-life' bearings with a motor of ¾hp giving a blade speed of 3,000ft (914m) per minute. The switch, which incorporates thermal overload and no-volt release, is placed close to the left hand on the body of the machine. Sawdust drops into the lower compartment of the stand, simplifying its removal.

SPINDLE MOULDERS

This machine has grown in popularity with all serious woodworkers, but it is quite a specialised tool that can also prove to be expensive. Much of the work carried out on this machine could, in fact, be done on a power router fixed to a reliable router bench.

The machine must be of stout construction, preferably with a cast iron table. The vital component is the spindle which must be very stoutly made and of large diameter; the cutters must be housed safely and locked in the head. Well-designed guards are essential together with a holding-down device as large amounts of timber are removed with some cutters. Fences must be strongly constructed, and for the end spindling of long boards a sliding extension table on the left of the cutter is needed.

Startrite Spindle Moulder
This is a very strongly made floor-standing machine with a machined cast iron table. It is fitted with a deep fence with two independent micro-adjustable faces that permit perfect settings. Standard fittings in-

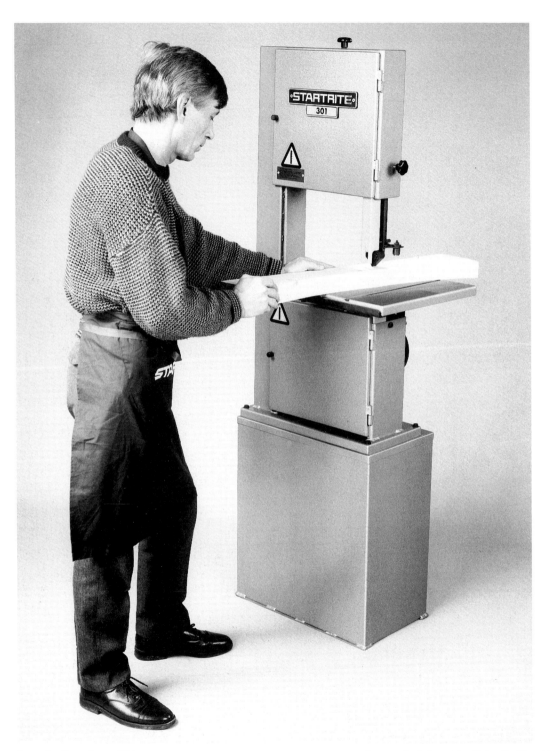

Startrite Bandsaw 301

(opposite) *Startrite Spindle Moulder*

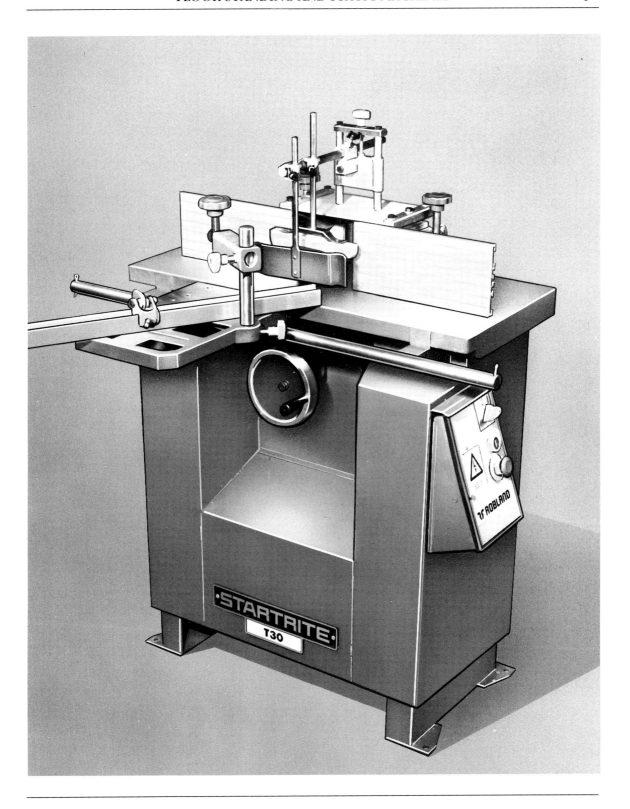

clude a hold-down and side-pressure spring unit, and sliding table complete with a long fence bar and an end stop. A large-diameter spindle with spacing collars runs in high-speed bearings at 6,000rpm, powered by a 3hp motor. Rise and fall is adjusted by a lockable handwheel. All the working parts are housed in a steel cabinet.

The table measures 360 × 800mm (14¼ × 31½ in), and the sliding table 240 × 375mm (9½ × 14⅞in) with a stroke of 710mm (28in). The cutter head is 95mm (3¾in) diameter by 45mm (1¾in) deep. It comes with a set of nine pairs of moulding cutters and two pairs of grooving saw segments. The cutters are held in safety-type wedge jaws and are of thick construction providing the ultimate in safety. An additional safety screw locates through a hole in each cutter and is turned with an Allen key. Recessed apertures on the periphery house the saw segments. The cutter head is set flush with the spindle to facilitate deep undercut work.

Cutterhead suitable for flush mounting on spindle head for deep undercut work.

Extra wide and thick cutters self-seating in safety type wedge jaw.

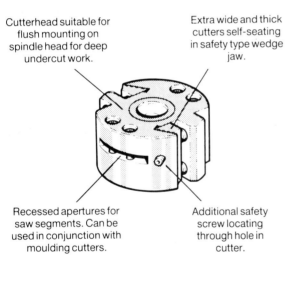

Recessed apertures for saw segments. Can be used in conjunction with moulding cutters.

Additional safety screw locating through hole in cutter.

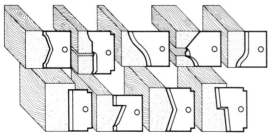

Startrite cutter head and range of cutters

THE MULTI-PURPOSE MACHINE or 'Universal woodworker'

It has been said many times that there cannot be a really perfect multi-purpose machine as it's bound to fail or be a poor substitute for the individual machine in one or other of its functions. With a number of these machines only one motor is fitted and belts have to be changed, and this is difficult and time-wasting. Sometimes one function partly obstructs or makes the use of another difficult, if not dangerous. A well-built machine, and there is no substitute for it, is extremely heavy and must have a permanent place in the workshop with plenty of working space around it. The safety arrangements must not be poorer than those on the comparable individual machines, and the capacity and scope of each function must also compare favourably. Unfortunately some machines look like individual items put together without much thought.

Startrite Super 260

This machine looks good; the tables are all at the same height, and each function is clearly divorced from the others, and at the same time it gives an impression of neatness and functional efficiency.

The machine incorporates the operations of a surfacer, a thicknesser, a circular saw, a spindle moulder, and a morticer. The three main tables are in finegrained cast iron accurately machined and ground. The planer block, saw, and spindle bearings are 'sealed-for-life'.

Three separate motors with selective switching enable you to move immediately from one function to another without belt-changing; each function is adequately guarded and fitted with accurately set fences, and a neat steel cabinet contains the motors, driving belts and electrical fittings.

The surfacer has extra-long tables, both of which are adjustable. The safety-type cutter block has three high-speed steel knives which are sprung for easier setting; the fence, which can be tilted, locks at 90° and 45°, and incorporates a rear guard.

The thicknesser requires the tables to be raised and the chip deflector automatically moves into position; an optional deflector can be fitted up to

Multi-purpose machine

connect with an extraction system – a very desirable feature as chips seem to fly everywhere. Power-operated feed rollers are operated by a clutch lever, and an anti-kickback device is fitted for safety and allows the machining of more than one piece of stock without their being ejected. All adjustments are by handwheel which can be locked against an easily read scale.

The circular saw has a quick lever-action rise and fall arbor and angles can be set against a clearly marked scale with position stops at 90° and 45°. A TCT (tungsten-carbide-tipped) blade is fitted to a ball-bearing-mounted spindle with a riving knife supporting the guard. A rip fence, a sliding table and a mitre gauge are supplied as standard.

The spindle moulder has all the features of the conventional individual machine. A spring-loaded locking device enables quick assembly of the various cutters; three removable ring inserts up to 180mm (7in) are set in the work table allowing large-diameter cutter blocks to be partly lowered into the table. The sliding table can be used in conjunction with the main table for long work.

The morticer has a quick take-off facility to avoid obstructing the planing operation. The chuck is mounted on the end of the planer cutter block, allowing left-hand mortice cutters and boring bits up to 16mm (⅝in) diameter to be used. The large table is raised, lowered, and locked by hand wheel, and a longitudinal and transverse movement on revolving

Radial arm saw

Multico morticer

slides gives a smooth and easy action. There are adjustable stops for length and depth with lever control handles which can be removed easily.

Radial arm saw

This is a useful machine in small and large scale production workshops and timber merchants' yards as it can be utilised as a cross-cut cut-off saw for cutting timber to length. However, in the small shop it can do any number of tasks because the sawing head can be angled on the arm and also set at right angles to it for use as a through-and-through saw. There are some disadvantages when it is used in the small workshop as it needs access space at both sides so that long lengths of timber can be dealt with free of obstruction; it also requires time for setting up, and it cannot be stored away easily as it needs a place of its own, although one model can be folded back so that it stores closely against a wall. The machine has a direct drive motor; its driving spindle can

Record floor-mounted morticer

accept not only saw blades, but also dado cutters, moulding heads, and even boring tools. The motor assembly moves along the arm which in turn can be raised or lowered, while the column allows the arm to be pivoted so that cuts can be made from the normal 90° cross-cut position to any other desired angle. The saw is fully guarded and is drawn towards the operator making for safe cutting as the main thrust is downwards and backwards.

Morticer

This consists basically of a hollow square mortice chisel which actually cuts the sides of the mortice with a twist auger revolving inside it to cut the waste away and pass the shavings through apertures in the sides of the chisel.

A *Wolf* drill can be set up in a drill stand which has been fitted with a morticing attachment to hold the hollow chisel and bit, and for the small workshop this is ideal. A similar assembly can be fitted with cramps to hold the material, with a depth-setting device mounted on the drill pillar. Many bench- and floor-mounted drill presses can also be fitted with morticing attachments and they work extremely well. There are also a number of machines using the hollow chisel and capable of cutting large and small mortices with great speed, while chain morticers are used in larger production shops.

By far the most important parts of the machine are the hollow chisel and bit. Great care must be taken in setting up so that the bit cuts just ahead of the chisel, the chisel finally taking out the corner and squaring the hole. The method of setting up is shown opposite. The first step is to open up the drill chuck, then insert the hollow chisel and the bit, locking the chisel in place. After placing a two-pence piece between the chisel shoulder and the face of the holder to act as a distance guide, tighten down on the chisel fixing screw. Now push the bit fully into the chisel and use the chuck key to tighten it down on the shank. Slacken the screw holding the chisel, then push it fully home into the holder, and remove the coin. The bit will now cut just ahead of the chisel.

Mortices can also be cut using a panel cutter in a portable power router; or by a side cutting drill fitted in any rotating head if setting and holding devices are present, and also by using a slot mortice miller bit instead of the hollow chisel in the drilling machine.

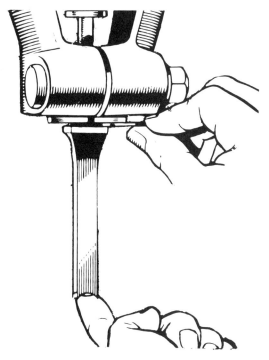

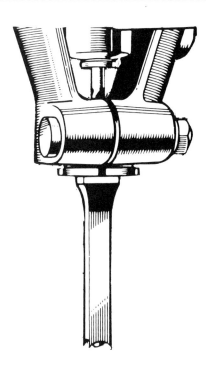

Setting the hollow mortice chisel and bit

Scroll saw

A useful tool for the model maker as well as the woodworker needing to make curved cuts in a range of thin materials. A well designed machine will accept a range of fret- and coping-saw blades with a number of options of throat depth. The *Multico Pro-Mex* scroll saws have three options of throat namely 18, 22 and 26in (460, 560 and 660mm). Constructed in grey iron with a precision-ground tilting work-table $17\frac{1}{2} \times 8\frac{3}{4}$in ($445 \times 224$mm) on the smallest machine. The worktable on this machine tilts to 30° and its depth of cut is 2in (50mm).

The $\frac{1}{8}$hp motor gives 1,720 cuts per minute; and the blade is fitted with a guard and also a dust pump to clear the dust at the point of work so that you can see to cut accurately. The arm is adjustable to accept different lengths of blade and a simple blade clamping device makes for speedy changing.

Bench and pillar drilling machines

Many will question the need for a large drilling machine in the woodwork shop, but it can not only bore holes but also act as a morticer. The choice of a bench or a floor machine will depend to a large extent on the amount of space available. The size of material to be bored and the diameter of hole will

also dictate the chuck and throat capacity. A choice of speeds is essential since large holes bored in timber will require slower speeds than smaller ones – probably four or five speeds will be adequate, but if the machine is also to be used on metal, then a wider range with higher speeds will be needed. The chuck should have a capacity of $\frac{1}{2}$in (12mm), and its jaws should meet perfectly so that the tiny drills can be held safely. The table should have a rack and pinion rise and fall system and be capable of being tilted; it should also be slotted to receive the bolts for attaching a drill press vice. In order to conform to the Health and Safety at Work Act the chuck must be fitted with a safety guard. *Startrite* offer two good examples of this type of machine, which can also be fitted with a morticing attachment.

Wet and dry grinders

There are many designs available and you need to consider the type and amount of work to which the machine is to be put before you make a choice.

The setting up of a small sharpening corner has been suggested, and you may wish to add a machine which will do the odd metal grinding job as well as

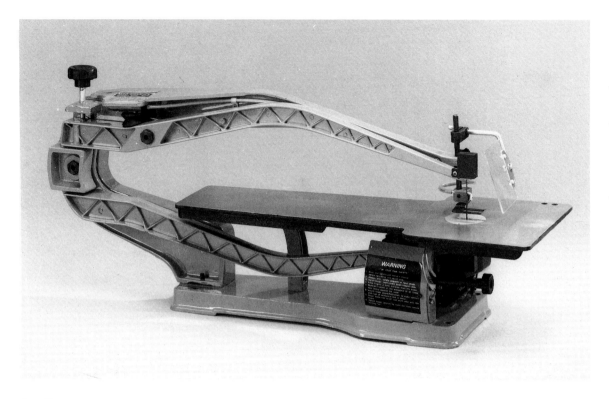

Scroll saw

grinding woodworking tools; if so you could consider the installation of a combination machine rather than the fast moving double-ended grinder. For wet grinding, a slow speed is needed as against the faster speeds needed to remove larger amounts of metal with dry wheels. The grinding wheel for a wet grinder must be of the correct material and have a suitable grit size, and differs considerably from the faster moving wheel.

One of the essential needs is a well designed toolrest to maintain the correct angle of grind. Safety guards must also be fitted, and the wet grinder must have a water trough which can be emptied after use; never leave a wheel standing with its lower half in water.

Drill press vice
Work which cannot be held safely in the hand should be secured in a vice before boring or drilling; the vice must be slotted so that it can be attached to the drill table with bolts. The *Record 414* vice is typical and has the advantage of a sliding jaw which is a non-lifting swivel type capable of holding any shape of workpiece. The jaw can be removed, and I have often substituted a wooden one with a vertical vee-slot to hold square blocks of wood for boring. The jaws have horizontal and vertical vees to hold round stock securely. The vice is strongly made in grey iron with accurately machined faces and screw, and has a jaw width of 4in (100mm), a depth of 1¼in (32mm) and opens to 3in (75mm).

Sawing table

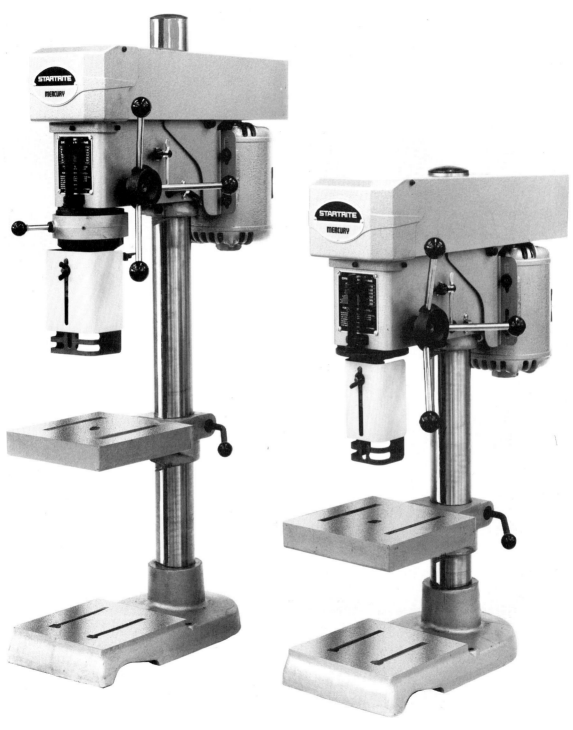

(opposite) *Metalwork vice stand*   (above) *Startrite bench and pillar drills*

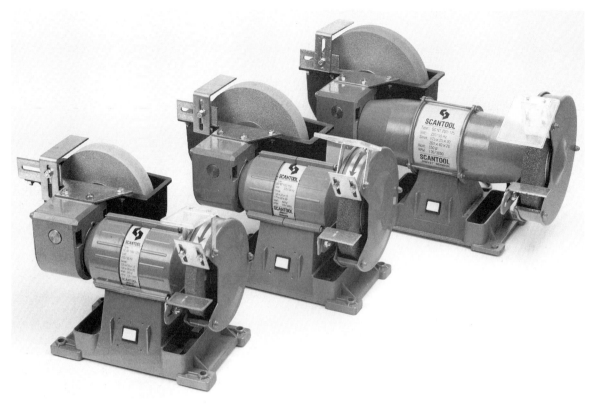

Scantool wet-and-dry grinders

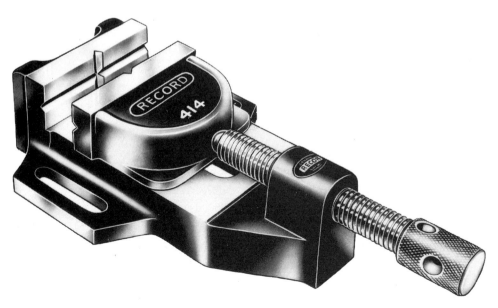

Drill press vice

8
WOOD CARVING

One of the most off-putting aspects of wood carving is the wide range of cutting tools available, and a glance at the pages of tool catalogues is enough to frighten the would-be carver out of his wits! The beginner would be wise to read one or two good books on the subject; he will then realise that there are so many different areas in which he can work that when it comes to the selection of tools he may not need very many.

The workplace need not be large nor complicated in its facilities, but there are one or two provisos which must be observed. The light, both natural and artificial, needs to be good; plus satisfactory ventilation and some form of heating for the winter. A concrete floor will need some form of covering such as sheets of hardboard which will be comfortable to stand on; further, any dropped tools will be less likely to shatter.

The bench

The most important piece of basic equipment is the bench. In Chapter 2 details are given of a number of commercial benches which are suitable for the carver. I have suggested that a special top be made for the work which has all the requisite holding options, plus additional equipment made in the workshop to make things easier.

The biggest problem in wood carving is that of holding the work firmly. The holding capabilities of the traditional English and the European style bench have already been discussed.

Three-dimensional work requires a deep vice, and the woodworker's vice fails in this respect: however, such work can be held by the carver's bench screw, a deep vice, or Scopas chops. If you are making your own bench, bear in mind that the bench holdfast must be able to pass freely through the

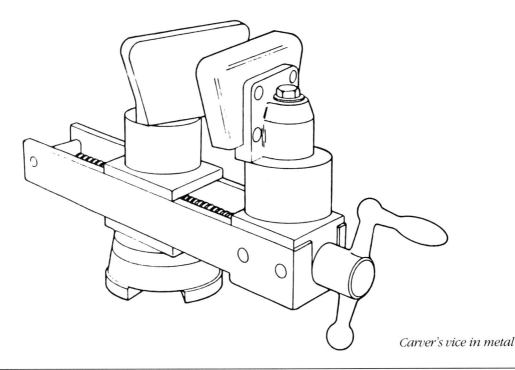

Carver's vice in metal

Scopas chops vice

benchtop, and the woodcarver's screw will need sufficient clearance under the bench to allow your hand to reach the butterfly nut for tightening. With an existing bench it may only be necessary to modify it to receive the holdfast and carver's screw.

Carving tools

The next step is to select the carving tools. Don't buy a complete set of tools as it will be prohibitively expensive and you may well be buying some tools which you will rarely, if ever, use so acquire only the ones which are necessary and add to them when required.

Carving tools from the best manufacturers carry numbers – Numbers 1 and 2, for instance, are chisels; the others which follow are gouges, starting with the flatter or slower gouges, moving along to the deeper gouges (quick gouges), and then on to the various bent patterns which repeat the shapes and sizes of the earlier straight ones. Frequently the tools are referred to by number only, with no other description (see illustrations).

The handles are also important as they should fit the hand and be comfortable. Many carvers use the octagonal shape, but I prefer the well-established carver handle seen in both carving tools and bench chisels. Tool handles can be made in beech, box-wood, rosewood or jarrah.

The blades vary in finish from the early black-and-straw (the outside is left black from the forge, while the inside is first ground then heat-treated and left straw coloured), to the normal brightly finished and very highly polished, almost plated-looking, examples. Obviously, the better the finish the easier it will be to keep them clean and bright.

Many tools are supplied already sharpened; while this is probably good for the beginner to make his first cuts, he will need to master the art of sharpening them as they are different from the tools of the cabinet maker in some respects. The curves are very accurately shaped and the bevels must be very accurate as to angle and also stropped like a razor.

Chisels are listed as square across, and skew: they are bevelled with rounded bevels on both sides and not flat as are normal cabinet makers' and carpenters' chisels. Bent chisels are square across or angled to the right or left; the latter are used to cut into difficult corners. The dog-leg chisel is for difficult situations, as is the fishtail spade which will slide into recessed work.

Gouges have the working classifications of slow (shallow curve) for finishing and flat work, and quick (deeper curves) for fast removal of waste and particularly deep curved cuts. They are also available 'straight' or 'bent' and in the same sizes and shapes as the straight variety; fantail shapes are included in this group and they are very useful, allowing you to work quite deeply without obstruction.

There are also spoonbit or backbent shapes with curves still related to the straight tool; the backbent enables you to deal with difficult convex shapes, and the spoon gives the reverse option. Vee parting tools are available in straight and curved patterns, and also in spoon shape with three different included angles and a number of widths. They are used for marking out, cutting letters, and for texturing work of all kinds. They are a little tricky to sharpen but a handy tool to have around.

| Chisel | Gouge | Fluting | Veiner | Parting | Macaroni | Fluteroni | Backaroni |

Standard edge sections

(opposite) *Carving tools – shapes and sizes*

SIZES AND SWEEPS OF

STRAIGHT AND BENT CARVING GOUGES.

Straight Gouges Nos.	Bent Gouges Nos.	Spoon-bit Gouges Nos.	Back-bent Gouges Nos.
3	12	24	33
4	13	25	34
5	14	26	35
6	15	27	36
7	16	28	37
8	17	29	38
9	18	30	
10	19	31	
11	20	32	

SIZES AND SWEEPS OF

STRAIGHT AND BENT V PARTING TOOLS.

Straight V Tool Nos.	Curved V Tool Nos.	Spoon-bit V Tool Nos.
39	40	43
41	42	44
45	46	

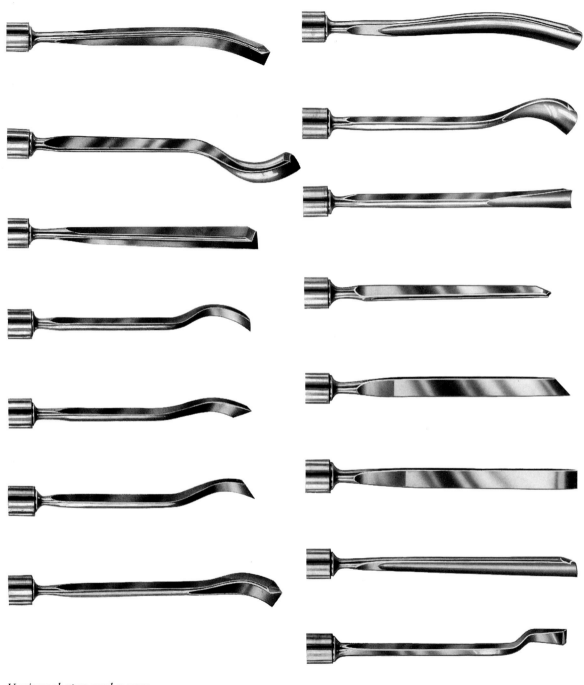

Various shapes and curves

Carver handle on Marples skew chisel

Another important tool is the veiner, which is a very tiny but deep gouge, and is most useful for texturing and lining out. Several special patterns are seen; the macaroni, for instance, has a spade-like shape with square upturned corners. It is used to cut cleanly into corners and is particularly useful in low relief work. The flutaroni is, again, spade-like with round upturned corners for cutting and finishing curved corners. Both are excellent tools for finishing ground work.

Should you want to work in the round and on a fairly large scale, you would be well advised to consider the tools designed specifically for the purpose. They are more strongly built. The *Marples* sculpting tools are fitted with the *Blue Chip* handle which is designed to fit perfectly into the hand; these tools also have a very strong bolster. The out-cannel gouges described in Chapter 5 can also be used for sculpting.

Dishes, trays, and small bowls can be carved with

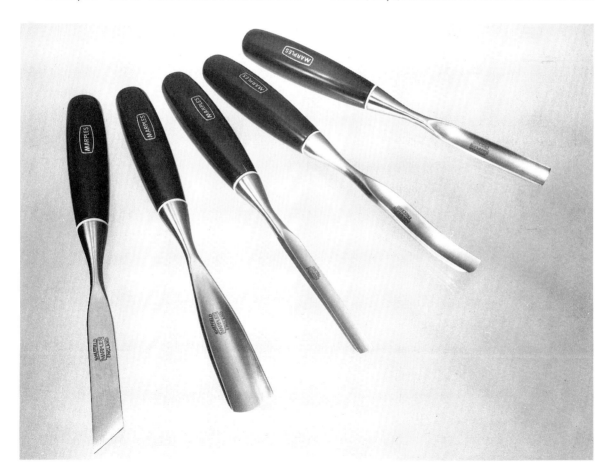

Sculpting tools

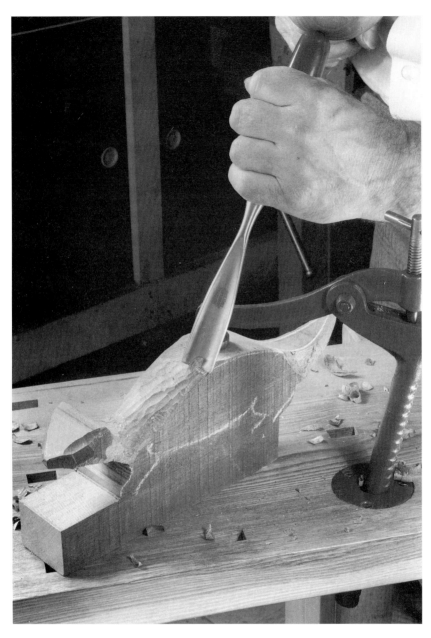

bent gouges and spoon bits, but many carvers prefer to master the art of using the carver's hook. Those illustrated have short handles, but the hooks of the old Welsh spoon and ladle maker had long handles which fitted under the arm and allowed him to pull large amounts of timber out in a curving cut.

Carver's planes are growing in popularity; they are made entirely in metal with curved or straight soles, with a lengthwise curve, or a spoon shape. The handle fits comfortably into the palm of the hand and they are really excellent finishing tools.

A smaller, shorter-handled version of the carpenter's adze can be obtained in several curves fitted with an ash or hickory handle about 9in (230mm) long. It is most useful for roughing out a job, but it can also be used for finishing.

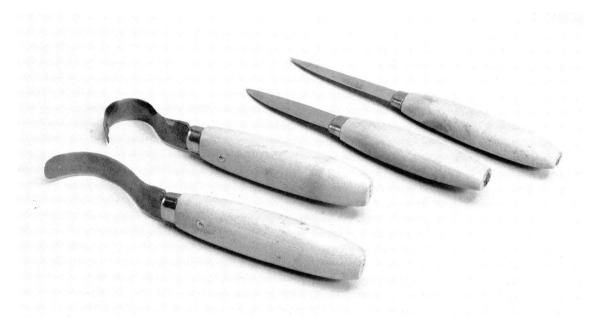

Carver's knives, bent knives and hooks

Another popular tool is the riffler file. This is available in a number of curved shapes and is made from square, round, or flat stock. The teeth can be fine, medium, or coarse and may have rasp-like teeth at one end and fine file teeth at the other. They extend about 2in (50mm) each side of the centre section of the tool, which is knurled to give a handle grip. It is fine for finishing, particularly those parts where the chisel cannot reach.

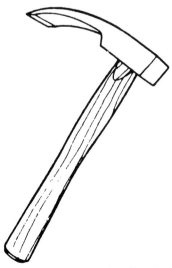

Sculptor's adze

Carver's plane

Specific holding devices

Work must be held securely for safe working and to protect it from damage; holding with the vice and bench dogs has already been described. Low relief panels can be placed in a frame and secured by folding wedges.

A similar arrangement can be set up on the bench top, but you may object to screwing battens to it. Another method is to use a board which has been bored to receive dowel pegs which can be inserted in many positions – the work is held between the dowel pegs with small wedges. A similar board uses an offset cam to hold the work in place. For very small pieces you can use an ordinary benchhook, placing the work against the upstand, and securing it with a touch of hot-melt glue.

Other expedients include small carvers' clips which can be used to hold down thin panels, or small wooden dogs, but again you may object to marking the bench with holes. Small and odd-shaped pieces can be held in purpose-made jaws which can be used in the woodwork vice.

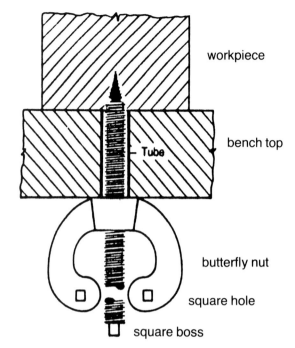

Carver's screw

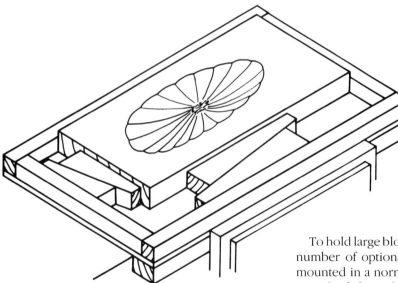

Holding a relief panel

To hold large blocks for three-dimensional work a number of options is available. The block can be mounted in a normal bench vice, but a spare piece must be left on the block to grip in the vice. The carver's screw is another method of holding a block, and this allows you to work freely around the work-piece; a hole must be bored in the bench top through which the screw can be passed and the butterfly nut screwed on to hold the work securely. To prepare the work, first bore a hole in the underside which is the exact diameter of the main screw; then bore another hole, half the diameter of the first one, into which the screw can be wound; the first hole will help to give extra support. The screw has a square head, and the butterfly nut a square recess, so that the latter can be used to wind the screw into the hole.

The Scopas chops was the traditional method used to hold large blocks, and has already been de-scribed. The screw can be of steel, or it can be made in wood, using a screwbox and tap after the piece has been turned on the lathe. The metal vice similar to Scopas is mounted on a swivel base, and the jaws swivel to accept awkward shapes.

Finally, the bench holdfast is a perfectly good method of holding, but the arm can be obstructive. There is also one with the nylon pad which will not mark the job.

Record bench holdfast

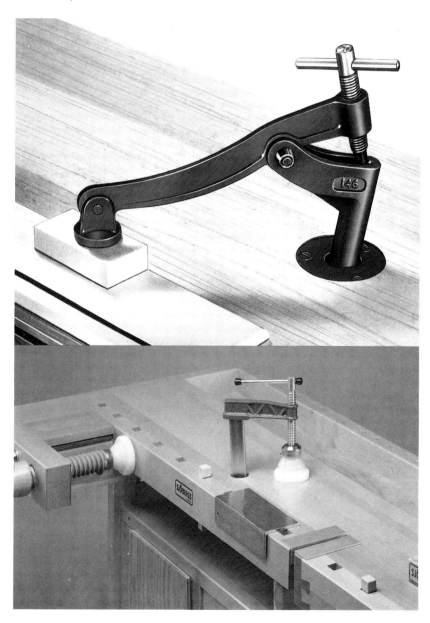

Sjoberg bench holdfast

Carver's beech mallet

You must have a carver's mallet; the head is round so that you can strike the work with the mallet without looking to see if the face is square with the tool, as you would in the case of a joiner's mallet. The heads are usually in beech but the best timber is lignum vitae which provides the weight without the bulk. A good mallet will probably weigh about 22oz (0.62kg), and the handle should be made of a good resilient timber like ash or hickory. The practice of having the mallet turned in one piece makes using it particularly hard on the hand. They are also made with hard plastic heads and also in bronze (see illustration). The plastic one tends to bounce a bit, and the handle of the metal one really does hurt the hand.

Tool kit

A starter kit of edge tools could comprise one each of the following: $\frac{1}{4}$in (6mm) square chisel; 1in (25mm) chisel; $\frac{1}{4}$in (6mm) vee parting tool, No 39; $\frac{1}{8}$in (3mm) veiner; $\frac{3}{8}$in (10mm) No 2 gouge; $\frac{3}{8}$in (10mm) No 5 gouge; $\frac{1}{2}$in (12mm) No 6 gouge, and $\frac{1}{4}$in (6mm) No 7. Also, a carver's mallet, plus the equipment for the bench depending on what has been chosen.

A recent addition is the *Arbortech* woodcarver which attaches to 4 or 4$\frac{1}{2}$in (100 and 113mm) angle grinders. The wheel is of carburised steel which has been heat-treated in a molten salt bath to achieve a surface hardness of Rockwell 62, giving long life to the cutting edges; these can be sharpened using a special stick supplied by the manufacturer. It will cut in all directions and removes quite a volume of material, but it can also be used to stroke the timber gently to produce a fine cut. The technique is quickly acquired and if only used as a time-and-labour-saving tool it is worth having; but no doubt in the future a range of carvings will appear where only the *Arbortech* has been used. The tool can also be used to make grooves, rebates and other cuts.

Finally store tools carefully; if they are in a roll, keep away from the damp and lightly oil the tip of each blade before sliding into its pocket. Don't have a heap of tools on the bench, only those you need. Keep them in a slotted tray with their edges pointing towards you so that they can be selected quickly.

Carver's mallets with plastic and metal heads

9

THE ROUTER WORKSHOP

The versatility of the tool and the multiplicity of uses to which it can be put calls for a section of the workshop in which the router can play a major part. During recent times the router with its range of cutters and the development of tables and other accessories has meant that practically every process formerly carried out on the bench using hand tools can now be done to perfection with a minimum of time and effort. Man-made boards which are often difficult to deal with using normal cutting tools can be worked as tungsten-carbide-tipped cutters are available in a wide variety of shapes, profiles and sizes.

Such a workshop must have a woodworker's bench preferably fitted with a tail vice and bench dogs so that work can be held safely. However, the woodworker who has very little space and may have to pack away each time after work should consider the *Black and Decker Workmate*, which will hold a worktable. There are also other ways in which timber can be held for routing without the use of a vice, so that working on the kitchen table or any flat top set up in the garage or spare room becomes practicable.

CHOOSING THE ROUTER

There are many machines to choose from and you must first consider the work to which the router is to be put, and whether it will be used for home projects or to meet the demands of a small production workshop. Two typical routers are shown.

Most modern routers are of the plunge type in which the router cutter is lowered into the work by bearing down on the body which slides on two vertical rods positioned in the base. This is the best type to choose and there are many examples to choose from. Other points to bear in mind are that the fence should enable both straight and curved cuts to be made, and the router itself should be fitted with a depth stop (preferably working in conjunction with a rotary turret) which helps when making deep cuts in two or three passes. Also, the depth of cut should be indicated in both metric and imperial measure, and it is essential that it should be read easily. One manufacturer has a magnifier fitted which is a great advantage.

The router must be held firmly but comfortably, and some attention must be paid to the handles both as regards shape and position; they should be fixed as close to the base of the router as is practicable. The depth-setting on some machines is fixed by twisting one of the handles. This can often be difficult to operate, particularly when releasing at the end of a cut or in an emergency. The best choice is the router which has a lever set close to the hand to allow instant cut-off.

The machine must be fitted with a collet chuck to provide effective holding for the cutter. The size of collet must be checked as many of the larger cutters for heavy duty have shanks up to $\frac{1}{2}$in (12.7mm) in diameter, and some of the larger machines have several sizes in both metric and imperial measure. Always remember that the cutter shanks are exactly to the size quoted, as are the collets, and diameters must be quoted in either metric or imperial as the equivalents will not apply.

The shape of the base or sole is important as it is very desirable to have at least one straight side which can be used against a strip of timber fixed to a board to act as a guide when the fence cannot be used. The forward edge of the base should be rounded to ease the passage of the machine over the work – sharp edges are a menace, and the base itself must be in a hard-wearing material.

The plunge is, of course, sprung to give instant return of the cutter, but the springs should not be so strong as to make plunging heavy and difficult. The locking screws on the fence should have springs and washers fitted to prevent slackening of the screws by vibration during cutting; also quick and effective

Festo router

CHOOSING A ROUTER BENCH

locking of the depth setting is important. Although there must be a guard around the cutter, there should also be good vision around it.

The router does create a lot of tiny chips, and, if possible an extraction system should be fitted; unfortunately many routers do not provide for this to be fitted easily. A number of machines provide a down draught which helps to blow the chips away but this tends to fill the air with dust. Look to see whether any provision is made to keep the dust out of the body of the machines – in some cases a gauze screen is fitted.

The router rating is important. A good one will have not less than 26,000rpm with an output of 600 watts; the plunge should not be less than 2in (50mm).

The router should have a flat top as this is useful when inverting the router on the bench to insert or remove a cutter. Spares and accessories should be readily available; a number of sizes of guide bushes are most necessary. Check that there are local arrangements for servicing; good routers rarely break down but it is as well to ensure that this is available.

There are a number to choose from, and you would be well advised to visit a good dealer or attend one of the major woodworking exhibitions where they can be seen. Most woodworkers have a number of power tools in their workshop and many router benches will accept these as well.

Triton Work Centre

Probably the most versatile router bench on the market. It will accommodate the router, plus a circular saw, and a jigsaw. All three machines can be inverted in the table to convert them to a bench mode, and a very clever system of moving tables allows the machines to be traversed across the work; or when in the fixed position, the work can be moved into or across the cutter. Also, the tools are well guarded, and the accuracy is extremely good. The bench top itself, with its several tables, can be fitted to a floor stand which in turn can have a set of wheels attached for ease of movement. The bench is fitted with a readily accessible knock-off switch for the electricity; the router itself is plugged into the back of the switch, so no looking or searching for the machine switch is needed.

(above) *Elu 177E router*

(right) *Triton work bench*

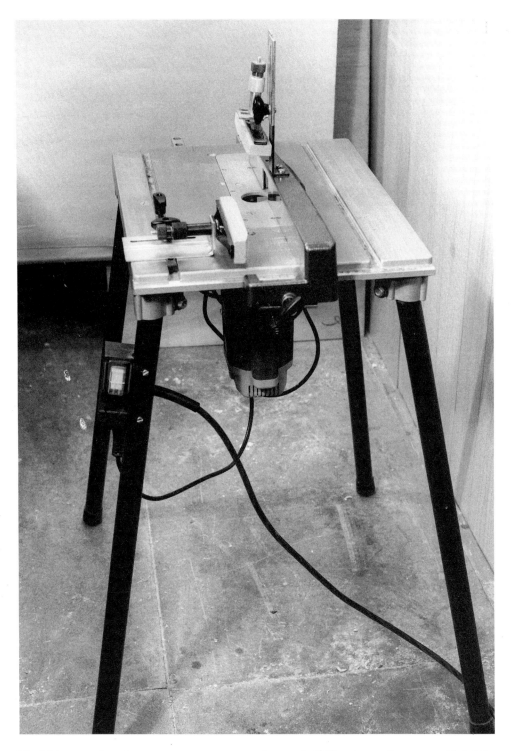

Elu 551 router bench   (opposite) *Wooden sash cramp with folding wedges*

Calvert Stevens smoothing plane

The Triton Work Centre – on the move

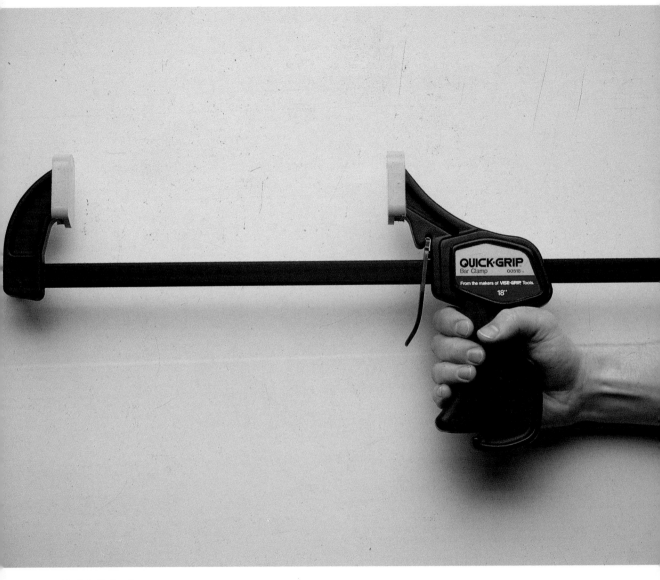

Quick-Grip clamp

Elu 551

This is a router table that can be recommended for a small production workshop. It will accommodate both a router and a circular saw.

It has an accurately machine-cast aluminium table fitted with sturdy tubular legs which have rubber feet to stop the table moving around; the fence is well designed so that much of the waste passes out through the right-hand side. A pressure guard is fitted directly over the cutting point and another pressure guard can be fitted to the left of the work-piece, both guards having micro-adjustment. A no-volt release switch is fitted to the leg and the router plugs into the rear of this switch.

All *Elu* routers fit this table, the smaller ones by using their fence arms, and the larger ones by means of the screws supplied. Check that your router will fit before buying the table. The *Elu 96* and *96E* can be fitted to an accessory kit table, converting it to a small spindle moulder.

*Elu accessory table with
Elu 96 router attached*

Black and Decker Workcentre

This can be fitted to the *Workmate* bench or to a purpose-made stand. It's made in a very strong and rigid plastic, has a fully adjustable fence, and excellent guards. *Black and Decker* routers will fit it, but check to see that other makes are suitable before buying.

CUTTERS

High-speed-steel (HSS) cutters are suitable for most timbers, except perhaps the very hard ones, but tungsten-carbide-tipped (TCT) cutters must be used with all man-made boards and tougher timbers. Where cutters are very small they are usually made in solid tungsten-carbide (TC).

A very wide range of both kinds of cutters is available, and it is best to choose a well known brand name, as the initial cost is fairly high; thus the source and the back-up from that source is important should problems arise. I use *Titman* tip tools which I select from a very comprehensive list. Store all cutters safely in stands so that the edges will not be damaged.

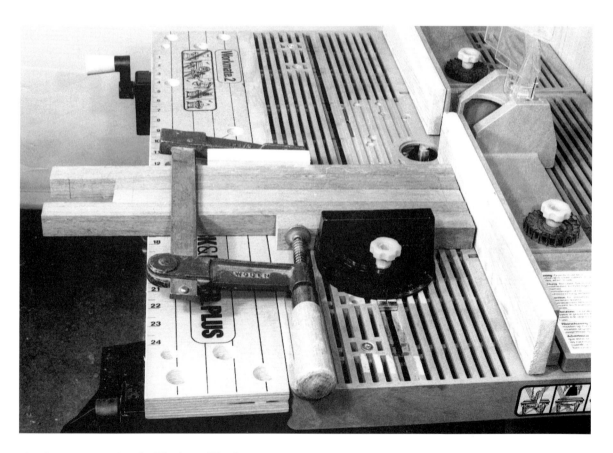

Cutting tenons using the Black and Decker workcentre

(opposite) *Router cutters*

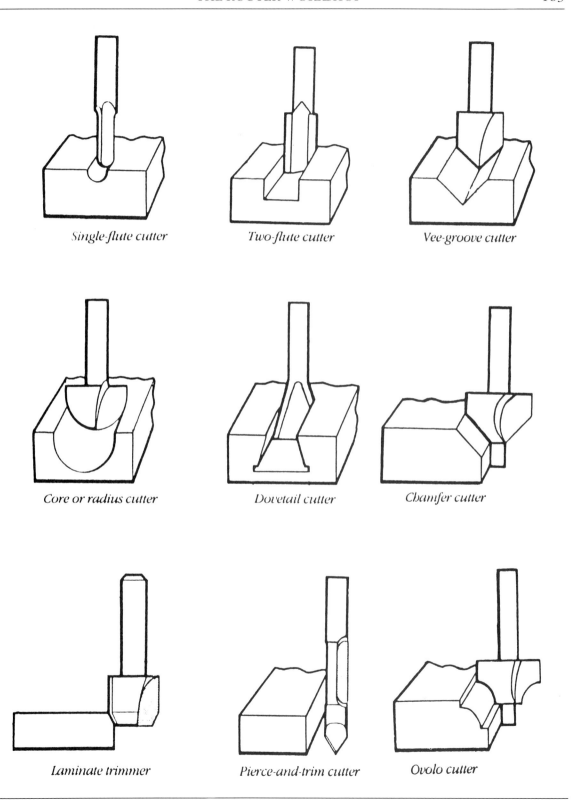

Single-flute cutter

Two-flute cutter

Vee-groove cutter

Core or radius cutter

Dovetail cutter

Chamfer cutter

Laminate trimmer

Pierce-and-trim cutter

Ovolo cutter

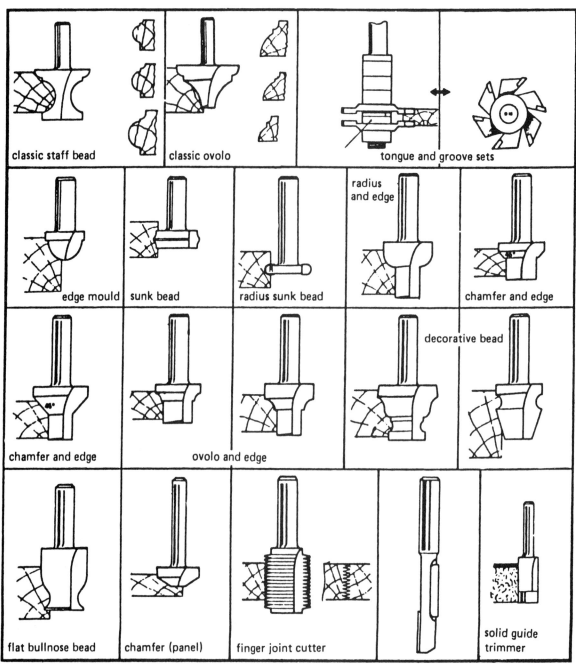

classic staff bead

classic ovolo

tongue and groove sets

edge mould

sunk bead

radius sunk bead

radius and edge

chamfer and edge

chamfer and edge

ovolo and edge

decorative bead

flat bullnose bead

chamfer (panel)

finger joint cutter

staggered edge cutter

solid guide trimmer

Router cutters

ROUTER ACCESSORIES

The router itself has its own fence which can be used to make straight or curved cuts, but for template work a guide bush must be fitted at the centre on the underside of the router base. The edge of the guide runs against a template which acts as a fence; usually the router is supplied with one of these, but small and large ones can be bought to use on slow or fast curves. They are included in the ranges offered by *Trend* and also by *Leigh Industries* of Canada.

Many other accessories are available, but you should only buy them if the need is a positive one. Probably the most important of these accessories is the fine-height adjuster which will be found extremely useful to ensure a really good fit when using a dovetail jig. Some routers are supplied already fitted with a fine-fence adjuster, but in some cases they are only available as extras.

ROUTER JIGS

There are a number of jigs that are worthy of serious consideration. One of the finest of these is the *Leigh* dovetail jig. The dovetail is an effective joint and when well made it can be a decorative feature as well as a strong joint. Cut by hand it can be varied in size and style, but most dovetail jigs can only produce one size of dovetail and are consequently not as popular as they might be. The *Leigh* jig, however, gives every kind of size option with variations in the length of the tail within the same joint. It is made with adjustable fingers which can be moved to any position across a board; the fingers are double-ended so they can be flipped over to cut both pins and sockets at one setting. Further, the jig can also be used for cutting housings, and, in spite of its cost, it's a jig well worth considering if a great deal of cabinet work is to be done.

A recent addition to this jig is an attachment which enables the router to cut multiple mortice and tenon joints in any size or arrangement you want. It replaces the finger attachment, or it can be bought as a separate jig complete in itself. Once the jig is set up for plunge-cutting the mortices, the setting for the tenons is automatically set, guaranteeing a snug fit every time. Flush or raised tenons with through or blind mortices can be cut and the mortices can either be left with rounded corners as they come

Detail of guide bushes

from the cutter, or squared-up with a chisel. Material capacities are from ⁵⁄₁₆ to 1¹⁄₂in (8 to 38mm), and there are two sizes of jig, namely 12 and 24in (305 and 610mm).

Elu dovetailing jig

This has no adjustment for the fingers but assists in the making of a good standard joint.

Special jigs

These include several types of dovetailing jig, a drawer and panel decorator, a letter and number template, a 'Rout-a-sign' device, a router crafter for use on the lathe, an edge crafter, a re-creator, a pantograph, a staircase jig, and edge guides. Studying a good book on the subject (see Bibliography) will pay dividends.

Leigh dovetail and mortice and tenon jig

10

VENEERING, INLAYING AND MARQUETRY

Veneering is an old craft, and there are some magnificent examples of veneered furniture in many museums and stately homes all over the world. Many exotic timbers would otherwise never be seen, as they come from small trees which produce insufficient timber to make them commercially viable unless used as veneers.

Veneers are produced by peeling or slicing the trimmed log and the latter method produces the best figure since the log can be cut along the medullary rays to produce the most beautiful grain formations. Timber from the crotch of the tree can produce wonderful grain – indeed, many fine examples can be seen in the mahogany furniture of past years.

Inlaying
This is closely associated with veneering as the skills are so often seen together.

Bandings
These are long thin strips of many coloured sections of veneer arranged to form a pattern and then laid into a veneered surface. The pieces are made by gluing long thin strips together, sandwiching them between covers of veneer, and then slicing across them to produce very thin and delicate strips. These can be inserted in shallow grooves cut in solid timber or made up as part of a veneered surface.

Stringings
Finely-cut strips of solid timber used in the same way as bandings, but also used to line the edges of fine table tops.

MARQUETRY

This craft uses pieces of veneers to make up pictures, and gives the craftsman (a 'marquetarian') the opportunity to use both the colour and the beauty of the grain to create beautiful effects. Some colours – green, for example – are not seen in timber, and can be introduced by dyeing; sycamore is a plain and undistinguished wood that is often used for this purpose.

The workshop for the craft can be anywhere where there is a flat-topped table and an electric point or gas connection handy for heating glue. If you intend to use a normal work bench it is advisable to make a cutting and sawing top from hardboard or MDF board, to be used only for cutting with the knife or saw to save wear on the main top; it can be replaced when both sides are badly scored or worn.

The tools can be divided into four main groups: cutting, laying, inlaying, and cleaning-up tools.

Cutting and trimming tools
Veneers can be cut with a knife, but it must be selected with care. The best shape of edge is a curved one which will give a slicing cut through the veneer with no chance of tearing it; the pointed knife used for marking-out should not be used. The veneer must be cut so that the edge cuts are vertical, and this is particularly important when joining long strips of veneer. There are many combination craft knives having a selection of blades which will be found ideal; the blade should be a thin one and for preference sharpened only on one side – which side depends on which hand you use.

Veneers can be sawn, but a specially thin saw is needed. The teeth must be very fine and the blade curved. There are two types of such saws; one has

(above) *Veneer saw*

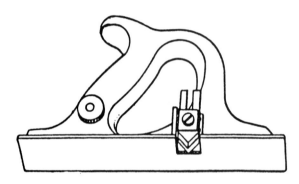

Veneer edging tool (above) *and strip and trim cutter* (below)

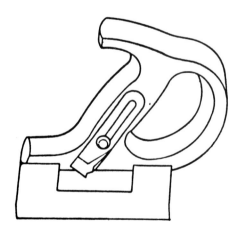

teeth that point towards the centre from both ends with a single tooth at the centre point and is used with a rocking motion to cut perfect veneers. The other type has one edge of fine teeth and the other of slightly larger teeth for more difficult work. They are both fitted with round wooden handles, and it is as well to practise on spare pieces before tackling an expensive sheet of veneer.

The small fretsaw can also be used to cut veneers provided a fine sawblade is used and the material held down flat on the table, particularly if you are using a machine saw.

The combination strip and trim cutter has a pair of cutters fitted on one side which can be adjusted by means of shims, with a small clamp to hold them in place. The blades are designed to cut on either the backward or forward stroke and will cut strips $1/12$ to $5/16$in (2 to 8mm) wide. On the opposite side a single blade is fitted which can be used for trimming a leaf or strip of veneer; the tool should always be used with a straightedge.

An edging tool is the one to employ for trimming veneer glued to a board as it has a single spear-point cutter for trimming in both directions. Another trimming knife has a small cutter with a nylon guide fitted.

A straightedge is needed to guide the saw or knife when cutting; it is best made of steel, but a number made from long straight pieces of hardwood can be good substitutes.

Veneer repair punch

Small blemishes can often spoil an almost perfect job, but can be made good using a specially made veneer punch. This consists of one punch which when tapped into the sheet will remove an irregularly shaped piece; another matching punch can be used to produce a perfect and exactly matching piece which can be glued in place. This is much better than cutting the defective veneer away with a chisel or a Forstner bit and inserting a hand-cut piece. Punches are available in a variety of sizes.

INLAYING

This job needs special cutters, and probably the simplest is the scratch stock. It consists of two small pieces of beech or similar hard wearing hardwood held together with some small nuts and bolts, or bolts and wing nuts. Small cutters can be made from scraps of old hacksaw blade and ground to size. The cutter should be set at the required distance from the edge of the work, and the tool is pushed away from you with the stock held firmly against the edge of the work.

Alternatively, small cutters can be made from scrap metal to fit into a cutting gauge instead of the normal cutter. They are held in place with a small brass wedge, and the stock can be set accurately along the stem of the gauge. Once again the gauge is pushed away from you while you hold the stock tightly against the edge of the work.

One of the finest inlay cutters comes from Germany; its hardwood frame has brass fittings with a steel cutting assembly which holds three cutters. The fence slides along the main beam and is adjustable up to 6in (150mm) from the edge of the work. The sides of the grooves for the inlays are cut with two blades, set with their bevels inside for cutting grooves and outside for cutting veneer. The waste is removed with a third cutter which is set in an adjustable holder for accurate setting. The grooves range in width from $1/12$ to $5/16$in (2 to 8mm).

The purfling tool is really a violin maker's tool, but it can be used by the inlayer to cut tiny rebates and grooves. It's quite a small tool with a knife cutter held in place with a single screw.

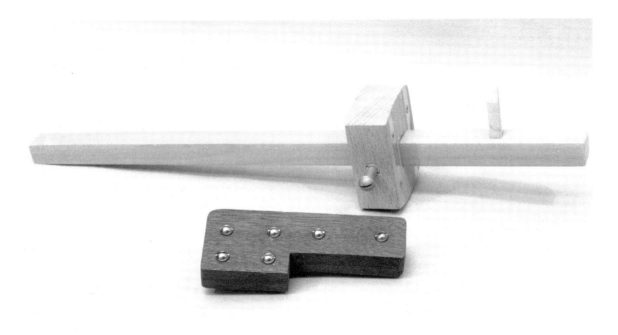

Scratch stock, and gauge-type scratch stock

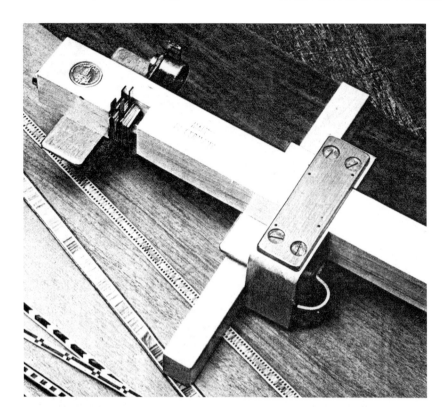

German inlay cutter

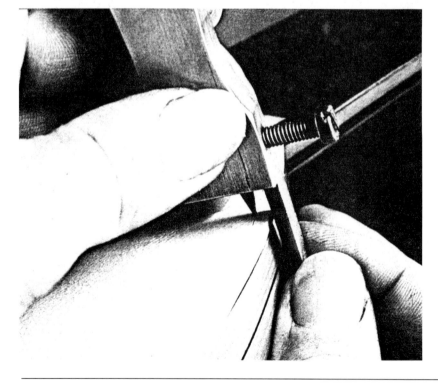

(opposite) *Cabinet scraper/ using the scraper*

Purfling tool

PREPARING THE GROUND

The ground or base for laying veneer is prepared by being scratched to roughen up the surface so as to give maximum grip to the glue, and a toothing plane is used for this. The modern toothing plane is usually made of beech with a sole of hornbeam; the cutter is set in an almost vertical position and is serrated along its flat face so that a series of teeth show through the mouth of the plane. The planing must produce a perfectly flat toothed surface which makes a perfect bond for gluing the veneer.

An alternative to this plane is to fit a special cutter to the *Stanley No. 80* cabinet scraper. This is serrated in the same way as the plane cutter.

Trimming and finishing

A small plane is a useful addition to the kit and when used in conjunction with a shooting board can be used to plane the edges of the veneers, and one of the shoulder planes or a bullnose rebate plane will do the job.

The small metal router plane ('old woman's tooth' plane) has a tiny cutter enabling it to be used if the width is suitable. Better still, a small wooden one can be made with a small body made from beech (see illustration). The cutters, which are taken from an old plough plane in this case, are held in place with a wooden wedge.

Workshop-made router plane

A cutting tool of a sort, but certainly an essential one, is the bench scraper previously mentioned and, indeed, the surface of veneered work can only be improved by using a scraper. They are made from sheet steel, are extremely thin so that they can be flexed in the fingers to present a slightly curved edge to the surface of the work. They are available in rectangular shapes or in various curves.

An alternative and better solution is the cabinet scraper. This has a double-edged blade which is set at the exact angle for best cutting and a screw which can be used to bow the cutter. It's easy to use and gives perfect results – it is, in fact, the only answer to renovating old veneered surfaces as well as cleaning up new ones.

A cork sanding block is a necessary addition as abrasive paper will have to be used at times, and when wrapped around the block it will ensure that the surface of the paper is kept flat.

Use of the power router

This can be used to cut grooves for banding and stringings by means of fine HSS or TCT cutters which are available in very small sizes to cut grooves. It is an extremely easy method to use and gives perfect results. A tiny lining cutter made by *Titman Tip Tools*

Small metal router plane

gives a $\frac{1}{16}$in (2mm) wide cut to a maximum depth of $\frac{1}{4}$in (6mm), and is available in shank diameters of $\frac{1}{4}$, $\frac{3}{8}$, and $\frac{1}{2}$in (6, 10, and 12mm).

TOOLS FOR LAYING VENEERS

Veneers have been laid for centuries using animal or fish glues and many craftsmen still prefer to use this type of glue. The glue is still available in bead or cake form and is prepared by adding water and boiling in a double glue pot. They are either thermostatically controlled or for heating over gas.

Lining cutter for the router

Workshop-made veneer hammer

The glue is applied hot, giving plenty of time to lay the veneer and to squeeze out the surplus glue. Should any come through the veneer it can easily be washed off. Modern glues can be used, but it is as well to check that they will not stain the wood, as some certainly do.

The glued veneer is pressed into place using a veneer hammer. The traditional hammer has a wooden head into which a strip of metal is inserted along its edge, and a cylindrical handle which can be made quite easily on a lathe. There is also a metal pattern in which the head is drop-forged and has a striking flat face and a spreading pane or pein similar to the metal strip in the wooden version.

A number of laying cauls need to be prepared, slightly larger in length and width to overlap the finished work. They should be of stout thickness and planed dead flat. Strips or battens of strong sound

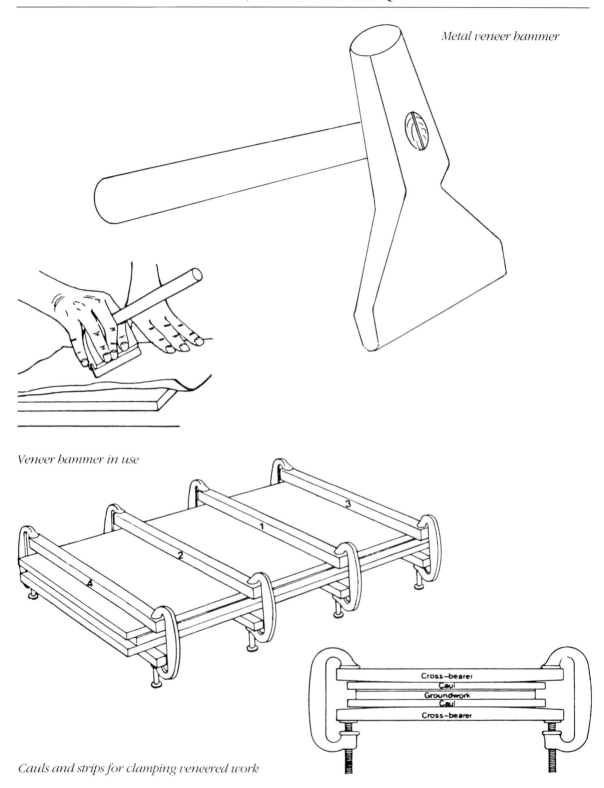

Metal veneer hammer

Veneer hammer in use

Cauls and strips for clamping veneered work

hardwood will also be needed to bridge across the cauls on both sides and be cramped together to hold the veneers in close contact with the groundwork, and to squeeze out surplus adhesive. An electrical veneering hammer is also on the market, and this has a rounded hammer edge for laying the veneer and one large surface for heating the glue. As it is expensive, it is really a tool for the professional who is constantly doing this work. A hardwood roller of the kind used in hanging wallpaper is very useful to run along the joins in the veneer and for laying the edges. It is also possible to use a press; the old metal presses are rarely seen now, but a wooden one could be made.

CRAMPING

There are a number of cramps which will be needed. Probably one of the best is the long-reach cramp (once called a 'veneer cramp'). This comprises a steel bar with an arm fixed at one end and another arm fitted with a handled screw fitting that slides along the bar. This gives instant action without having to pre-wind the screw or insert pins as in the case of bar cramps. A number of types are currently available any of which will be found suitable.

Types of cramps
Deep-throated G-cramps are very efficient, but are unfortunately only available in one size from *Record*. Edging cramps are invaluable for applying pressure to the edge veneers. They are available with two and three screws, the latter being preferable. The large edging cramp – similar in construction to the veneer cramp, has a side screw similar to its main screw.

The *Jet* cramp is an extremely versatile tool as the heads can be assembled on any length of standard bar, and the variety of jaw shapes is also useful.

Where round work is being veneered, one or other of the Band cramps will be invaluable. They can be obtained with steel, nylon or pre-stretched canvas bands; in each case the band goes round the work and is attached to a screw which can be wound up to exert pressure.

The Joiner's bar cramps can also be used in some circumstances, and ordinary G-cramps are ideal for smaller sizes of work.

SUNDRIES

A good quality glue brush is essential, and it should be washed after use and not left in the glue pot to go hard. A soft dusting brush will keep the veneers free from dust and the worktop clean.

Veneer pins are often needed to fix the veneers down and if they have to be cut, small end nippers can be used. Also, a pair of small pincers will be handy for withdrawing them.

Ready-gummed, brown paper tape or masking tape will be needed for holding down veneer at the joints, or for holding down protective paper.

11
WOOD TURNING

Wood turning is one of the fastest-growing crafts, and this is probably due in no small part to the fascination of watching the moving work, and the speed with which a simple block of wood can be transformed into a desirable artefact.

THE WOOD TURNER'S WORKSHOP

This needs just as much careful planning as any other having machinery in it; a badly planned workshop can be a dangerous one and greatly reduce one's enjoyment of the work. The working space must be a comfortable one and the provisions already outlined for a general woodwork shop are equally applicable.

The lathe must be positioned to provide access to both ends, and if an outboard attachment is to be set up, then the lathe must be away from the wall so that the turner can move easily and safely into any cutting position. There should also be space for a small work bench to use for wood preparation, and for tool sharpening.

Cupboards for chucks, accessories and associated equipment will be useful, if only to keep them free from dust and a small cupboard marked with a red cross should house the simple first aid requirements which hopefully will never be needed. It can also contain safety equipment such as the dust masks, the ear defenders, and the safety spectacles. All of them should always be kept free from dust; so often they are found smothered in waste in some dark corner and are as much a hazard in themselves as is the dust they are intended to keep out.

CHOICE OF LATHES

We can now look at the equipment bearing in mind the various requirements when choosing a lathe. The two lathes selected to illustrate these are typical, and they have also been chosen because they are newly on the market; in the case of the bowl-turning lathe it is purpose-designed.

The lathe should give you a lifetime of service and there is every chance that it could be used by your grandchildren, so it is as well to consider every aspect before making a decision. Lathes are designed to be either floor-standing, or to be mounted on an existing wooden or metal bench, or on the manufacturer's own bench stand which is usually offered as an optional extra.

The bench-mounted type can have a fixed head or one which can be rotated and set at any angle, and there is one model where the headstock can be moved along the bed to the right-hand end to give a trouble-free position for bowl turning. The fixed-head machine can have an outboard attachment fitted for large bowl work; unfortunately this type of machine will need both left- and right-hand chucks and faceplates. Pedestal lathes usually house the motor, the belt drives and switch gear, and this keeps it free from dust and shavings. The great advantage with the rotating headstock, apart from being able to set the head at any angle, is that only right-hand equipment is needed.

The bed can be of solid cast iron, which is preferable but a little more expensive than those using double or single steel tubes, solid section, round bar, or square steel tube. Machined beds are best for accurate setting up of components. The main point to bear in mind is the accuracy of the bed, and a test should always be made to see that the centres line up – if they don't, is there any provision made for adjustment to bring them in line?

The drive can be by single or multi-vee belts, or flat multi-vee belts, the multi-vee giving the best performance. All drives should be fully guarded, and it would be good to see manufacturers fitting a micro-switch to break the power when the belt is being changed. The ultimate in convenience and efficiency is the 'Varispeed' type lathe where infinite variations of speed can be set without belt changing.

Tailstock and tool rest assemblies are best secured with a lever-operated cam as in the *Graduate* lathe; some are not positive. The introduction of the ratcheted lever is an improvement on the drop bar which sometimes got in the way.

The capacity of the lathe must be matched to the type of work and the maximum sizes anticipated as well as the possible limitations imposed by the workshop itself. There are a number of national exhibitions where most of the current machines can be seen as well as exhibitions by the larger trading companies, which are worth a visit. Look to see which machines are used by the demonstrators, and talk to the representatives on the stands.

Secondhand machines

If you consider buying one, examine it closely, ask the age of the machine, how many owners, and the reason for the sale. Run the machine and listen for unusual noises. Look to see if there is a large amount of oil or grease around the machine which might indicate wear or that the sealed bearing units may be cracked.

Ask if very heavy work has been carried out on it, and if it is in a workshop take note of the conditions, looking particularly for damp which may have resulted in harmful rust. Check the spindle for wear, as a replacement may be difficult or impossible to obtain if the machine is an old model. Check the bed for wear, and see if all components slide easily along it. Make quite sure that the spindle threads are in good condition; and if there are any faceplates or chucks with the machine, run one on to check for slack and ease of assembly. Take a look at the condition of the belt and, at the same time, see if the fitting of a new one will cause any problems. All the electrics should be free from loose or frayed wires, and switches should operate instantly. The lathe should preferably be from a reputable manufacturer.

The paintwork may tell you a lot as a re-painted job may be hiding a multiplicity of problems; badly scarred paint may well indicate misuse.

Finally compare the asking price with the cost of a comparable new machine, not forgetting to make allowances for any accessories.

ACCESSORIES

Most manufacturers supply their lathes complete with motor, switch, driving fork, and tailstock centre, together with at least one tool rest and the necessary spanners. Full assembly instructions will be included if the machine isn't delivered already assembled.

Where the headstock is of the swivelling kind, a right-angled attachment is needed to cater for large bowl work; *Tyme Machines* supply theirs as standard. A short tool rest and a bowl rest are almost essential; a running centre will avoid the use of oil or grease at the tailstock end, and a good multi-purpose chuck together with a screw fitting is a real necessity.

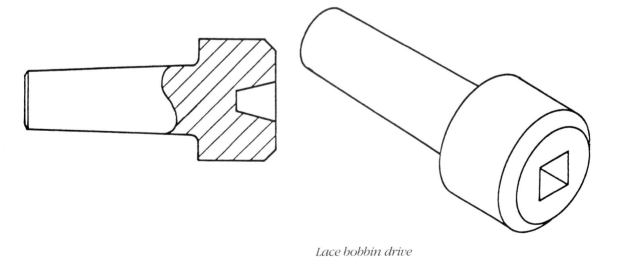

Lace bobbin drive

The screw chuck is also a necessity but if a combination chuck is being considered they usually already have a screw chuck accessory.

Driving forks are available for large or small work, and if you intend making small pieces between centres such as lace bobbins, you should consider buying a lace bobbin drive. A recent innovation is the *Turnbry Twin-dog* driving centre which uses two round dogs and a small centre which engages in the workpiece to centre and drive it. There is no necessity to make saw cuts or prepare the piece in any way other than to mark its centre with a bradawl. The head of the centre is longer than most others giving much better access at the left-hand end of the work.

The most efficient type of centre has four chisels, while most of those supplied by the lathe maker have two. The running centre is needed for the tailstock and several are available. There are also several combination running centres which offer a number of options – solid and cup centres, a double-cone centre, an extended solid centre used with tiny work, and a screwed fitting to which a turned wooden disc can be added and inserted just inside the cup to support it while cutting the thin stem or pedestal. The *Teknatool* centre system has a stepped cone which will accept round or square stock up to 2in (50mm).

Tool rests are best when made dead straight with a rounded edge to ease the movement of the tool along the work. A number of sizes are needed. Curved rests for bowl work will be found useful, and care must be taken in their selection as a number are made which can only be used with scraping tools. An adjustable one is advisable for deep work.

Equipment for holding bowls, cups, and similar work has changed a great deal in recent times – indeed, the ideas seem unending. Certainly a screw

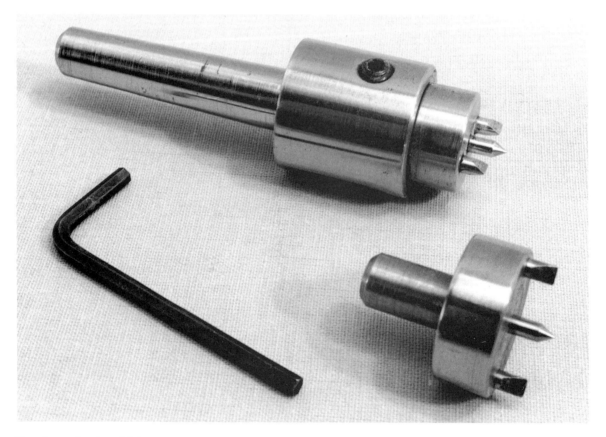

Turnbry twin-dog driving centre

Four-prong centre

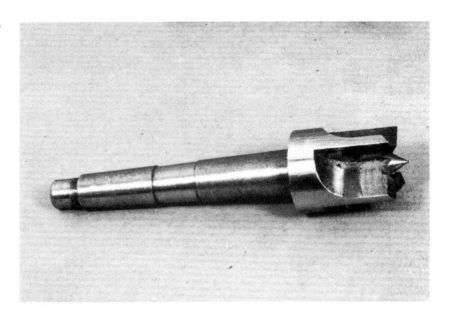

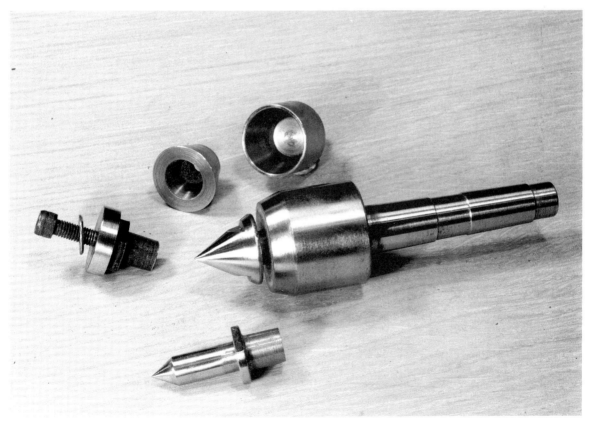

Craft Supplies Multi-purpose centre

Teknatool centre system

Tool rests

Glaser screw chuck

chuck is needed and you should choose one with a parallel threaded screw. A popular one is the *Glaser* which offers two sizes in one; as does the *Tyme*. A wood screw was normally fitted to most of the chucks, the best of the old ones being the *Coronet*, the screw of which could be changed at will and adjusted for length within the chuck. A company called *Turnbry* are offering a conversion kit or they will convert the chuck for you, which turns the *Coronet* into a perfect screw chuck with a strongly threaded parallel screw.

Few wood turners will quarrel with the statement that the greatest advance in equipment is seen in the multi-purpose chuck. There are a number of these and space will not permit a detailed discussion but the following points are given so that chucks can be compared to see how they match up and whether they will meet your particular needs.

(a) The chuck should completely eliminate the problems of chucking, for example the centring when the job is reversed.

(b) In one basic chuck as many advantages as possible should be included to reduce the cost, to offer plenty of working options, and also to be readily available.

(c) The workpiece should be held positively and strongly with no possibility of its running off centre.

(d) Accuracy of running of thin walled items to be turned, and accuracy of fit to permit thin base sections.

(e) No holes should be left in the completed work.

(f) Protection of components against rust and staining.

(g) The chucks should preferably be available in most countries and compatible with the lathes of well known manufacturers.

(h) Chucks should be made as light as possible commensurate with strength, but the jaws should be of machined steel to offer a high degree of accuracy.

(i) Interchangeability of all components in one chuck body, for both left and right hand, to reduce cost.

(j) Spanners and keys should be well made.

(k) Sizes must be clearly stated as components such as pin chucks must be matched with boring tools.

(l) The price must be competitive.

A typical lathe

The *Myford* company is well known to turners all over the world; for more than forty years the *ML8*

Turnbry screw chuck conversion set

(left) *Precision combination chuck*

(right) *Precision chuck, 3-jaw conversion*

Spigot collet chuck

lathe has been distributed world-wide and gained a great deal of respect. The new *Mystro* is, however, entirely different from it in design.

The machine is well built with a headstock in grey iron. The spindle runs in tapered roller bearings, and speeds of 350, 566, 916, 1,483 and 2,400rpm are available through a five-step multi-vee pulley which can be reached by lifting a hinged lid. The motor is housed on a hinged platform with easy access to a locking lever for speed adjustment. The headstock swivels and can be locked in any position between 0°

and 90°, with three indent positions of 0°, 45°, and 90°; the latter is for use with the optional bowl-turning attachment. A plunger locking device for the spindle is fitted which makes for easy removal of components and at the same time permits the indexing of the spindle through 24 positions for dividing work. All locking levers are ratcheted which eliminates the need for spanners.

The lathe is available in a long-bed design with a distance between centres of 1,016mm (40in) on the standard model and 316mm (12^7/16in) on the short-

Myford Mystro lathe

bed version. The swing over the bed is 282mm (11⅛in) and over the bowl-turning attachment (when set at 90°) 508mm (20in). Steel and timber constructed stands are available for both models.

The continuously rated fan-cooled motor is supplied with a stop, start, and reversing switch: the reversing facility involves locking the faceplates and chucks to prevent spinning off – a groove is cut to enable this to be carried out.

The bowl-turning attachment is an optional extra. It has two arms to support the rest assembly and these slide in channels on either side of the headstock, which is a very sturdy arrangement. The spindle and tailstock sleeve are bored No 2 Morse taper. A full range of accessories is available.

Short-bed lathes

Where spindle turning is not required it is worth

Myford bowl-turning attachment

examining the purpose-designed short-bed lathe. These are generally compromises to the extent that a manufacturer takes a standard lathe and modifies it, and this is the case in the *Graduate* range. An Australian company, *Woodfast,* have made a study of the problem and come up with the answer. The machine has a solid cast-iron bed which has been machined to a very high standard and can be supplied with a tailstock giving 450mm (17¾in) between centres. Swing over the bed is 210mm (8¼in). It can be fitted with a rear turning attachment which allows a 610mm (24in) diameter. The motor is totally enclosed within a strong metal cabinet: four speeds of 370, 650, 1,200 and 2,000rpm are available through a four-step multi-vee pulley. The spindle nose is offered in both metric and

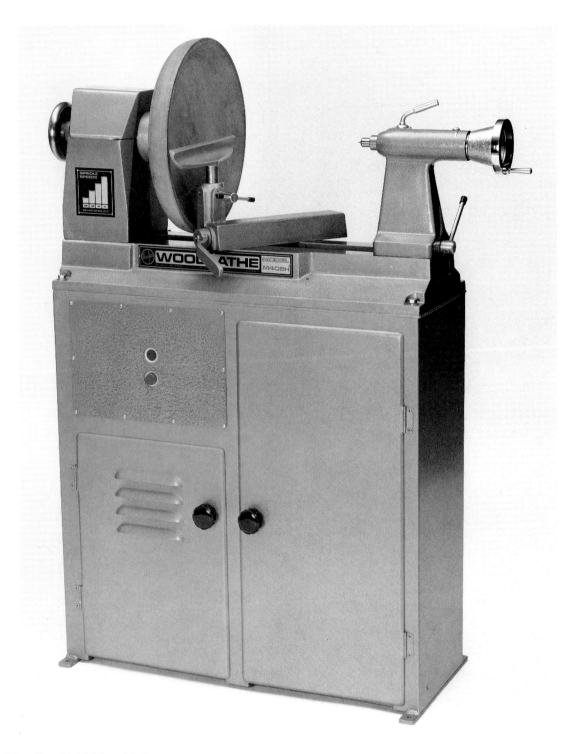

Woodfast BL 300 bowl lathe

imperial options and is bored to receive a No 2 Morse taper, as is the tailstock. The cabinet would permit the addition of a sand box if you need add further weight to the machine which is one of the quietest I have used. A wide range of accessories is available including two special chucks.

When making your final choice, choose the additional equipment at the same time. Consider carefully whether you need the bowl-turning attachment immediately, or if the inboard will accommodate the pieces you contemplate making at first. Certainly get a running centre, a *Turnbry*-type driving fork, and a short tool rest.

When you have gained some experience you could add the following: a combination chuck complete with a ¼in (6mm) screw chuck; an outboard turning attachment if the size of your work merits it, or if you feel that working outside completely free

from any bed problems will suit you best; and a long hole-boring auger complete with an attachment to suit the lathe if lamp stands are to be turned.

The essential cutting tools are best chosen in high-speed-steel (HSS) for long lasting cutting edges. The basic tools are all from *Robert Sorby Ltd* and comprise: one ¾in (19mm) deep roughing gouge – for roughing a square down to the round; one 1 or 1¼in (25 or 32mm) U-section skew chisel for planing and shaping between centres; one ⅛in (3mm) parting tool for marking out and cutting off; one ½in (12mm) U-section skew chisel for small work and beading; one ¼ or ⅜in (6 or 10mm) round-nose spindle gouge for coving and similar shaping; one ⅜in (10mm) bowl-turning gouge; one 1in (25mm) round-nose scraping chisel. All should be fitted with standard size handles except the bowl gouge which needs a longer one.

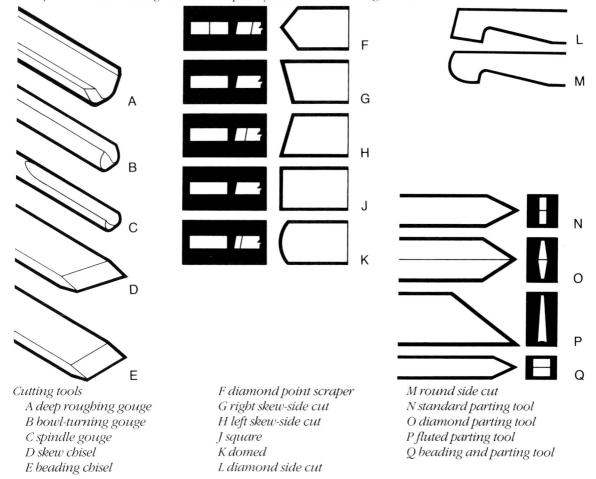

Cutting tools
  A deep roughing gouge
  B bowl-turning gouge
  C spindle gouge
  D skew chisel
  E beading chisel

F diamond point scraper
G right skew-side cut
H left skew-side cut
J square
K domed
L diamond side cut

M round side cut
N standard parting tool
O diamond parting tool
P fluted parting tool
Q beading and parting tool

12

ABRASIVES AND FINISHES

Finishing your work will demand the use of abrasive papers, and possibly some of the abrasive tools which can be used in the shaping or improving of curved work. The earliest of the latter type of tool is probably the rasp, which is made from flat, round, or half-round steel and has teeth which were originally cut with a punch. They are available in a number of lengths and are usually supplied without handles which must be bought and fitted before the tools are used. Probably the most popular shape is the 'cabinet' in half-round shape and 10 or 12in (250 or 300mm) lengths. It is a tool for roughing out and the surface has to be finished with a finer-toothed file.

Files have teeth made by machined cuts made across the tool: they are graded as coarse, bastard, second-cut and smooth. The teeth are either in single cut for smoothing, or double-cut, where the teeth are cut across the file in two opposed directions. Special files for carving work are called 'rifflers'. They are shaped to file areas which are normally difficult to reach and usually have rasp teeth at one end and file teeth at the other. They are available in round, flat or half-round.

A tool which is similar to the file is the *Aven Filemaster*. This has curved teeth on one side which produce shavings almost as good as those of a plane;

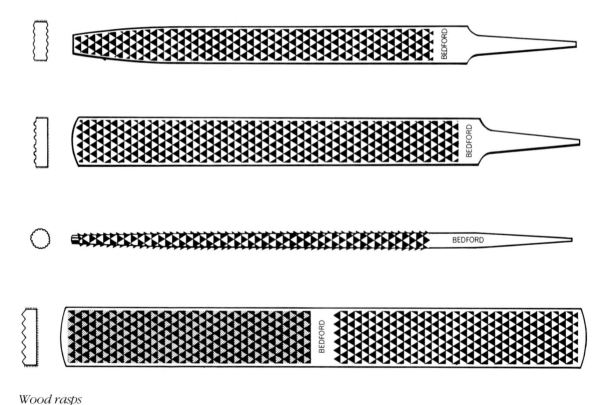

Wood rasps

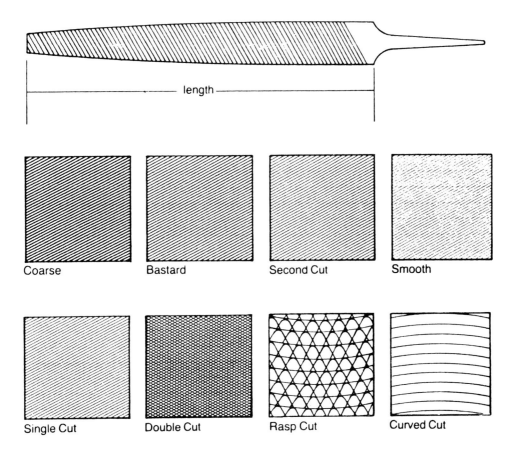

File and types of teeth

while the other side, which has crosscut teeth, can be used for roughing out. The *Filemaster* is supplied in flat or half-round section. The *Trimmatool*, which can be used for the same purposes, is fitted with a front and rear handle similar to a plane, and it is possible to flex the blade to convert it for curved work.

The *Stanley Surform* tool has teeth of unique and distinctive shape, first patented by a Sheffield company – *Firth Cleveland*. The blades are pierced to form rows of rounded cutting edges which remove a considerable amount of timber at a stroke. They are available in a shape that lends itself to a planing action, and also as double- or single-handled files, the blades being flat, flat-curved, or round. In action the blade cuts small shavings which pass through the blade itself and out at the back.

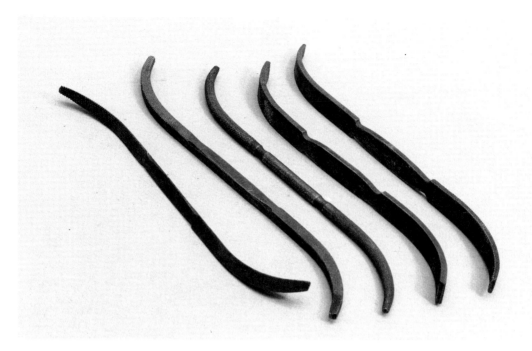

Rifflers

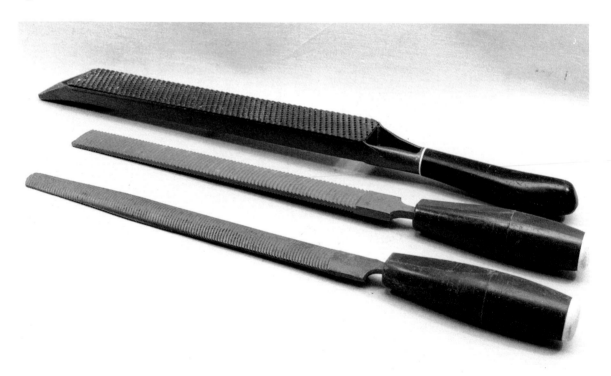

Aven Filemasters and Stanley Surform

DRUMS, WHEELS, AND DISCS

There is a number of abrasive tools which can be used with an electric drill. One of the most popular and fairly cheap to buy is the abrasive drum. This consists of a cylinder of plastic foam with a centre boss of steel through which passes a central spindle, usually ¼in (6mm) in diameter, which fits into the drill chuck. Abrasive bands of various grit size can be

fixed around the drum to make an excellent cutting tool.

Another long-lasting tool is the abrasive flap wheel. This consists of a number of flaps of abrasive paper attached to a central boss of plastic which is itself fixed to a central spindle. Larger patterns can be fitted to a bench grinder. Grit sizes are between 40 and 320, and wheel sizes 1½ to 3in (37 to 75 mm) in diameter. As the tool wears, more grit is exposed

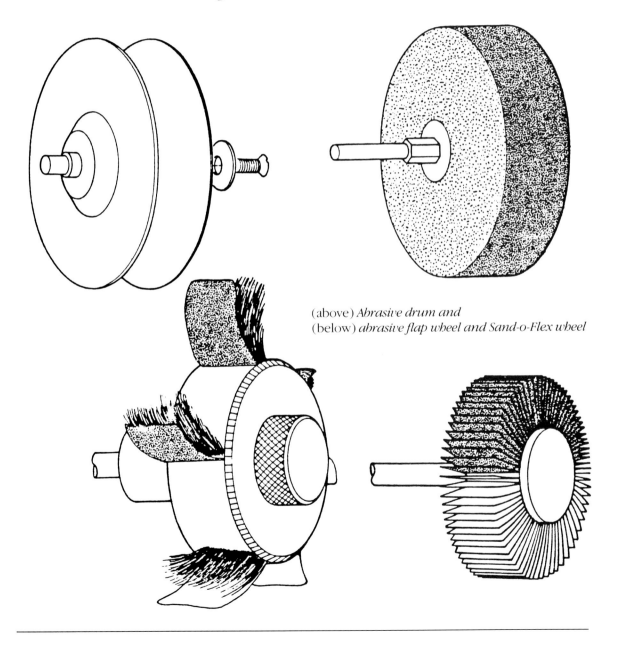

(above) *Abrasive drum and*
(below) *abrasive flap wheel and Sand-o-Flex wheel*

since the flaps are coated throughout their length: do not push the wheel but let it cut at its own rate.

A more refined abrasive wheel is the *Sand-o-Flex*. This consists of a hollow drum with several slots around its periphery through which pass abrasive-coated strips which are cushioned against backing brushes. The cushioning allows the cloth to work into and around shaped surfaces, and when the abrasive strips become worn further lengths can be fed through by turning the outer cover. There are several sizes available with coils of 50 to 150in (1,270 to 3,810mm) capacity. The tool can be used fitted to an electric drill or mounted on a stationary power unit.

Abrasive discs are made with a rubber, metal, or plastic backing plate and the abrasive discs are available in several sizes of grit.

Another type of disc is made from perforated plastic charged with abrasive grains, while the *Cintride* disc has abrasive particles brazed to the thin metal sheet.

Take care when using these abrasives to wear protective spectacles or goggles. Also, always apply a revolving disc carefully as its edges can badly score or burn the timber.

ABRASIVE PAPERS

There are several varieties of abrasive paper, the most familiar one being glasspaper. This is very strong and is coated with man-made grit which is available in many sizes; a quicker-cutting paper is coated with garnet.

Another paper is coated with aluminium oxide, a man-made grit that gives long life, and this is also used on machine belt sanders in the furniture industry. Broken belts can be a fruitful source of free supplies for the home worker!

The best quality papers use silicon carbide grit which is considerably more efficient than glasspaper. Wet-and-dry paper is gaining in popularity, particularly for work on the lathe and for cutting back polished surfaces. The grit is silicon carbide, and both the bonding adhesive and paper are waterproof. The great advantage with this paper is that clogging is reduced and there is very little dust.

All papers should be used with a block of cork or a wooden block faced with felt when used in the hand;

often you can glue the sheet to a block of plywood or timber strip.

Fine grades of steel wool are particularly useful for cutting back polished surfaces and for fine-smoothing surfaces on the lathe or bench. Abrasive disc and belt life can be extended by cleaning with an abrasive block, which is a kind of plastic which removes pieces of metal and loose grit. An alternative is to use a tightly rolled up plastic shopping bag.

Abrasive Papers

	Fine	Medium Cutting	Coarse
Glasspaper For all woodworking and general work	00-1	1½-M2	S2-3
Garnet paper For soft or hard woods. Longer lasting than glass paper	5/0-3/0	2/0-1/0	½-1½
Aluminium oxide Hard and softwood, also metals	180-120	100-80	30-12
Silicon carbide The finest – can be used for wet sanding and is ideal for cutting back polish	220-120	100-80	30-12

Velcro sanding system

This power sanding system is now in common use and finds special favour with the wood turner. It consists of a flexible pad fixed to a steel pin which fits into the chuck of the electric drill and there is a *Velcro* fixing on the pad to which abrasive discs can be quickly fixed. There are four sizes of disc, namely 1, 1¼, 2, and 3in (25, 32, 50, and 75mm) and they can all be supplied with 60, 80, 120, 180, 240, and 400 grit. The *Velcro* fixing surface on the pads can be renewed and the abrasive discs can be cleaned using a plastic pad.

The device can be used directly in the power drill or in conjunction with a flexible drive. When used on the lathe, the running pad is held below centre when working between centres, and between half-past and a quarter to the hour on the clock face when working on bowls and other faceplate work. The rotation of the work and the drill pad eliminates scratches and gives an excellent finish and the technique is soon mastered. Do use a dust mask. In addition to its use by wood turners, there are many applications in general woodworking.

NOTES ON FINISHING

Preparation

The finest of finishes applied without perfect preparation of the work will only bring disappointment and often only highlights marks and blemishes.

Generally, whenever a piece of cabinet work is glued up, all pencil marks are removed with a very finely set smoothing plane and a scraper, the latter being particularly useful for large flat surfaces. Surplus adhesive should have been removed while still wet – as it is difficult to remove when hard; it can also be harmful to cutting edges on tools. Veneered man-made boards, if badly scored, can only be scraped as the veneers are too thin for planing, and the careful use of the cabinet scraper with a fine setting is the only answer.

After cleaning up abrasive paper can be used (see table for information on types and grades). Abrasive grits and even the paper to which the grits are applied have changed a great deal in recent times. With the increasing use of machines both in industry and in the home workshop, the need has arisen for stronger papers with sharper grit and controlled distribution of the grit on the paper. At the present time I am using a silicon-carbide paper called EAC 177 made by *English Abrasives* and obtainable in hand sheets, orbital sander sheets, rolls, and discs. This uses a high quality latex backing and the grit is set in a specially developed lubricated flexible bond. In use this paper keeps sharp longer and certainly doesn't clog or crack as quickly as conventional papers.

Abrasive papers should always be wrapped around a cork block, or a wooden block faced with felt. Fold and cut the standard size sheet into four or even six sections for real economy, keeping the sheet flat and working with the grain. Periodically shake out the dust by slapping it against the bench top. If the work is well finished from the plane, there is little chance of picking up grease and other clogging; but with some timbers there will be an oil content which may cause loose grit to stick to the paper and eventually score the work. Be careful never to paper across the grain, and whenever crossgrain is adjacent to long grain a strip of timber or masking tape should be used to prevent scratching. Curved work may require scraping, in which case the curved scraper can be used. If the paper has to be used without a block, take care not to spoil the sharp corners and other features by over-rubbing.

The orbital sander is a great help in cleaning up, but it must be followed by a number of grades of paper to remove the tiny circular scores it leaves behind. Start with 180 grit paper, and then change to 240; but where wood fibres have to be cut back a smaller grit number will be needed, such as 150 or 120.

Cleaning up can also be carried out, with care, using 0000 grade steel wool. Wrap a piece into a small ball and rub the work gently; the sharp edges will cut the very tiniest of shavings. Carefully brush down the work after this, and don't get fragments of steel in your fingers. Steel wool may also be needed at a later stage for rubbing down some kinds of polish. Clean off the work with a brush or a lint-free cloth before applying any finish.

Polishing of any kind should be carried out in a well-ventilated and dust-free atmosphere since any grit may spoil the finished surfaces and some finishes may spoil your health, unless you read the maker's instructions: he knows best and it is incumbent on him to inform you of any dangers to health inherent in the material.

FINISHES

Most timbers have a beauty of grain and colour which makes one ever appreciative of the wonders of nature. Few need the application of colour, although many will be enhanced by the application of an oil.

Stoppers

Many timbers have very open grain and if french polishes or similar finishes are to be used the grain will need to be filled. There may be the occasional flaw or indentation in the timber which cannot be removed with abrasives, and here a stopper must be used. One of these is beaumontage which is supplied in stick form and obtainable in a variety of colours. Warm a small knife to melt the tip of the stick and apply, leaving a little surplus which can be removed when set with abrasive paper. A mix of *Araldite* epoxy resin and fine wood dust makes the very best of fillers and if made up in the same colour, the blemish becomes almost invisible and the epoxy resin and wood dust mixture has a polish of its own. Alternatively, you can heat a mix of beeswax and natural resin in equal quantities, add some colour pigment to match the work, and apply it with a heated knife.

Stains

There are any number of proprietary brands of stain available in a range of acceptable colours, but you may have to choose a special colour to match an existing piece. There are a number of companies who stock every conceivable kind of staining and polishing materials.

Water-based dyes are probably the cheapest and the most commonly used, but unfortunately they are extremely difficult to apply evenly. The method is to dissolve the dye in boiling water, adding sufficient to produce the requisite depth of colour.

The work must be carefully prepared before applying the stain. First wipe the surfaces with a warm, wet cloth; this will raise the grain which, when dry, must be papered off. Brush away any dust, and if necessary wipe with the wet cloth once more; the necessity for this second application will depend on the type of timber. Stain the work using a sponge, this gives a quicker and more even stain than a brush, and also helps to avoid the darker lines where the applications overlap. A number of coats may be needed, and each should be rubbed down with 300 paper or a finer grade before polish is applied.

Oil stains can be made by mixing colour, turpen-tine (or turpentine substitute, also called 'white spirit') and linseed oil, but it is best to obtain a proprietary brand if possible. They are less difficult to apply than water stains, they do not penetrate quite so deeply, but take just that little while longer to dry while producing a more even spread of colour.

Some woodworkers use aniline dyes which are soluble in turpentine substitute (white spirit). They are available in a very wide range of colours, but dry quickly and can sometimes react with other finishes to ruin the job.

The stains of my youth were pretty standard be-cause they were cheap. Bichromate of potash dissolved in warm water was a very popular one, giving a walnut colour, while Vandyke crystals were used to produce an oak effect.

Always try out any stain on a piece of scrap wood before applying it to the finished job.

Filling

This may be needed with some very open-grained timbers such as oak. The standard method is to use plaster of Paris and water; dip a cloth in the water and then in the powder and rub into the wood using a circular motion. Use a piece of hessian to wipe away the surplus and, when dry, paper down using a very fine grade. Another filler can be made by mixing plaster of Paris with linseed oil and adding a colour pigment.

With less open grain the best filler to use is a sand-ing sealer which can be bought from most stockists. This is shellac in a petro-chemical base and several coats can be applied to seal the work effectively, and is popular with wood turners. If the work has been oil stained, then it will be wise to fill with a shellac-type filler. Where the final polish is to be lacquer the filler should be of the same material, indeed the lac-quer itself can be used as the filler, each coat being cut back when dry.

Oil finishes

There are a number of excellent oil finishes on the market. They all vary in drying time, but most are acceptable since they serve to enhance the colour and grain without changing them. Linseed oil was the most popular of these in times past. The raw lin-seed oil was mixed with turpentine in the propor-tion of 8 to 1 and applied with a cloth. Unfortunately, drying is slow and it takes quite a long time to get a good finish. Mahogany was treated with linseed oil which was dyed with Alkanet root.

Linseed oil has been largely replaced by Danish oil, and this is one of the best. It dries very hard and fairly quickly, giving a trouble-free surface with very little tendency to show finger marks or accept grease, and it is perfect for wood turning.

Tung oil is another which is ideal for the more oily timbers like teak, but it does seem to have a rather oily look about it. Teak oil is in common use and is a popular one for teak furniture, as its name would suggest. They are all good to use and can be touched up from time to time should they become scratched.

Wax polishes

Wax has long been a favourite of mine and for many years I melted a mixture of beeswax, carnauba wax, and turpentine in a double heater to produce a fine hard wax. Applied over one coat of sanding sealer this produced a really finely polished surface after rubbing with hessian. Wax can of course be applied over almost every kind of modern finish to revive the polish.

Probably the best polish I have ever used is *Briwax* which was first mixed by *Henry Flack* at Beckenham in Kent. It is a mixture of waxes softened in a petro-chemical base which evaporates quickly, and burnishing with a hessian strip brings up a very high polish without great effort. It is widely used by wood turners and is also available in colours. There are any number of high quality proprietary wax polishes and some of those in liquid form are good for re-polishing dull surfaces.

Shellac polishes

Shellac forms the base for traditional french polish and there are a number of bottled polishes available some of which are classified as 'friction polishes' and these are basically for use on the lathe. Shellac is

Burnishing with shavings before applying polish

dissolved in alcohol to produce french polish; unbleached shellac gives button polish while the bleached is cream coloured and is the most commonly used. The application of french polish is an art in itself but some woodworkers apply it with a brush and cut back each coat to produce a glass-like finish. All these finishes can be removed or touched up as the need arises.

Synthetic finishes

There are a number of these which are clear finishes such as polyurethane; they can be used to produce a coat of polish rather like a coat of paint. They usually have a petro-chemical base and dry quickly, and have various qualities depending on the type – general durability, heat resistance, and suitability for interior and exterior use. They are not easy to apply evenly, and the surface can often disappoint. Use only a minimum of brushing; indeed, they are probably best applied with a spray gun which will of course preclude them from use in a home workshop.

A finish recommended for use on the lathe and one which is particularly useful for vessels designed to hold liquids, is a two-part mix acid-catalyst polish called *Rustin's Plastic Coating*. It is applied, allowed to dry, and then cut back with steel wool dipped in wax polish which eliminates the tendency of the polish to pull. The final polish can be cut back to an eggshell finish, and the result is a lasting one provided the instructions are followed exactly. Another method of cutting back is to use wet-and-dry silicon-carbide paper wet, and grade 320 usually does the job well. Melamine lacquer is applied in the same way as *Plastic Coating*.

Varnishes

The old fashioned copal varnish had much to recommend it, particularly for household use on both internal and external woodwork. The modern synthetic is a poor substitute in my view, and the craftsman is advised to read the notes about any proprietary brand which he is tempted to buy as many cannot be universally applied.

Bleaches

It may often be necessary to bleach or change the colour of a piece by bleaching. A proprietary brand from a reputable manufacturer is the best bleach to use as using the old standby of oxalic acid can be harmful to both skin and clothes. The bleaching action must be controlled after the bleach has been applied with a brush, and the manufacturer's instructions regarding neutralisation must be followed scrupulously; always store the bleach in a bottle.

General notes

Always use thinners supplied by the same manufacturer as the polish so that they are compatible and do not react.

Clean brushes immediately in thinners before storing them.

Do not use too much polish of any kind. Wax, especially, should be used sparingly.

Indentations or bruises in timber can often be raised by using a damp cloth and a domestic electric iron, but great care must be taken. The iron can often be used to remove blisters in veneered work because the glue is usually Scotch or animal type and will soften with the heat: this does not, however, apply to veneered man-made boards which are bonded with a urea-formaldehyde adhesive.

13

SHARPENING AND MAINTAINING TOOLS

The maintenance of good cutting edges and the servicing of machines and other equipment rarely seems to get the priority it deserves, in fact many woodworkers seem to hate the whole idea and avoid it whenever possible. Yet the enjoyment and success of one's work depends very largely on the condition of one's equipment. Most reputable manufacturers give guidance in the use of their tools and almost always give some guidance about sharpening.

The cutting edges of most tools are perfectly ground before leaving the factory, and many are sharpened, but every edge will at some time need attention. A wide range of equipment for the purpose gives the woodworker plenty of choice.

BENCH OIL STONES

These are used to sharpen plane irons, chisels, spokeshave cutters, plough plane cutters, and other sharp edges, while slip stones are supplied in shaped forms needed to sharpen gouges and other curved cutters.

Oil stones fall into two groups, the man-made and the natural. The most famous and best of the quarried stones come from Hot Springs in Arkansas, USA. These are in a variety of sizes and the most popular for the woodworker is 8 × 2 × 1in (200 × 50 × 25mm). They come in four grades – Hard Black Arkansas (which is the finest), Hard, Soft, and Washita.

Man-made stones are available in Coarse, Medium, and Fine grades and carry the names of *India* or *Carborundum*. There are also combination stones with a coarse face on one side and fine on the other.

The range of Japanese water stones is becoming popular. These are divided into Coarse stones – (*Toishi* 1,000 and 1,200 grit), and Finishing stones – (*Shiage Toishi* 6,000 and 8,000 grit); these grit numbers do not relate to the grit sizes used in the western world. The stones should be used wet, but not flooded as the floating grit helps in the sharpening. They should be stored wet. I use a 1,000 stone for speedy sharpening and fine up on a 6,000. The bevel has a beautiful shine which is particularly important for carving and turning tools.

A range of stones called *Diamond Whetstone* is manufactured in the USA but is available worldwide. It is not really a stone but consists of a perforated steel sheet which has a surface made up of tiny diamond particles held in a nickel coating. The plate is attached to a hard plastic base, and water is used as a lubricant. Coarse 325 (diamond mesh) or Fine 600 (diamond mesh) stones are available complete in wooden boxes.

Rubberised abrasive stones are becoming popular for producing very fine edges. Again, these are not stones but silicon-carbide grit bonded in neoprene rubber. They are available in blocks, round sticks, or as slips for use on gouges.

SHARPENING THE CHISEL

The oil stone is best kept in a close-fitting box which can be gripped in a vice or set against a bench stop when actually being used. Put a small amount of thin non-drying oil on the stone; place the chisel bevel side down, rest it on the ground bevel then raise it through five degrees to bring it to the sharpening angle. Move the chisel backwards and forwards in a figure-of-eight movement along the length of the stone until a wire edge forms on the flat side of the

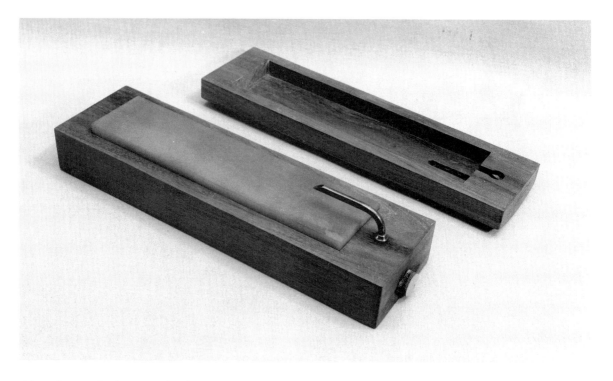

(above) *Boxed oilstone with oil reservoir*

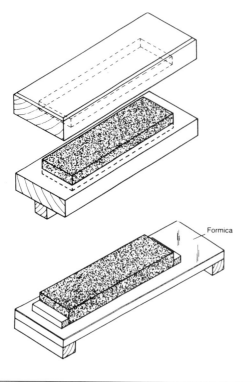

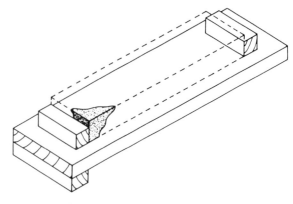

Various oilstone blocks: boxed oilstone with vice strips; formica-faced oilstone block; and oilstone block with vice strip

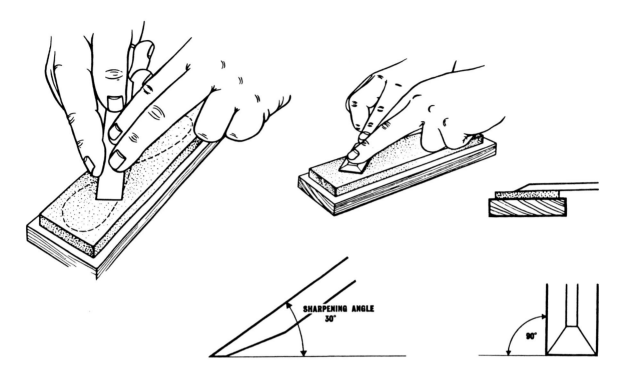

bevel along its entire width. Reverse the chisel so that it is bevel side up and lightly move it along the stone to remove the wire edge. Viewed across the edge an unbroken black hairline of cutting edge should be seen.

Sharpening the plane cutter is similar to that of the chisel but some woodworkers prefer not to have a sharpening angle and sharpen exactly on the ground bevel. Plough cutters are treated in a similar way, being sharpened on the ground bevel – this actually helps in keeping the cutting edge square with the sides which can be quite difficult with small cutters.

Spokeshave cutters are best held in a wooden holder while being sharpened.

SHARPENING GOUGES

The out-cannel gouge is sharpened on a flat sharpening stone. Place the ground bevel on the stone, raise it to produce a 30° sharpening angle, then rub it forwards and backwards along the stone while at the same time rotating it so that the whole of the cutting edge comes in contact with the stone. A wire edge will be created and this must be removed by rubbing

Sharpening: figure-of-eight movement

a slip stone along the inside of the gouge, keeping the slip flat. Put the final touches to the gouge by placing it at right angles across the stone and rotating it as you move it along.

The in-cannel gouge is sharpened using a round-edge slip stone which must be selected with a profile to match the gouge. The stone should be carefully placed in a vice, or, alternatively, in a specially prepared block. Oil the stone, place the gouge carefully in place, raise it to give it an angle off the ground bevel, then rub backwards and forwards along the entire length of the slip stone. When a wire edge appears on the flat side, remove it by rubbing it along the flat oil stone. Honing guides are a useful addition, particularly where the user experiences difficulty in maintaining the correct sharpening angle.

SHARPENING TURNING TOOLS

There are a number of schools of thought concerning the sharpening of turning tools. The professional

(above) *Sharpening the cutting iron*

(left) *Sharpening the spokeshave cutter using a wooden holder* (right) *Sharpening the out-cannel gouge*

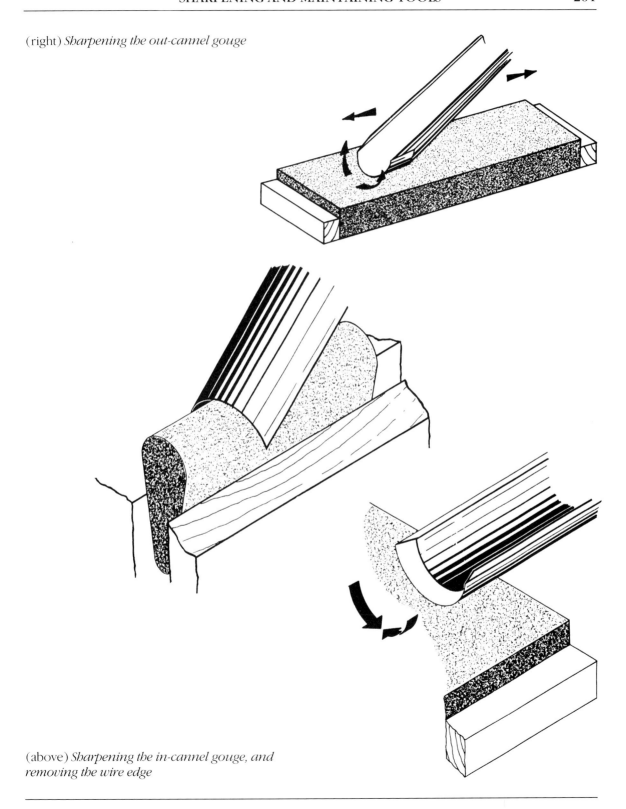

(above) *Sharpening the in-cannel gouge, and removing the wire edge*

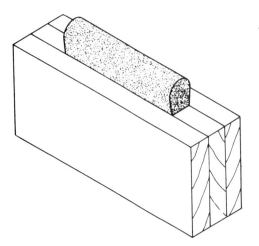

Slipstone holder

Footprint honing guide

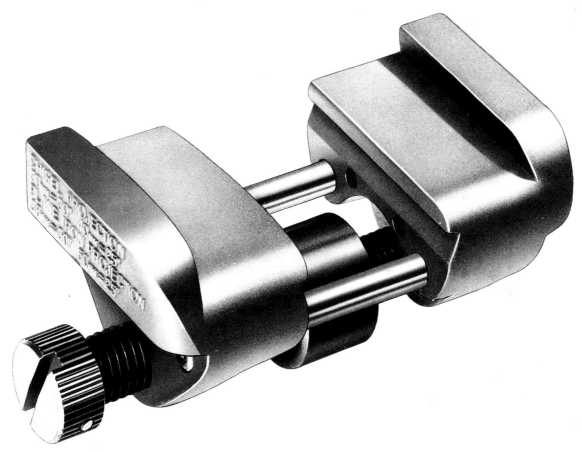

Eclipse honing guide

tends to sharpen on the ground bevel using a double-ended grinder, but care must be exercised to prevent the temper being drawn by excessive heat. Rest the gouge on the wheel with its heel rubbing the stone, rotate the tool from side to side so that the bevel·will rub evenly as the handle of the tool is raised. Some users use an oil stone to remove the wire edge which forms, while others leave it to break away on contact with the timber.

A better method is to use an abrasive disc set up in an electric drill which is itself held in a stand to present the disc horizontally. An alternative is to use an abrasive belt either in a small linishing machine or a little machine called the *Tantec* which is driven by an electric drill. These enable you to grind chisels and gouges without producing a great deal of heat to draw the temper of the tool, and the shape and angle can clearly be seen; the quality of the bevel cannot be faulted. The wire edge on the gouge can be removed by a slip stone held flat in the inside of the gouge and

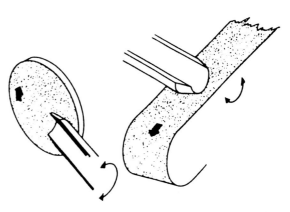

Sharpening on the disc or belt (note direction of rotation)

Picador linishing machine

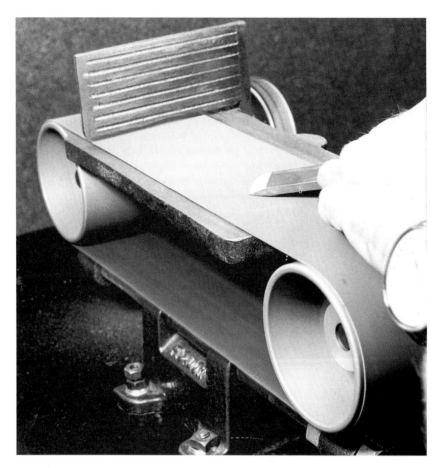

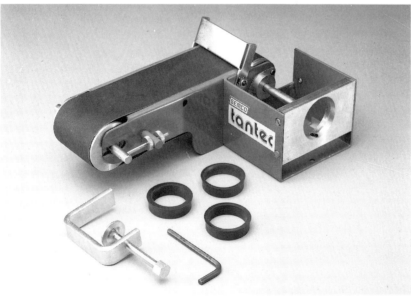

Tantec sander and grinder

moved around the curve. The chisel can be treated similarly using a flat abrasive block or a normal oil stone. These edges last far longer than any other and the polished bevel is a bonus.

Scraping chisels require a different treatment since they are ground at 80° and need a turned edge to scrape/cut the work. The flat side and the bevel must be flat. A burnisher, which can be bought or made from an old triangular file with its teeth removed and its corners rounded over, must be used to rub the flat side of the chisel in order to consolidate the metal at the hairline of the cutting edge, but this time it will be turned over to form a hook.

SHARPENING CARVING TOOLS

Carving tools consist of chisels, gouges and vee-parting tools. They cut and, at the same time, polish

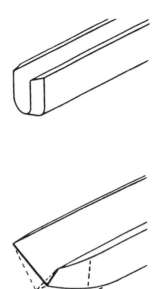

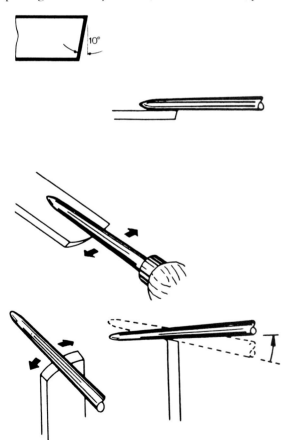

Sharpening the scraping chisel using the burnisher

Sharpening carving tools: veiner and vee-parting tool

the work after the point of cut thus eliminating the need for glasspaper. The gouges are sharpened in the same way as the out-cannel gouge, and particular care must be taken to maintain the shape, to sharpen on the ground bevel, and to finalise the edge by stroking it with a rubberised sharpening slip stone. The chisel has a rolled or curved bevel unlike the flat bevel of the carpenter's chisel. Sharpen as with the normal chisel but before finishing raise and lower the handle so that the back of the bevel is rolled. Again, finish with the rubberised stick.

Veiners are very tiny gouges with deep flutes; great care must be exercised in sharpening, and veiners are best done with a slip held in the right hand and the veiner held, sharp edge upwards, in the left hand. The vee-parting tool, if newly bought, must have much of the metal removed from the outside of the vee by grinding. Both sides are in turn sharpened equally by holding flat on an oil stone; when a wire edge appears, remove it with a very fine slip stone held flat in the vee. Any small hook formed at the outside of the vee during sharpening indicates too much metal which must be removed.

A leather strop with a dressing of rouge can be useful to produce the final edge and give an extra polish to the bevel, but the rubberised slipstone does just as good a job without the mess. Always store carving tools in trays or in a proper roll – if the latter, be sure there is no damp present or, alternatively, wipe them with a very lightly oiled rag before storing.

SHARPENING SAWS

This is a specialised job, but many woodworkers like to sharpen their handsaws even if the small teeth of the tenon and dovetail saws defeat them. Saw sharpening is carried out in four stages: topping, shaping, setting, and sharpening.

Topping is the levelling down of the teeth if they have become irregular due to careless use or poor sharpening. It is carried out with a flat file set in a clamping block and rubbed along the points of the teeth.

The teeth are then shaped with a thin triangular file with a width about twice the depth of the saw teeth. The saw should be held in the vice for this; a makeshift one can be made using two strips of timber the length of the saw blade, which is cramped between them. Place the file in the gullet and file at right angles, shaping the teeth so that any flattening on the teeth points will be removed. File so that the teeth are of exact shape.

Setting. Before a saw can be used the teeth must be set alternately to the right and left. This must be done accurately so that the teeth cut a groove slightly wider than the thickness of the saw blade to enable it to move easily through the timber. A saw-set can be used to do this job.

Sharpening can be carried out using a file. For crosscut saws, position the file so that it works on the front edge of the first tooth set towards you – the file will also be cutting the back edge of the left tooth which is leaning away from you. Move the file so that its handle makes an angle of 65° to 75° with the

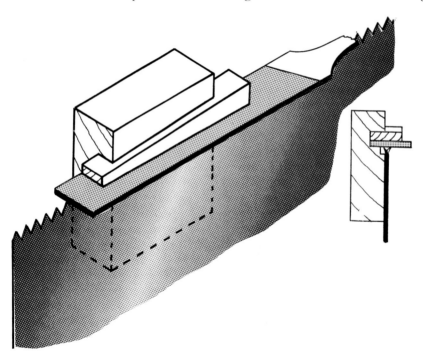

Topping the saw

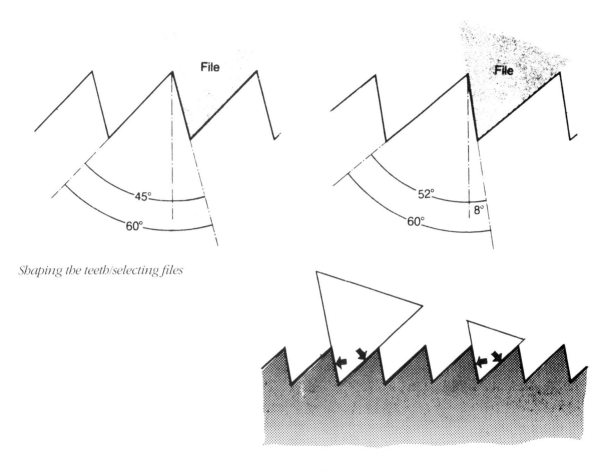

Shaping the teeth/selecting files

Setting the teeth with the pliers-type saw-set

Sharpening the hand saw

blade. Work through alternate teeth, then reverse the blade and file the alternate teeth to complete the job. Ripsaw teeth are filed in the same way, but the file is kept at 90° to the blade.

A saw guide sharpener does this job perfectly. Any slight burrs can be removed by lightly passing a sharpening stone across the sides of the teeth.

SHARPENING BORING TOOLS

Sharpening auger bits is done using a small fine file which will move easily between the working parts of the bits. The rule should be to remove as little of the metal as possible and maintain the shape of each part carefully.

The Jennings-type bit must have its spurs sharpen-ed on the inside; do this only sparingly and keep the slight curve on the inside. The lifters or cutters must be sharpened on the underside, and the auger must be held head down on the bench to do this. Sharpen on the original angle, and keep the two at equal levels working through the throat of the bit. The Scotch nose bit cutters are sharpened in the same way, but this bit has wings instead of spurs and care must be taken to sharpen these on the inside, main-taining the shape. The solid centre auger bit is sharpened in the same way as the Jennings pattern.

Special machine bits like the Forstner should be returned to the maker, but the saw-tooth cutter is easily sharpened with a fine file. In this instance we file the ripsaw-like teeth with the file, taking care to

(opposite, above) *Crosscut saw: set and shape of teeth;* (below) *cutting action of crosscut saw*

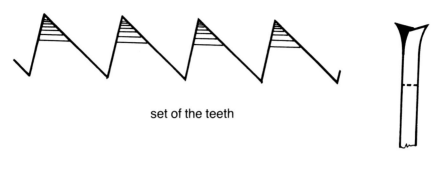

set of the teeth

teeth filed to knife edges

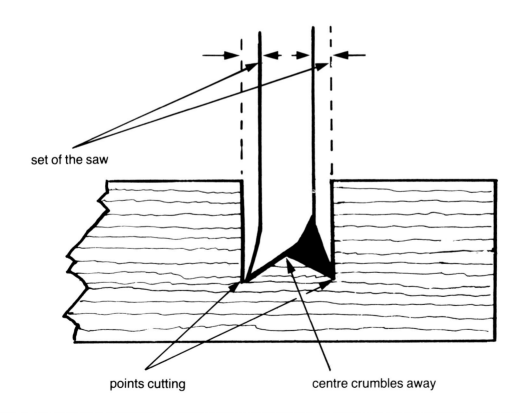

set of the saw

points cutting

centre crumbles away

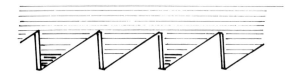

sharpen each tooth equally. Invert the cutter to sharpen the two lifters, passing the file through the mouth to file equally. Remember that the teeth must be slightly higher than the lifters or cutters to ensure that they scribe and cut the periphery of the hole before the cutter engages.

SCRAPERS

The scraper is an essential part of the woodworker's kit. It is used to clean up finished work, to remove tiny blemishes, to clean up veneered work and even to remove old polish. There are two types – the single sheet of thin steel which can be rectangular or shaped, and is called a 'cabinet scraper', and the handled or stock scraper which has a bevelled blade and is held like the spokeshave in use.

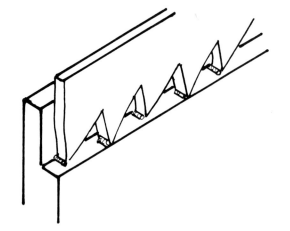

(left) *Ripsaw: set and shape of teeth, and the chisel cutting action*

JENNINGS BIT
Sharpening the Cutters.

JENNINGS BIT
Sharpening the Spurs.

CENTRE BIT (New Pattern)
Sharpening the Spur.

FLATBIT
Sharpen with slip stone
or dead smooth file.

Sharpening the boring bits

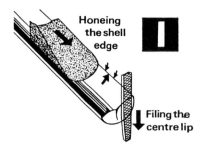

Honeing
the shell
edge

Filing the
centre lip

**LAMP STANDARD
SHELL AUGER**

BASIC RULES FOR SHARPENING

- KEEP THE SHAPE
  AND ANGLES
- KEEP THE BALANCE
  OF THE NOSE
- FILE BOTH SIDES
  EQUALLY
- USE A SMOOTH FILE—REMOVE
  AS LITTLE AS POSSIBLE
- ALWAYS SHARPEN FROM
  INSIDE OR UNDERNEATH

Sharpening the saw-tooth machine bit

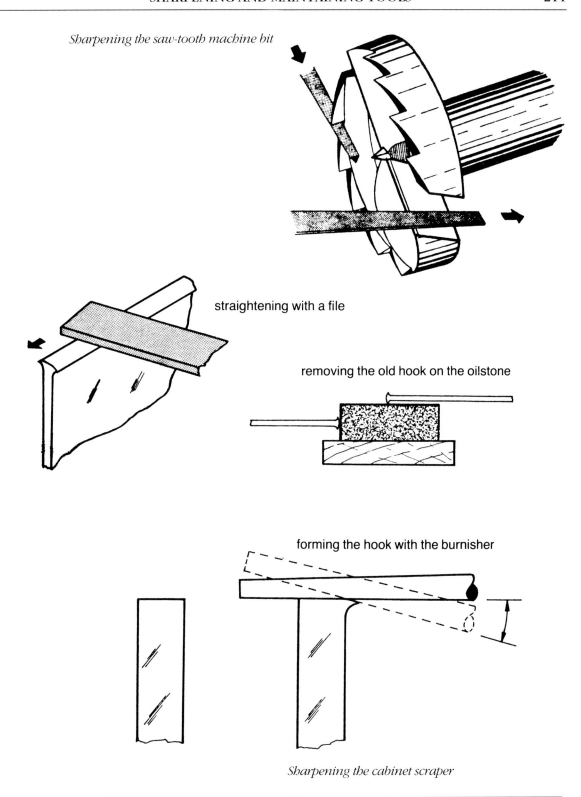

straightening with a file

removing the old hook on the oilstone

forming the hook with the burnisher

Sharpening the cabinet scraper

Unlike the plane the cabinet scraper has a hooked cutting edge which engages the timber when the tool is pushed forward at an angle. It cuts fine lace-like shavings, leaving a smooth and polished surface.

The scraper edge should be straight and flat and an old one may need filing by rubbing the edge on a flat oil stone to bring it to perfection. A burnisher or ticketer is needed and this can be bought; it is made from tapered hard round steel. The one I use is made from a 4in (100mm) triangular file with the teeth removed and the corners slightly radiused. This has the correct degree of hardness needed and when finely polished and buffed makes the ideal tool.

First lay the scraper flat on the bench and with the burnisher make twenty or thirty passes along the edge with the burnisher held dead flat. This is called 'consolidating the metal' and produces a strong edge. Place the scraper in the vice with the edge on top, place the burnisher flat on top and at right angles to it. Draw it forwards and backwards pressing down quite hard. As you proceed, drop the handle of the burnisher progressively until it makes an angle of 15° with the face of the scraper. The edge will then be turned over to make a hair line of a cutting hook. A woodturner's scraper should be sharpened in a similar way.

The handled scraper blade is ground at an angle of 45° along both top and bottom edges. The blade edge is consolidated in the same way as the ordinary scraper and its edge turned over with the burnisher.

Draw knife

This is a particularly awkward tool to sharpen on the oil stone. The best method is first to make a holder in wood which consists of a long block with a slot cut at

Sharpening the draw knife

Sharpening the bradawl

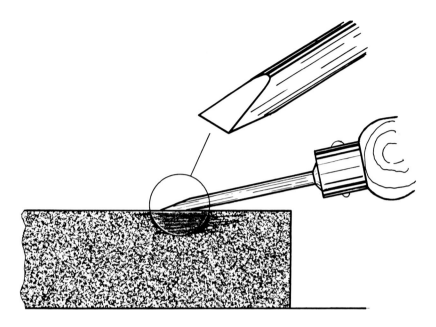

an angle to house the knife so that a flat oil stone can be rubbed along it. A sharpening angle of 30° should be aimed at, and the wire edge formed on the flat side will need to be removed with the draw knife taken out of its holder.

Bradawl

Unlike plane cutters, the bradawl is sharpened on both sides at an angle of 30°. This is best done on an oil stone, keeping the blade close to the edge to avoid uneven wear at the centre of the stone.

GRINDING

Grinding equipment can be very expensive, and unless the workshop is a very busy one, it is probably advisable to send tools away to be ground by a professional. Early grindstones were quarried in sandstone quarries, and water was used to keep the metal cool.

There are a number of modern versions which are motorised and are extremely efficient. The *Tormek* is one of these, and there are two models, one of which has an integral motor, and the other can be driven by an electric drill. In addition to the normal tool holder, the machine can be fitted with a grinding jig for planer blades up to 12½in (320mm) long. It affords complete control of the grinding angle and grinding depth to an accuracy of 0.1mm. An easy angle guide is available for accurate setting of the different grinding angles for numerous tools.

Possibly the most popular sharpener/grinder at the present time is the Japanese wet grindstone which can be obtained with several grades of stone for both sharpening and grinding. These often carry the name *Samurai*, and have a reservoir of water; the 1,000 grit stone produces a first class edge with a polished bevel quite quickly, while the 180 grit wheel can be used for grinding. A silicon-carbide stick can be used for flatting the stone and levelling off any highspots.

Grinding can also be carried out using a double-ended grinder, the combination machine, or the *Electra-Beckum* combined wet-and-dry grinder. The disc or belt methods already described provide the cheapest and most trouble-free form of grinding for the smaller workshop.

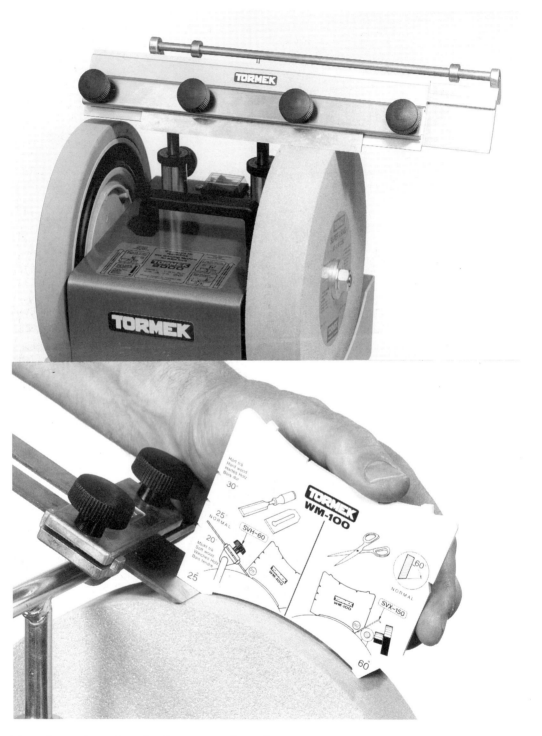

Tormek grinder with jig for sharpening planer knives

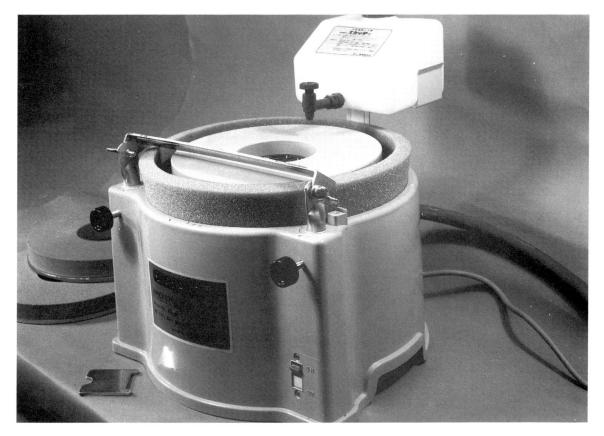

(above) *Japanese wetstone grinder*

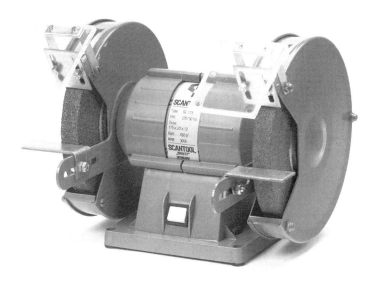

(right) *Scantool double-ended bench grinder*

(above) *Elu belt-and-wheel grinder*

(opposite) *Sharpening corner, showing a drill driving the Tantec grinder, and a drill fitted with a rubberised wheel and held in a Wolfcraft clamp*

(left) *Electra Beckum wet-and-dry grinder*

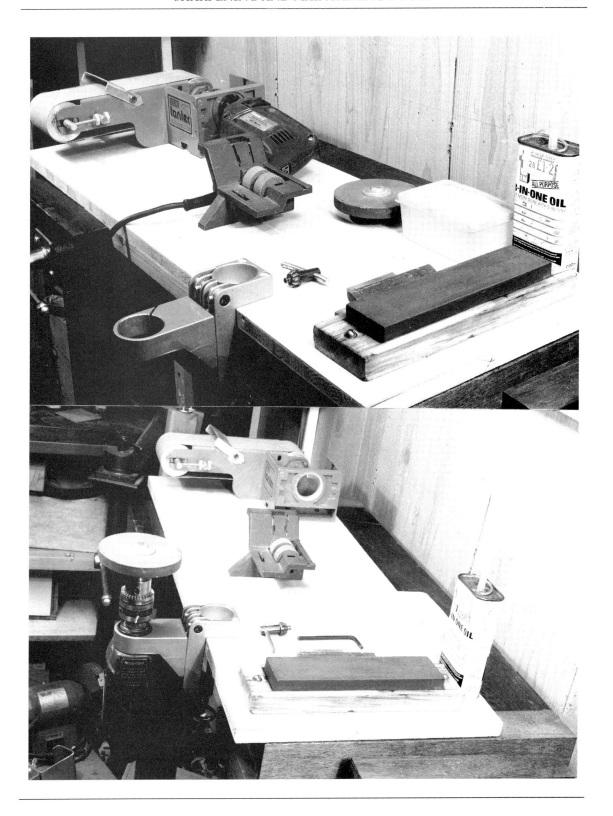

SHARPENING CORNER

In many workshops the sharpening and grinding equipment may have to be packed away immediately after use and it may not be possible to find enough space to have a small bench devoted to sharpening. To this end it is suggested that a small top is made which can be brought out and set up on the work bench when sharpening is needed. A sheet of man-made board serves as a base, and, using a *Wolfcraft* drill clamp, the drill can be set up to hold small flat discs of board with abrasive paper glued to them; the discs are fitted with an arbor which is held in the drill jaws. You can use 120 grit aluminium-oxide paper, but silicon-carbide would be better for all grinding. A slightly larger stepped disc could offer two grit sizes, one for grinding and the other for sharpening; the latter could be 320 grit. The second clamp is set so that the drill can be slipped into the horizontal position to accept small timber drums covered with abrasive paper similar to grinding wheels. This provides the cheapest and best grinding for the home worker; the quality of the bevel is superb, and very little heat is generated.

Sharpening can be carried out on a small rubberised abrasive wheel fitted with an arbor and running horizontally – this will produce a perfect cutting edge with the added bonus of a polished bevel.

A sharpening stone can be positioned alongside, but it must have a cover to protect it against grit and dirt. A box at the rear of the board houses the small slip stones and oil stones when not in use.

For many years I have used a *Picador* linisher fitted with a ¼hp motor to do my grinding. It is fitted with 120 grit aluminium-oxide belts; it is a little expensive to set up, and as an alternative you could consider the *Semtex* machine which is designed as a belt sander and is driven by an electric drill. This can be fixed to a board with sharpening facilities situated alongside; either using the drill, as previously described, or sharpening stones. Both the foregoing can be used for grinding and sharpening gouges, but in-cannel gouges provide a problem which can best be solved by using one of a variety of shaped grinding points, the shape of which is selected to suit the curvature of the tool. Rubberised points can also be used to carry out the sharpening.

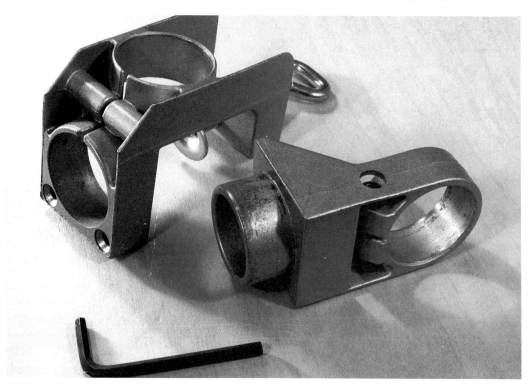

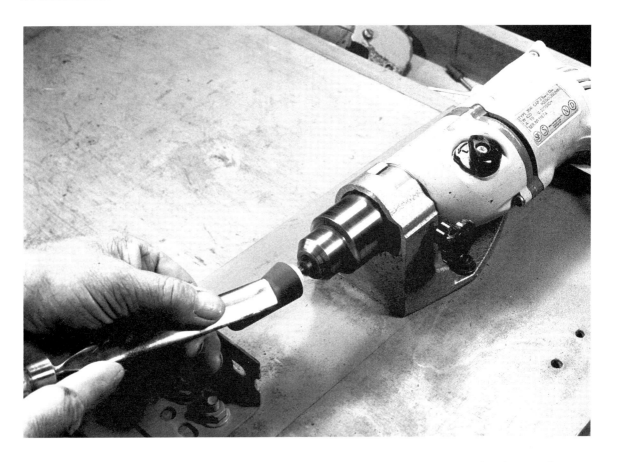

Rubberised abrasive cone used to sharpen the in-cannel gouge

(opposite) *Wolfcraft drill holder and clamp*

14
GLUING-UP AND CRAMPING

The great moment when all the jointing has been done and a dry run indicates that all is well and gluing up can commence is always to be savoured. Preparations for gluing must be made as carefully as for any other of the constructive processes, and bad work at this juncture can ruin an otherwise excellent piece of work.

In a big workshop it may well be possible to have a gluing-up table which will have a flat top and where the cramps can also be stored. The best solution for the small shop is to make up a cover for the workbench. This cover should be made of hardboard with battens around the edges on the underside to locate it, the front and end battens being held in the vice. This cover will prevent the top being smeared with glue while at the same time providing a good flat surface on which the cramps will stand firmly.

Glues are discussed later, but if a heated glue pot is being used it should be brought to the bench and should not stand on it. Cold glues, if in powder form, are best mixed and poured into an empty plastic washing-up liquid bottle so that the glue can be squeezed from the nozzle directly on to the joint. You will need the right type of cramp to suit the work and some guidance is needed as there are a great number of all shapes and sizes.

Bar cramps
Cabinet work will need bar cramps which are seen in two styles: one has a straight steel bar while the other uses a bar of T-section. The bar cramps are available with capacities of 18 to 48in (460 to 1,220mm) and an additional lengthening bar can be obtained to increase capacity by 36in (915mm). The T-bar cramps have capacities of 42 to 84in (1,066 to 2,132mm), again with a lengthening bar which adds 48in (1,220mm) to each one.

The bar cramp is of excellent construction with grey iron fixed and sliding heads; the latter is located by a pin which is attached by means of a welded chain and can be inserted in any one of a series of equidistant holes. It's a good cramp for most small work and is the one most seen in the smaller workshop.

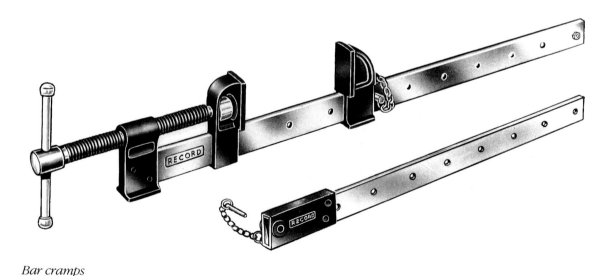

Bar cramps

The T-bar cramp, having great resistance to bending, is the one for large work requiring extra cramping strength. The head is bored to receive screws for permanent fixing to a gluing-up bench. A cramp which is an extension of the earlier veneer cramp is the *Speedcramp*, which has a steel bar similar to the traditional bar cramp on to which two sliding clamp arms can be fitted and placed in any position along it. This gives fast cramping and releasing, and 4½in (115mm) of cramping depth is a welcome bonus. They are available in lengths of 18 to 48in (460 to 1,220mm).

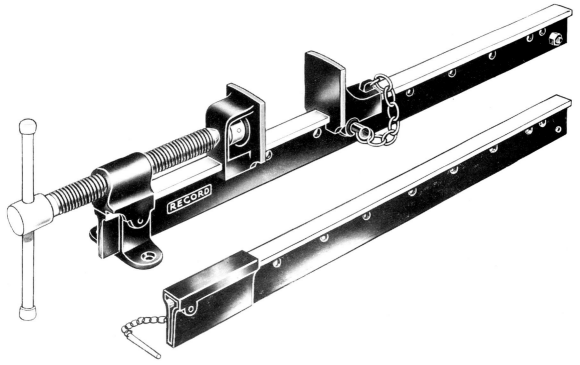

T-bar cramp and lengthening bar

Speedcramp

Cramp heads

Probably the cheapest cramp can be made by purchasing cramp heads. These are similar to the heads used in the bar cramps, with large thrust surfaces. They are designed to locate over a length of timber 1in (25mm) thick, giving you the opportunity to have any number of cramp capacities within the limits of your timber and your capacity to store it. The cramp heads are secured by steel pins which locate in ³⁄₈in (10mm) holes bored through the rail.

Another cramp which uses any standard steel pipe with an outside diameter of 1in (25mm) has two cramp heads, one of which is fitted with a screw and drop handle. They can be located at any position along the length of the pipe and locked by a one-way clutch mechanism which operates when the heads are placed under load. There are a number of variations where the head slides and the tail is fixed, or the reverse, where the head is screwed to the rod which has been threaded to receive it.

The *Jet* cramp uses a straight bar which can be fitted with two deep-reach arms, one of which is fitted with a thumbscrew which brings on the pres-

Pipe cramps

(opposite) *Jet cramp and its applications*

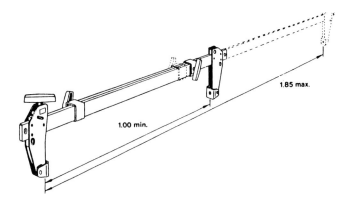

STANDARD EXTENSION BARS

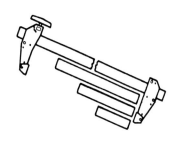

POWER APPLICATION

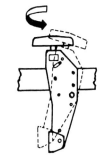

WORK-HOLDING ADAPTORS

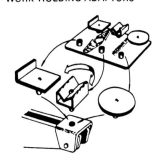

EDGE CLAMP

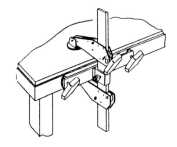

SWIVEL UNDER LOAD

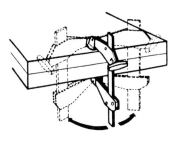

LOCKING WORK-PAD

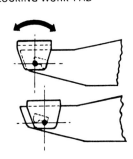

MACHINE CLAMPING

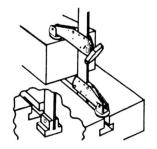

JAW COMBINATIONS

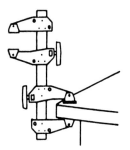

sure and locks the arm at the same time. This is a very versatile cramp since the arms have a number of different pads offering serrated, plain, rubber-faced and right-angled options. The arms can be reversed on the bar so that the cramp can be used in reverse to push joints apart. There are many situations where this cramp is invaluable and it is probably the most versatile of them all.

G-cramps

These are the most used and probably the most abused of all the cramps. They come in many sizes and in several forms – the most popular one being for general purpose use, having capacities from 4 to 12in (100 to 305mm), the best are in cast steel and are fitted with fast-action screws. The heavier ones are usually drop-forged and have similar capacities. A smaller drop-forged one from *Record* can accommodate work from 1⅛ to 3in (28 to 75mm); they are amazingly strong and ideal for small work. Other G-cramps are obtainable with a capacity of 4in (100mm) and with a deep throat of 1⅛in (28mm)

A variation on the G-cramp is the *Record* edging clamp especially designed for cramping edging strips on straight or curved work. It has a capacity of 2⅜in (61mm) with a throat depth of 1¼in (32mm) from the centre of the screw. Another version has three screws instead of two and is also faster to set up.

Handscrews

Years back the craftsman often made his own handscrews from beech, turning the wood screws on the lathe and threading both components using a screwbox and tap and this is still done.

This type of handscrew can be bought, but the screw is made in steel. The handle end of the front screw runs in an untapped hole, while the opposite end of the screw runs in a threaded hole in the other jaw, and the second screw is the reverse of this. The

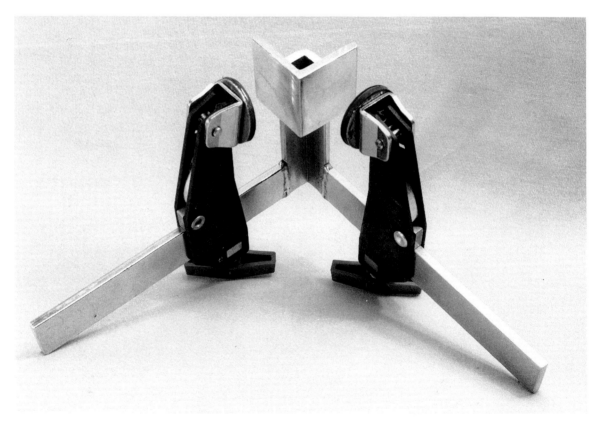

Jet cramp: corner mode

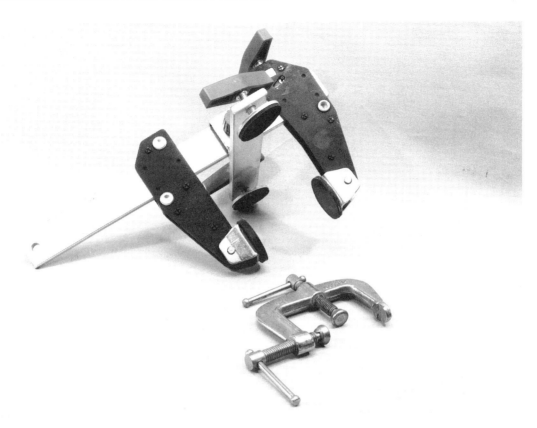

(above) *Jet cramp: edging clamp*

G-cramp and edging clamp

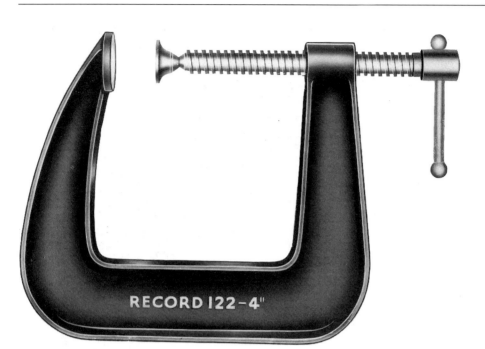

Deep-throat cramp

steel threads reverse direction at the half-way point so that each of the jaws can be advanced or retracted at one and the same time; they also adjust automatically to accept angled work. My woodcramps are heavily waxed to prevent glue from adhering to the jaws and care must be taken to avoid surplus glue running over them.

Special cramps

The spring cramp looks rather like a pair of pliers and has a similar action, with a capacity of 25 to 76mm (1 to 3in). The handles are squeezed to open the jaws and released when in position to give sufficient pressure for small work to be glued, or to serve as an extra hand.

For picture framing and other frame and corner work the corner cramp will be found most useful. The *Record* pattern will accept material up to 4¼in (108mm) in width. It can be used when holding work for gluing and pinning. For convenience in use it is best to screw the cramp to a batten which is held in a vice, and holes are provided in the casting for this purpose. There are a number of alternative cramping aids for the picture framer. *Wolfcraft* have an excellent band cramp that has a steel mechanism which applies tension to a nylon webbing which is wrapped around the frame when cramping. Further tightening is effected by pulling on the webbing at its free end, while additional cramping is available through a ratchet nut which can be turned with a spanner.

Another cramp uses corner blocks which are placed under tension by a cord which passes through them and around the frame, the tension being maintained by a cleat. A similar cramp has corner blocks connected by threaded rods which are tensioned by turning knurled nuts; care has to be taken to apply equal pressure at all four corners to maintain squareness.

Quick-Grip bar cramp

This is a new and quite unique cramp which can be applied with one hand. Available in 6, 12, 18, 24 and 36in (150, 305, 460, 610 and 915mm) lengths, the comfortable pistol grip and trigger action allows the operator to adjust the cramping distance and tighten the jaws securely to any job, using only one hand. The jaws and handle are made from strong, light-weight glass-filled nylon. The cramp jaws also have resilient pads to protect wood and other materials from damage. They are infinitely adjustable and release quickly and easily from the work. It can also be fitted with a corner clamping jaw.

(right) *Corner cramp*

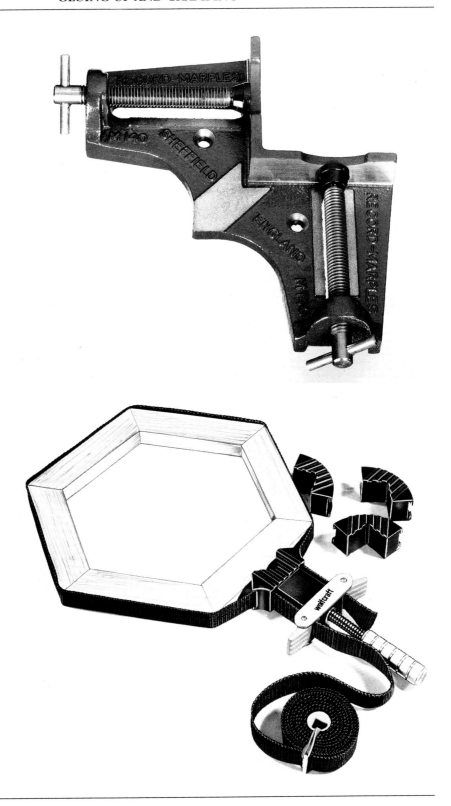

Wolfcraft band cramp

Cord cramp

Quick-release cramps (speed-type)
There are a number of these which are based on the old veneer cramp pattern and those illustrated are typical.

ADHESIVES AND GLUES

Woodworkers are almost spoilt for choice when it comes to selecting the type of adhesive to be used on a particular job. Certainly some guidance is needed because some adhesives, which have been designed for joining specific materials, are useless for others. You must also consider the setting time of an adhesive as gluing up a carcase needs time for cramping and checking for squareness. As many bonded joints

are 100% stronger than the wood itself, in some cases the strength of the bond may well be the deciding factor as to whether a joint needs to be used at all. It is generally accepted that an adhesive is a synthetic product of the chemist (examples are polyvinyl acetate, casein, epoxy resins), while glues have an animal origin, such as Scotch and fish glues. An adhesive bonds, while a glue sticks.

Conditions must be perfect for gluing up which means that the work must be free from dust, oil, or grease, and the timber must not have an excessive moisture content otherwise the adhesive may be useless. With some timbers which have a large oil content, the surface may need to be de-greased before gluing. The surfaces of the timber should not be highly polished, and in the case of veneering must

(opposite) *Quick-Grip clamp*

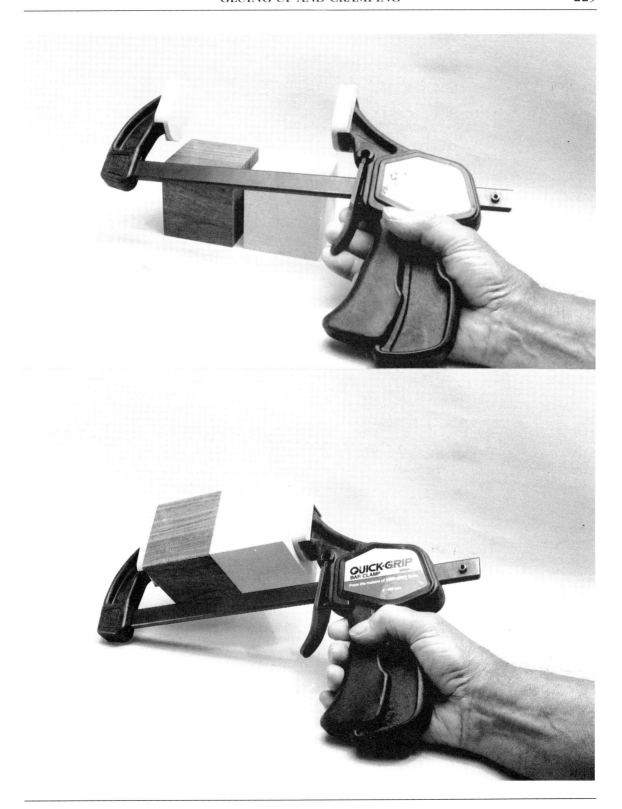

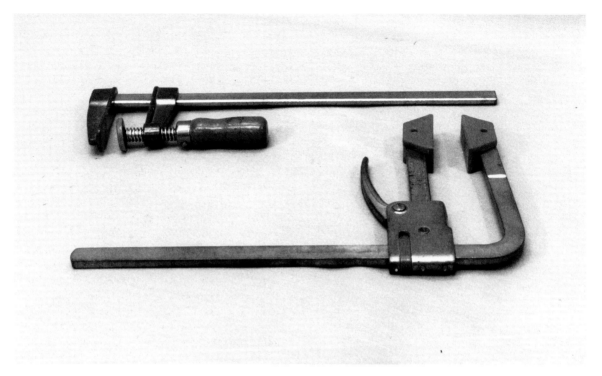

Speed-type cramps

be keyed to provide a grip for the glue; joints left from the saw also provide an excellent key. If end grain that is absorbent has to be glued, a coat or two of thin glue applied a little time before final gluing will seal the pores.

Animal or Scotch Glue

This has been used for centuries and is still the popular choice of many woodworkers and particularly those using veneers. It is available in cakes or granules and must be heated in a double boiler glue kettle. Electric glue kettles are more reliable and usually have an inbuilt cut-out to avoid boiling dry. Alternatively, the glue can be bought in the can, and a good proprietary glue is sold by *Croid;* it is ready for use after having been gently heated and a radiator often suffices to provide this.

Animal glue makes an excellent bond, but it must be remembered that it is not water- or heat proof and is not gap filling. It will take upwards of 24 hours to become hard, although this will vary a little depending on the surrounding air temperature. It can be washed off with warm water.

Polyvinyl acetate or PVA adhesive

This is one of the most popular liquid adhesives in use, and there are many proprietary brands. It gives a very strong bond, but care must be taken to avoid joint slip, and it is good practice to rub the mating surfaces together wherever possible to get a little initial 'stick'. It will take up to twenty minutes to harden initially and complete setting takes several hours; it cannot be used as a gap filler and is not resistant to heat or moisture. Any surplus on the work can be removed with a wet cloth, and it is best to do this immediately after cramping.

Urea-formaldehyde adhesives

These are some of the strongest, and one of them – *Aerolite* – was used in the construction of Mosquito aircraft in World War II. They are heat proof and waterproof and can be used in damp outside conditions; they are also excellent gap fillers. The adhesive has to be used with a hardener which smells strongly like vinegar, and as it has a limited shelf life it should be bought in small quantities. Setting time depends upon the type in use, and can vary between 3 minutes and 24 hours, any excess can be washed off with warm water before it sets. *Cascamite* is a well known brand name and in its case no hardener is needed.

Epoxy (thermosetting) adhesives

Most versatile because they can be used on wood, some plastics, glass and metal. They are obtainable with various setting times; *Araldite* in its Red Pack is probably the most popular, and it sets in 20 minutes. These adhesives are in two parts, the resin adhesive requires the addition of an equal quantity of hardener with which it must be well mixed prior to being applied. They resist heat and moisture and are very good for all outside work. They can also be used as a gap filler; care must be taken to keep the skin free of the adhesive as it can be an irritant. Wash down with white spirit or methylated spirits and then with hot soapy water to avoid problems.

Impact adhesives (elastomeric)

Evostik is a well known make of this type of adhesive which is largely used for gluing plastic laminates. The adhesives need no mixing and must be distributed over both surfaces to be joined using a spatula. When the adhesive is touch-dry and appears transparent, the surfaces are placed together and as there is an immediate grab, location must be exact. Highly inflammable fumes are given off which can act as a drug, and bonding should therefore always take place in a well ventilated room. The adhesive takes about 15 minutes to set; it has very poor gap-filling qualities and is unsuitable in hot conditions. Remove surplus with white spirit.

Hot-melt adhesive

This is used in hot-melt glue guns which have become increasingly popular. I have used one for the last twenty years to hold pieces on the lathe for woodturning and there is nothing better.

It is useful for gluing tiles to wood and for many other applications where instant adhesion is needed. Unlike most adhesives it never gets really glass hard and softens at temperatures around 200°C(424°F) taking a bare minute to grip. It is fairly strong with average resistance to moisture, and is difficult to remove without applying heat and scraping; it can be re-melted using the heat gun designed to remove old paint. There are a number of proprietary brands and the sticks come in several sizes up to 12in (305mm) long.

Super Glues

Cyanoacrylate glues are now in limited use in woodworking. The glue is particularly useful for the woodturner who can use it for attaching workpieces quickly to wood chunks for turning on the lathe as it bonds in a few seconds. The glue can also be used for stabilising loose knots and for bonding wet timber, but is too expensive for general use. There are several types. *Hot Stuff* has a consistency similar to water and is used mainly for gluing up close-fitting parts. *Super T* looks rather like syrup and will serve as a gap filler when parts don't fit closely and cures at a slower rate than *Hot Stuff* – generally in about 10 to 25 seconds, but this will depend in part on the type of material being bonded. *Special TM* has the consistency of cold honey, and is a better gap filler: it also gives time for the positioning of parts, generally between 30 and 50 seconds. The action of these glues can be further speeded up by the application of an accelerator called *Hot Shot* and this is particularly useful when bonding unusual materials, greasy and oily timbers, and when working in low temperatures. Special ingredients actually clean the bonding surfaces and act as catalysts to start the thermal reaction. Two well-known British brands are *Loctite Superglue 3* and *Bostik Superglue 4.*

The glues can also bond human skin and you must avoid getting it on your fingers. If you do, immerse them in warm soapy water and use something like a spoon handle to ease them apart gently.

WOOD SCREWS

If timber has to be joined without the use of joints, then screws are a better answer to the problem than nails. Screws are far stronger and can be inserted easily without splitting the timber and offer no problems if they have to be removed at any time. They are mainly available in steel or brass, although other materials are used. Brass screws are to be preferred if they are visible on the finished piece, and in any case must be used in oak, since steel reacts with the tannic acid and stains the wood. Aluminium alloy, stainless steel, and silicon bronze screws are also obtainable, and there are several finishes.

Three styles of screw heads are in wide use, namely the countersunk, the raised countersunk, and the round; of these, the countersunk head is the most widely used. The head may be left flush with the surface of the work, slightly sunk below the surface, or housed in either a surface countersunk cup, or one which is inserted flush with the workpiece. Raised heads are mostly used with door and other cabinet furniture such as lock escutcheons where they are seen but are not obtrusive. Round heads are used in assembling shelf brackets, outside gate hinges, and similar metal fittings.

Many of the screws can be obtained in a variety of finishes and chromium-plated, sherardised, electro-brassed, and japanned are the most popular. Screw heads are usually slotted but the use of *Pozidriv*, *Philips*, and other cruciform types is increasing.

Screw thread configuration has remained the same for decades, but in recent times, largely through the efforts of *Nettlefolds Stock-Point* in the UK, a whole new range has been created.

First came the *Twinfast,* which unlike the traditional screw is threaded throughout its length and has a self-centring point and a double thread giving an easy start. It keeps its centre and only requires half the number of turns and the grip in the timber is also much better. They are made with countersunk and round heads, and also *Pozidriv* cruciform recesses and are made in stainless steel.

A further development is the *Supafast,* which has an unthreaded shank like the standard screw and is made in steel. The *Mastascrew* has a countersunk head and is slotted, while the *Supascrew* is countersunk with a *Pozidriv* recessed head; a slotted round head is also available. All these threads are parallel and not tapered as with the traditional screw. They can be obtained in diameters 4 to 12 and in lengths up to 4in (100mm), depending on the screw.

With the increasing use of particle and other man-made boards a range of chipboard screws has been developed. They are in high quality carbon steel which is heat treated for toughness and fast driving. The thread is cut at a 40° angle for fast driving and good resistance to pull-out, a feature which is very necessary when using this material. They have a *Pozidriv* recess and can also be used in natural timber. These screws have no number but are quoted in diameter size – 3 to 5 in half sizes (also in millimetres); the lengths are from 12 to 70mm depending upon the diameter and they are boxed in 200s. With all screws the box carries a label giving size details and description of the screw.

PREPARATION FOR SCREW FIXING

It is essential when using screws to prepare the timber by boring a hole of shank size and countersinking it if necessary. If one piece is being screwed to another a hole approximately half the diameter of the shank is bored in the piece underneath into which the thread winds. It is suggested with *Twinfast*-type screws that the hole underneath is not needed, but use your own judgement depending on the hardness of the timber as with very hard stuff the screw may need some help. Holes for very tiny screws can be made with a bradawl.

Always select the correct length of screw remembering that at least six threads should engage in the timber. When a fitting is being attached, the gauge of the screw will be determined by the holes already bored in the fitting, but when wood is being attached to wood the thickness of the timber must be considered – certainly, small and narrow timber will require smaller gauge screws.

Where screws are to be used in end grain it may be necessary to insert a dowel cross-wise into the timber to provide long grain for the screw to wind into so that it obtains a good purchase. When using chipboard, plastic plugs can be inserted into a pre-bored hole for best results.

When it is impossible to sink the screw head below the surface of the work, the head can be hidden by threading the screw through a collar and snapping a plastic cap into place. When screwing mirrors in place, special screws are obtainable which have a tapped head into which a chromium plated dome can be screwed.

Coach screws are rarely used by woodworkers but whenever a bench is to be fitted with a vice, these bolts can be used to hold it firmly in place. The timber must be bored to receive the shank of the screw and its tapered thread and a spanner selected to fit the square head.

The table in Appendix D gives the size of hole needed to suit both hardwood and softwood. The sizes are quoted in metric followed by imperial.

NAILS AND PINS

Nails are rarely used in cabinet woodwork but at times they are indispensable. Most nails are made from steel wire, the round wire pattern with a round flat head being the most common. Since nails hold by friction, the fixing can be improved by first gluing the pieces to be joined, or by using one of a number of styles of round nail which has a type of integral spiral thread.

Nails are available in sizes from 1 to 6in (25 to 150mm) long and are used in work where the sight of the nail head is unimportant.

The oval brad has an oval shank with a small head which can be punched below the surface and covered with a filler. They are available from ½ to 4in (12 to 100mm).

Panel pins are often needed and are made in wire gauge sizes, the most popular being between 18 and 21 gauge and between ½ and 2in (12 and 50mm); the head is extremely tiny. A veneer pin is similar to the panel pin and is used to hold veneer in place until the glue has set. The brass or brass-plated escutcheon pin is used to hold keyhole and similar plates in position; it has a round shank and a shallow domed head. Cut and improved tacks are used by upholsterers, although they have been largely superseded by staples inserted by an electric or hand-trigger stapler.

Many nails can be galvanised to prevent rusting. When nailing always choose a nail of a length three times the thickness of the timber being fastened. Always stagger the nails and never insert them in a straight line as this will encourage splitting. A small hole cut with a bradawl will help to avoid splitting, particularly if the awl is used like a chisel to cut the fibres across the timber.

15

PURCHASING TIMBER

Most of the timber which you will use in your workshop must be bought and rarely will you be in a position to convert from the log, except perhaps in the case of the wood turner where this sometimes is practicable.

Timber comes in planks or scantlings all of which conform to standard sizing. Softwood planks vary in lengths from 1.8 to 7.2m (approximately 6 to 23 ft) and usually come in increments of 300mm (1ft). Hardwoods vary in lengths which are largely dictated by the species of tree. Planks of softwood can be in standard or random widths, but hardwoods vary, again depending on the species.

All timber is offered as sawn, and should planed material be needed, the instructions to the supplier must be clear. It must be remembered that planing will reduce the size by approximately 1/8in (3mm) in both width and thickness. Lengths under standard are usually termed 'shorts' and sold as such. Many of the exotic timbers are fairly rare and only come in small sizes; they can often be quoted as sold by weight in kilogrammes or pounds. In prepared sizes they can be quoted by the millimetre or inch of length.

The following table shows the abbreviations used in the trade:

PBS or P2S	Plane both sides
P1S	Plane one side
P1E	Plane a single edge
P2E	Plane both edges
PAR or P4R	Plane all round.

A combination of these will give one edge, one side etc.

SE	Square-edged
1in.ft.	Foot length
t and g	Tongued and grooved.

There are also a number of trade abbreviations which the average buyer will not need to know.

Timber is very carefully graded by experts, but it is as well to examine every piece carefully. Look particularly for bad and loose knots, long end splits, and splits within the length; also take a look along the edge to see how straight it is, and also look for curvature across the board. Always allow for waste at the ends as most boards will have some short splits. If a piece has to be bent and subjected to stress it will be as well to check with the supplier whether the timber will be suitable.

MOISTURE CONTENT AND SEASONING

Usually the timber you buy will have been seasoned to a known moisture content, but it is as well to check this out because in drying, timber will often shrink and also lose its shape as a result of shrinkage across the grain.

There are a number of small moisture meters which can measure water content, and you can always ask for this be done, particularly if the cost is high and the job an important one. Domestic furniture in a centrally heated atmosphere should be constructed of timber having a moisture content of not more than 12%, but garden furniture, worksheds and similar structures can be between 15 and 18%.

It is as well to remember that timber cannot be completely sealed, and it will lose or gain in moisture content according to atmospheric change. It must be appreciated that a newly felled log is full of water; the cells are saturated and the walls which form them will also contain water. These cells dry out after they have been fully seasoned and shrink, but in a wet situation the cells will still tend to absorb moisture.

Timber for wood turning can often be taken from freshly felled logs and turned wet. If the walls are left quite thick the work can be immersed in a solution of PEG; then removed and left to dry before final turning. PEG (polyethylene glycol) 1000 is really most effective in green timber. The PEG molecules take the place of those molecules of water which are held in the cell walls. Read the supplier's instructions carefully and remember that the time of immersion will vary according to the size of the timber. The turner can avoid this by turning his workpieces down to very thin walls and carefully allowing them to dry naturally in a home atmosphere.

Woodworkers always look around for timber, and often a hedgerow or garden tree, or one brought down by the elements will come his way. If such trees can be taken to a sawmill they can be converted by sawing and seasoned naturally. The sawn logs should be stacked with each plank separated with stickers to keep the surfaces apart and allow the air to circulate. The planks should be laid flat, off the ground, stacked as sawn so that matching of the planks is preserved. The stack should be weighted down, and be placed out of direct sunlight. For each plank allow one year for each one inch of thickness.

Always cover the ends of the planks with thick paint or paraffin wax to seal them, and this will also help to reduce splitting. Softwoods will take less time to dry. The stickers should be cut from timber which will not stain or harm the drying timber in any way and should be not less than 1in (25mm) square in section and be placed at regular intervals along the length of the stack, starting close to the end, and also arranged vertically above each other.

Remember to look at the timber from time to time

– it should never be allowed to grow fungae which may cause serious discoloration. Logs which lie on wet ground over a long period can suffer from a white rot fungus which will in the end completely destroy the wood. This infection at one stage produces spalted timber which is much prized by wood turners and others because it forms many beautiful lined patterns in timber. Very old timber should be closely examined for beetle attack as wood infested with live beetles can be destructive to existing timbers in the workshop or the home.

MAN-MADE BOARDS

These are utilised a great deal in modern woodworking and the present day worker needs to know as much as possible about them and the way in which they behave under the tool and the different forms of construction.

Plywood

The long-established three-ply boards have three sheets of veneer thickness timber with the centre one running at right angles to the other two. Usually all three thicknesses are equal, but the centre ones can vary, while the outer ones are always of equal thickness. Multi-plyboard has up to 19 layers with the grain of each lamination alternating at right angles. This type of ply is extremely stable, has little ten-

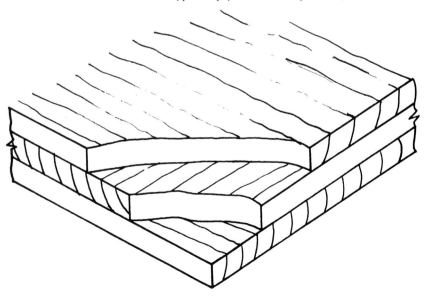

Plywood construction

dency to warp or twist, and is not affected by temperature changes.

Battenboard and blockboard
Consist of two outer layers of veneer with an inner core of timber strips with the grain running at right angles.

Laminboard
This is similar to the above but the strips are much narrower.

All the foregoing are graded for quality and durability; some are available for outdoor and marine use. The type of adhesive used has a great deal of bearing on the suitability for a specific purpose.

Particle boards
In the last fifty years a great deal of thought and research has gone into the re-cycling of wood waste and the use of timber which is not suitable for constructional work. Early particle boards used chips and shavings of random size and with little attention given to the type of timber. Modern technology has brought an exactness into the industry so that chips and fibres are accurately sized, and the strength qualities of the various boards can be specifically determined. Great attention is also paid to the bonding

adhesive which is basically urea formaldehyde, already mentioned in the chapter on adhesives, but various other additives are used depending on the intended use. Generally the boards are not waterproof and can have different facings added such as melamine, PVC, printed paper, or veneers.

There are various kinds as follows:

Single-layer chipboard, which generally has chips of equal size throughout:

Sandwich or three-layer board, which has an inner core of large particles while the outer layers are made up of finer chips.

Graded density chipboard, which again has a central core of large chips, but the chips between are graduated in size so that the face layers are extremely fine. Some of the better boards have sawdust quality chips and are very smooth.

The extruded board where the chips are aligned at right angles to the board faces.

FIBRE BOARDS

These use the smallest chips of all as the wood is reduced to very small fibres. Solid timber is placed in a vacuum chamber and the pressure is removed to form a vacuum, whereupon the timber explodes

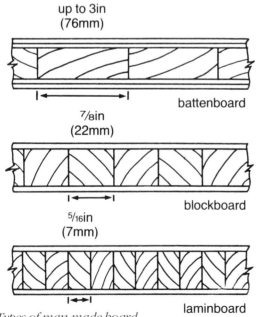

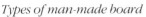

Types of man-made board

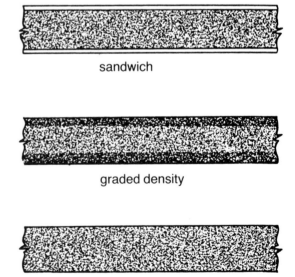

into a multiplicity of minute fibres. These are then mixed with water and the mixture passed over a wire mesh and pressed with a heated roller or platen to produce a bonded sheet impregnated with additives; it is a similar process to that used in the making of paper. The top side is smooth while the underside has the impression left by the mesh.

Variation of pressure determines the density and thickness of the boards; the faces can also be impressed with various designs or impregnated with heat-resistant materials.

Standard hardboard
Is supplied in thicknesses from ⅛ to 3/16in (3 to 5mm) and has a multitude of uses. Sheets are usually in sizes 4, 8, and 12ft by 4ft (1,220, 2,440, 3,660mm by 1,220mm).

Pegboard
This is hardboard with holes drilled at regular intervals in the face.

Medium-density fibre board
This is one of the latest products and there are also boards of low and high density used for every kind of panel and partition work. MDF, which is the trade abbreviation, is an extremely fine material which often machines better than timber, and it can be sawn, planed, routed and spindled.

Caberwood is a well known brand of medium-density fibreboard; the makers use the term 'homogeneous precision-made resin-bonded fibreboard'. It can be sawn, routed, drilled and edge-profiled, all with a high quality of finish. Further, it can be painted and lacquered, and laminates, veneers, and foils can be easily bonded to it.

Due to the fine distribution of adhesive and material there is little undue wear on high-speed-steel cutting edges, but tungsten-carbide-tipped tools are recommended. Circular saw blades should be adjusted to give increased clearance angles and increased hook angles to reduce the build-up of resin in teeth and gullets to lengthen the time between sharpenings. Parallel screws are needed for fixing, and they should be threaded throughout their length for screwing up thinner boards. The boards can also be nailed or stapled, but where dowels are used they should be grooved and the holes given 1mm clearance.

Boards can also be tongued-and-grooved, lap-jointed or butt-jointed, and can be edged with a tongued lipping. Mitred, tongued-and-mitred, and dovetailed joints are practicable, but care must be taken to cut the joints a trifle on the loose side to avoid an 'interference fit' which may split the material. Polyvinyl acetate (PVA) or urea-formaldehyde (UF) adhesives should be used for bonding under pressure. Finally 120–150 grit abrasive paper should be used for finishing, and the finished work is best sealed before colouring or polishing.

CHOOSING TIMBER

Obviously you will be influenced by the use to which the timber is to be put, and take into account any characteristics that influence your choice.

The grain of many timbers (particularly hardwoods) can be straight, curled or wavy, very irregular, spiral, or interlocking. Some timbers have characteristics of their own; thus one of the maples is distinguished by its 'bird's eye' figure which is caused by a fungal attack in the cambium layer of the tree. This breaks up the annual rings to create tiny indentations in the surface of the timber when cut. Sycamore, when cut on the quarter, has a unique ripple appearance known as 'fiddle back' because matched boards of quarter-sawn sycamore are used for the backs of fiddles. Often a timber will have streaks of colour – the black streaks in Imbuya and the pink stripes in Parana pine are caused by minerals present in the soil. Timbers like oak and maple show their medullary ray patterns to a striking degree; these are radial markings which show up in very few timbers when they are cut on the quarter.

Timbers can also show a marked stripe, as in the case of Macassar ebony, while many of the mahoganies appear to have a stripe when light is reflected across them; this is a characteristic of growth which affects the colour. Burrs are highly prized in timber and are caused by an injury to the tree; many small shoots form tiny knots which over a period cover up the injury uniting the cambium layer once again. Burrs are very difficult to machine and are mainly utilised in veneer form, although solid burrs are prized by the woodturner.

Resin cells and gum streaks appear in many timbers, and some are very decorative, although those in softwood can ooze resin which can be a nuisance.

Take care to avoid serious flaws when selecting your timber. Wood which is to be bent or curved to carry weight – as it must in chairmaking – must have long grain, and in such circumstances it must be checked for bending capabilities. Strength factors have always to be considered; poplar, for example, is not strong while most oaks are the opposite.

Timber pests create havoc, and much of this can be seen, so badly marked and infected timber should be rejected. The common furniture beetle is the most common pest and can ruin a fine piece of furniture over a period of years. Knots can be decorative, but loose ones should be avoided as they can be an indication of dead wood. Often shakes can occur in the growing tree – thunder shakes, for example, are caused by trees striking each other and show as interlocking streaks across the grain.

Many of the faults arise during seasoning; if a board is dried too quickly it will twist and warp and be quite useless. Such boards can be said to be in winding, twisted, curled, bowed, and sprung. Badly kilned timber can become case-hardened, which means that the outside has the correct moisture content while the inside is still heavily loaded with moisture. Be careful, therefore, to examine each board. A log of timber can show various types of shakes which can either appear as radial cracks or cup shakes, and these may occur along the length of a log which, when sawn, will yield poor grade timber.

Obviously it is well worthwhile to read books on timber, a number of which are usually available in the public libraries.

APPENDICES

FITTING A
WOODWORKER'S VICE

The top edge of the body jaw of the vice should be set approximately ½in (13mm) lower than the bench top. The jaw may either be placed on to the bench edge or, better still, let in so that its face is flush with the edge.

A packing piece will be required to fit underneath the bench top and the vice is screwed firmly to the top by coach screws which pass through the packing piece. The length of screws is determined by the thickness of the piece and the bench top.

Once secured, wooden jaw plates should be fitted to the vice.

These are made of strong hardwood, preferably beech, with the grain running vertically to give a hard wearing gripping edge. The top edges are made level with the bench top, and where the body jaw is not let in flush, the wooden plate must cover it to prevent possible damage to the tools.

It is not absolutely necessary to cover the top edge of the sliding jaw, but further protection is given if this is done.

Jaw plate thicknesses are preferably ½in (13mm) for vices with 6in (153mm) jaws, but ⅝in (16mm) or ¾in (19mm) is more suitable for those larger. A greater gripping area is obtained by making the plates wider than the jaw widths. These are fixed with ⁵⁄₁₆in Whitworth countersunk set screws.

If the wooden plates are fitted fractionally higher than the bench top they can be planed perfectly level later.

In order to achieve a firm grip at the top edge of the jaws there should be a gap of about 2mm at the bottom edges when the top edges are just touching.

CARE OF THE WOODWORKER'S BENCH VICE

This is often one of the most neglected of tools; the fact that they are generally well built seems to give the impression that no maintenance is necessary. The screw and nut must be kept free from dust and woodchippings, and kept lightly oiled. Vices of quality generally have a protective cover over the screw with a hole provided for oiling when necessary. Wear will certainly occur if the screw is dirty. The wooden vice screws also need the same attention. Wooden jaws should always be fitted to metal woodworking vices, to prevent damage to timber. The security of the jaws should be checked from time to time and their toe-in must be maintained to ensure perfect gripping. When checking the vice first open it fully, then oil behind the main screw head, the side slide bars, and the entire screw assembly.

VICE FITTED WITH APRON BELOW BENCH TOP

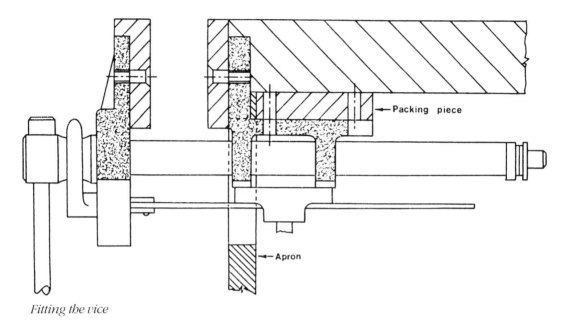

Fitting the vice

VICE FITTED BEHIND APRON ON BENCH TOP EDGE

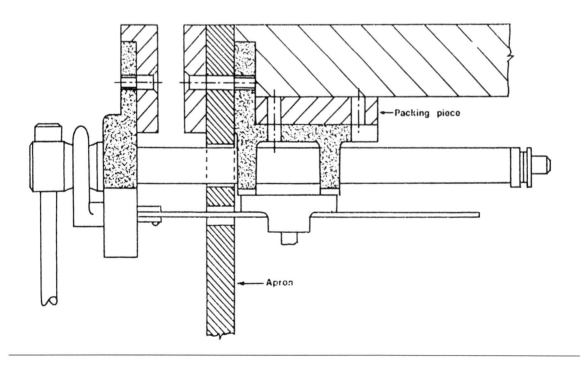

VICE FITTED WITH APRON ON BENCH TOP EDGE

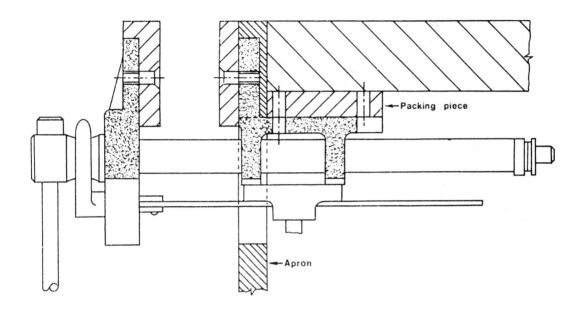

Packing piece

Apron

VICE BODY JAW FITTED FLUSH WITH BENCH EDGE

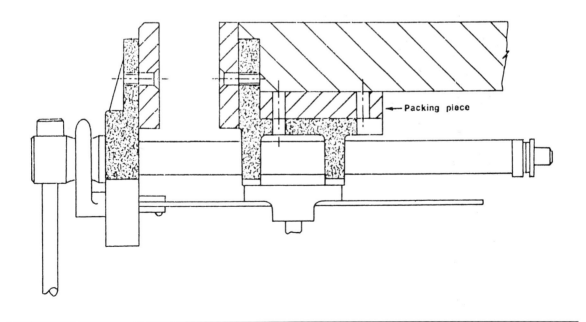

Packing piece

VICE BODY JAW SET IN MORTICE UNDER BENCH TOP

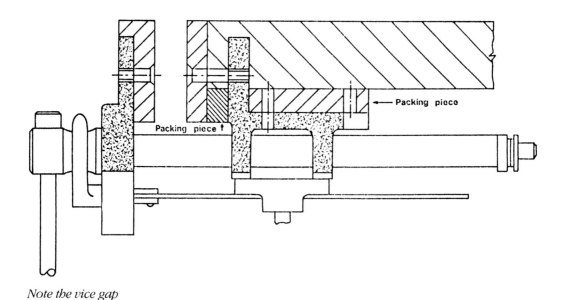

Note the vice gap

SECTION SHOWING GAP AT BASE OF WOODEN JAWS

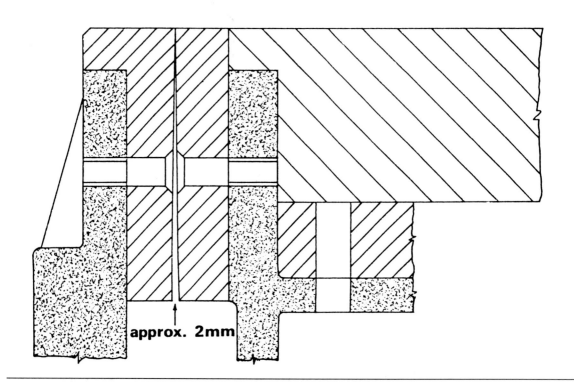

approx. 2mm

NOTES ON SAFETY

DUST EXTRACTION

Dust is one of the biggest hazards at the present time, especially given the wide variety of timbers. Some timbers can have a most irritating effect on the skin, nose, throat and lungs. If the craftsman has any doubts about the suitability of a particular timber, he should make an enquiry of the Products Research Laboratory or one of the government health departments.

Whenever possible, suitable dust extraction should be available in the workshop. Even with such equipment, fine dust will always be present, so a suitable dust mask is recommended. If working long hours in a very dusty situation, a power-assisted filter mask may well be the only answer. The use of a mask introduces another hazard, that is, the misting over the eyepiece. Use some form of spray to eliminate this.

The ideal situation is to have an extractor fitted to each machine, or ducting which takes the waste away to a central filter and waste collector. The dust-

The Mite wall-mounted extraction system

extraction system illustrated is ideal but, unfortunately, it requires floor space which might not be available, particularly for each machine. I have a wall-fitted unit which collects the waste from several machines in my small workshop.

Many portable power tools are now fitted with extraction nozzles which can be connected to a main hose. With a tool like the router, extraction is vital, since the head is often quite close to the action and the dust, particularly from man-made boards, is really fine and could be dangerous.

HAND TOOLS

Many hand tools have sharp edges which can be

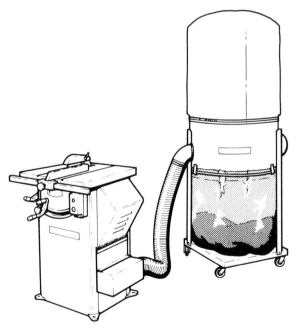

Startrite dust-extraction system

lethal. When chiselling, both hands should be kept behind the chisel edge. The workpiece must be secured in the vice, under a clamp or against the upstand of a benchhook. Always use the correct chisel for the job and use a mallet if it has to be struck. Chisels must be sharp; blunt ones are dangerous.

When sawing, make the piece secure; use a benchhook for the tenon saw and a trestle when using the hand saw. Always draw the saw backwards to start the cut, then push forward – and keep the other hand away from the teeth.

Whenever boring tools are in use the timber should be supported in a vice, and, if the holes are to be bored completely through the work, a waste piece must be placed behind the point of exit to avoid splintering.

Work for planing should be securely held either between dogs or in the vice. Always keep the bench top free from obstruction. Most metal bench planes are made of cast iron which can fracture if dropped or struck. Never check the setting of the plane by running the fingers across the sole.

POWER TOOLS

Power tools can be dangerous if carelessly handled or incorrectly wired. Always check that the supply voltage available in the workshop is the same as that of the machine. Follow the wiring instructions given by the manufacturer. Although most machines have double insulation, a faulty body or switch, or poor wiring can create a lethal situation.

Tools manufactured in Europe may carry a two-pin plug and whenever possible this should be changed to one common in the country of use.

Always use the correct fuse in the plug. Tools having 110 volts should have the correct fuse to suit the particular wattage of the power tool; 15amp for tools under 1,500 watts and 20amp for those over 1,500 watts.

Avoid carrying a power tool with your finger on the switch, and never connect to the supply before checking that the tool switch is in the off position. After use, switch off and wait for the machine to stop before putting it down on the bench or handing it to someone else. If extension cable has to be used, be sure that it is approved for use with power tools and

it is correct for the amp rating of the tools with which it is to be used. It is advisable to use a cable specified (and possibly supplied) by the manufacturer of the power tools. Take the plug out before fitting a cutter or blade, or attending to a fault. Never use power tools in the rain or very damp conditions. Use the tools in good light and do not use them near inflammable liquids or gases.

Do not touch earthed items like radiators and water pipes when using the tools. When using 110 volt tools, connect them to an approved transformer with an earth leakage circuit breaker.

Don't overload the tools, keep them away from children, don't use them in an untidy or very cramped situation and always put them safely away after use. Never carry a power tool by the cable, and never disconnect it from the socket by pulling on the cable. The cable should be kept free of oil, heat or abrasive edges.

Use correct safety wear, including goggles and masks where conditions are dusty. Keep clothing away from moving parts of the machine and, if your hair is long, wear a cap or net or safety helmet. Stand comfortably, and secure the workpiece whenever possible. Never work beyond a normal reach and, if you are working on a slope, stand above the workpiece (this particularly applies when using the chainsaw).

Don't leave spanners or keys in the machine.

Check regularly that the moving parts are free and undamaged. Check the safety guards constantly. If you have any doubts return the tool to an accredited repair depot.

THE BANDSAW

Complete familiarisation is necessary before beginning work on this type of machine. Read the instructions and obtain advice and training from a qualified operator. Check that the saw fitted is suitable for the task and that is sharp. Check the blade tension and adjust if necessary. Be sure that the top and bottom saw guides are correctly set and secure. Check that the guards are in place, the table is correctly set and fixed, and the fence positioned and locked. Use a pushstick, and keep fingers well away from the saw blade. Keep the top guides as close to the workpiece as possible.

The bandsaw makes a great deal of fine dust and should be connected to an extraction system whenever possible. Use a roller support or trestle to receive long timbers. Never leave the machine running, always shut off, and if possible lock.

THE CIRCULAR SAW

Check the machine before switching on: guards should be in place and all adjustments perfect. Never make adjustments with the saw running.

Keep the hands well away from the moving sawblade and use a pushstick. Always be sure that cutting is taking place freely.

Excessive force indicates a blunt blade, or twisted timber, or timber not flush on the table. The splitter to the rear of the saw should maintain the kerf thickness and prevent the timber closing as it clears the back of the saw. Wet timber may close up and be thrown towards the operator. The sawblade may also be damaged by overheating. Take care when cross-cutting to length to avoid pieces becoming cross-locked, thus jamming the blade and throwing the piece out. Take the greatest care to avoid touching the moving blade by carelessly handling the timber.

Timber should never be withdrawn from the machine by pulling it backwards. Ideally, a second person should stand at the rear of the machine to take the timber as it leaves the sawblade. If tiny rebates or other cuts are being made in small section timber, the operator would be well advised to make a slide or tunnel and fix this to the machine table. The timber can then be passed safely through with no danger to the operator or indeed the workpiece.

Keep the workplace clear of obstruction and follow the general rules which apply to the safe use of machinery.

THE JIGSAW

These are usually of the table variety, and should be bolted to the bench top or table. Make sure that all the adjustments are made and that a suitable blade is fitted. If a blower is fitted, this should be set so that the dust will be blown away from the line at the point of cut.

Since any guard fitted to this type of machine cannot completely protect the fingers, great care must be exercised when cutting. Hold the work down on the table, preferably using some form of clamp.

Be sure that the correct tension is set on the blade. Don't force the cutting, otherwise the saw may break, endangering both the workpiece and the hands.

These rules also apply to the Fretsaw machine.

RADIAL ARM SAW

The guards and anti-kickback device should always be in place and the saw should be operated with the hands completely free of the blade.

In the ripping position with the motor assembly turned through 90° the hands must be kept well away and a pushstick used. There is also the danger of the timber kerf closing and tending to throw the timber towards the user, although with the splitter and kick-back devices in place the risk is lessened. Always keep the guard as close to the work as possible to ensure safer working and direct the shavings away from the worker.

Don't use a blunt saw, or force the saw into the cut. Where possible the saw should have a footswitch fitted.

DRILL PRESS

Check that the belt is correctly tensioned, and the speed is right for the material to be cut and the size of the drill bit being used. Adjust the guard to give maximum safety.

Hold the work in a drill press vice or a hand vice, in such a way that the drill cannot strike the vice jaws and suffer damage. Set the depth stop in order to avoid cutting beyond the depth required. When using the hand vice, rest the workpiece on a piece of scrapwood.

This machine is best fitted with a footswitch, since both hands are usually in use. Check the security of the drill itself from time to time.

THE PLANER/THICKNESSER

Machines such as this one can be quite complicated

so read the instructions carefully and, if possible, obtain instruction on the use of the machine, its care and maintenance. Before using, always check to see that there is no obstruction to the movement of the knives, that all adjustments are perfect, and that the guards are in position and secure. Do not leave a running machine. Isolate it always and lock it whenever possible.

Adjustments should never be made when the machine is running. Always switch off and isolate the machine.

Whenever possible, and certainly with short lengths of timber, a pushstick should be used. If making one, use straight-grained timber, preferably hardwood.

Observe the usual dress precautions, and keep hands well away from the revolving knives. Knives must be sharp, blunt ones are dangerous and produce unsatisfactory results.

When planing long lengths use a trestle or roller support table to support the overhang. Keep the floor clear of waste and other obstructions. Connect the machine to an extraction system for long jobs.

WOOD-TURNING LATHE

Avoid loose clothing and use eye protection. For very dusty timber, a dust mask is essential.

The lathe should be bolted to the floor or weighted down, if very heavy and offset work is contemplated. Electrics must be correctly connected and complete cut off must be possible for adjustments to the machine. The switch should be close to hand; a foot or knee switch is preferable. If the lathe has an outboard attachment access on the left-hand side is needed, and access at the right-hand side is necessary to allow room for long hole boring through the tailstock.

There should be adequate standing for the turner, with both artificial light and daylight available. A flexible-arm tungsten light will provide light and shadow where it is needed. Check that all component parts are in good order and chucks etc, correctly assembled before use. Always use sharp tools and apply them correctly to the moving work. Set the tool and hand rest at the correct height and don't move it with the machine running. When glasspapering or polishing between centres, hold the paper or cloth underneath the moving work; when working on the inside of bowls and boxes hold it between half-past and quarter-to the hour. Always keep the rest in good condition, straight and true. Never use tools with loose handles.

MAINTENANCE EQUIPMENT

The safety of the operator cannot be overemphasised when using grinding and sharpening equipment. Here we are removing dangerous particles of steel so goggles must be worn. Safety guards must be placed in position so that there is protection against fine steel dust.

Double-ended grinders should be well illuminated and fitted with approved guards. The tool rests should be strong and capable of being held firmly in place.

Stones and wheels should be kept true, and the sides of the grinding wheel should never be used. If an extended spell at the grinder is envisaged, wear a mask.

If a belt linisher or abrasive disc is used for grinding and sharpening, the tool should be applied with the abrasive material moving away from the operator.

If a tool holder or guide is provided with the machine, use it. Always move the tool across the stone or belt to ensure even wear over the whole surface.

Use only the recommended oil on a sharpening wheel, or water, as specified. Never use the wheel dry.

When making a stone or wheel true, apply the tool with care and don't overcut to remove an excessive amount of wheel.

NOTES ON ELECTRICALLY
POWERED MACHINES

Too often electricity is taken for granted; some of us are not too sure what it is, or how it arrives in our homes. Although there is no need for the average woodworker to be an expert electrician he should be aware of matters that could be disastrous if not dealt with properly.

General considerations for static machines

Most woodworkers will be using machines with single-phase motors of either 110 or 240 voltage. Many of these are connected to the mains supply using insulated cable of one sort or another via a thirteen amp plug, which is inserted into a wall socket. There is nothing wrong with this system, but the correct grade of cable must be used to carry the load adequately. If the machine is to be moved from time to time it may be advisable to house the cable in a flexible conduit. In any case the cable should be constantly checked for abrasion and wear, and changed should any fault be found – do not repair cable by wrapping it with insulation tape. Always fit the correctly rated fuse and check that all connections are electrically and mechanically sound, as loose connections can lead to arcing, overheating, and eventually fire. Be sure to fit only best quality plugs as cheap ones are often made of poor materials which quickly give faulty connections.

Machines should never be plugged into the lighting system; always use a correctly fused ring-main system if more than one machine is being used. Earthing should always comply with the IEE regulations, 15th Edition; if in doubt consult your local electricity board.

Switch gear

Ideally the machine should be connected to the mains supply with an isolating switch firmly secured to the wall. From this isolating switch a cable should be taken to a switch placed in a convenient position on the machine. The location of this switch is of primary importance, and it should be near to the hand, indeed, so conveniently placed that it can be reached by either hand if possible. All too often a manufacturer places the switch in a position dictated by the design of the machine, and often this does not take into consideration the need for an instant shut-off in case of emergency. In these instances, and also where both hands are in use, the addition of a foot or knee switch is well worth considering.

All switches are purpose-designed; thus tumbler switches are designed for lighting circuits, and wall and similar switches are unsuitable and should never be used. When switching on an induction electric motor of the type used for static machines (usually a 'squirrel cage' motor) a current is induced in a rotor which causes the motor to start, and it is recommended that you fit switches designed to handle such loads. Complete protection for the user and the motor must be provided, and a no-volt release feature to prevent possible injury to the user resulting from unexpected restarting of the motor following a mains interruption or failure, is vitally necessary.

The *Mini-Start*-type switch supplied by *Cutler Hammer* is typical, and is designed for the control of woodworking and bench-type machinery powered by electric motors up to 4hp (3.0kw) at 250 volts, single phase. They are small hand-operated starters and comprise a green start button and a red stop button. The red button should stand proud of the other so that it is instantly located by the hand without the prompting of the eye. It has a complete measure of protection for both motor and user, and included in the starter is an adjustable thermal-type motor protection device. This is set to monitor the motor current and thereby switch the motor off before permanent damage can be done. Always fit a switch close to the left hand in the case of a right-handed person and the opposite for the left-hander; you should never have to bend down or search for it.

Whenever a machine is being used where both hands are likely to be in use and the power may need to be cut, an additional switch must be fitted. This is particularly important with some operations on the wood-turning lathe, essential with the drill press, and desirable also with the bandsaw. *Cutler Hammer* make a spring-return foot switch which permits remote stopping of the motor, so that your hands are both freed for working. These switches are supplied in metal housings for floor use, or with a surface plate for mounting on the machine itself; the floor pattern has a non-slip base. They can be obtained singly or in banks of two or three, and can be used with the *Mini-Start* and similar switches, or for direct mounting to the motor. The maximum rating is 240 volt, 4 amps and ¾hp (0.558kw). All these switches are oil- and dustproof (very necessary in woodworking) to IP 65 standard specification. A guarded type is also available which cannot be switched on accidentally by falling objects.

Selection of motor

Machines bought with motors fitted will almost invariably have the correct motor rating. If there is any doubt check with the manufacturer of the equipment before purchasing a motor or fitting one which is already available.

Motor maintenance

This is often greatly neglected, yet there is a positive need for regular checks when motors are used in woodwork.

Although motors rarely give trouble, a few moments given to periodic maintenance will help to avoid any difficulties.

Most motors are cooled by movement of air through the casing, although there is a growing use of ventilator fans operated by the motor itself and fitted at one end of its casing. While cooling is essential it does tend to suck wood dust into the windings of the motor and as a result it may run excessively hot, a fault which in the end may well cause a breakdown in the insulation of the windings, with resultant short-circuiting and burn-out.

Dust size will vary, as finer dust is created by a bandsaw, for example, than a wood-turning lathe; thus some motors may need attention more frequently than others. Use a brush as far as possible or use a vacuum cleaner and if it is possible partially to cover the motor against dust without interfering with the cooling, then do so. If using compressed air to blow dust away be sure the air is dry and the blast not too powerful otherwise you may damage the windings. If it is an old neglected motor, or even one which is badly choked it is advisable to have the job done professionally.

Earthing of machines

Hand-powered portable equipment has double insulation which renders earthing unnecessary. Older tools should however be checked out; do not assume they have double insulation. If an earth connection is needed, use an earth wire in the wiring, and be sure that the source of your supply is also earthed. Earthing is vital at all times, but never more so than when there is a suggestion of dampness, or when moisture is likely to build up for whatever reason.

Bearing lubrication

Many electric motors have 'sealed-for-life' bearings, but some will require lubrication with either grease or oil, grease being injected through grease nipples and oil through oil cups. Lubrication will remove some of the heat generated by the moving parts and at the same time reduce friction; it will also protect perfectly machined surfaces against rust, but careless and excessive lubrication can attract dust and contamination.

It is extremely important that the lubricant used is one recommended by the manufacturer and there is usually information about this in the instruction book supplied with the motor.

Brush motors

These are the motors generally used in power tools and are constructed having a commutator, and brushes which ride against it under the pressure of small coil springs. The brushes should be changed regularly; they are housed in small holders diametrically opposed to each other on the inside of the motor casing. Regular changing will reduce wear on the commutator. If possible keep the commutator clean, but if this is difficult it may be necessary to return the machine to a service centre.

USEFUL TABLES

Metric Conversion Table

INCHES – MM

Inch		MM	Inch		MM	Inch		MM
¼"	—	6 mm	7¼"	—	185 mm	40"	—	1015 mm
⅜"	—	10 mm	7½"	—	190 mm	41"	—	1040 mm
½"	—	12 mm	7¾"	—	195 mm	42"	—	1065 mm
⅝"	—	15 mm	8"	—	200 mm	43"	—	1090 mm
¾"	—	20 mm	8¼"	—	210 mm	44"	—	1120 mm
⅞"	—	22 mm	8½"	—	215 mm	45"	—	1145 mm
1"	—	25 mm	8¾"	—	220 mm	46"	—	1170 mm
1⅛"	—	30 mm	9"	—	230 mm	47"	—	1195 mm
1¼"	—	32 mm	9¼"	—	235 mm	48"	—	1220 mm
1⅜"	—	35 mm	9½"	—	240 mm	49"	—	1245 mm
1½"	—	38 mm	9¾"	—	250 mm	50"	—	1270 mm
1⅝"	—	40 mm	10"	—	255 mm	51"	—	1295 mm
1¾"	—	45 mm	10⅛"	—	257 mm	52"	—	1320 mm
2"	—	50 mm	11"	—	280 mm	53"	—	1345 mm
2⅛"-2¼"	—	55 mm	12"	—	305 mm	54"	—	1370 mm
2⅜"	—	60 mm	13"	—	330 mm	55"	—	1395 mm
2½"	—	63 mm	14"	—	355 mm	56"	—	1420 mm
2⅝"	—	65 mm	15"	—	380 mm	57"	—	1450 mm
2¾"	—	70 mm	16"	—	405 mm	58"	—	1475 mm
3"	—	75 mm	17"	—	430 mm	59"	—	1500 mm
3⅛"	—	80 mm	18"	—	460 mm	60"	—	1525 mm
3¼"	—	85 mm	19"	—	485 mm			
3½"	—	90 mm	20"	—	510 mm			
3⅔"	—	93 mm	21"	—	535 mm			
3¾"	—	95 mm	22"	—	560 mm			
4"	—	100 mm	23"	—	585 mm			
4⅛"	—	105 mm	24"	—	610 mm			
4¼"-4⅜"	—	110 mm	25"	—	635 mm			
4½"	—	115 mm	26"	—	660 mm			
4¾"	—	120 mm	27"	—	685 mm			
5"	—	125 mm	28"	—	710 mm			
5⅛"	—	130 mm	29"	—	735 mm			
5¼"	—	135 mm	30"	—	760 mm			
5½"	—	140 mm	31"	—	785 mm			
5¾"	—	145 mm	32"	—	815 mm			
6"	—	150 mm	33"	—	840 mm			
6⅛"	—	155 mm	34"	—	865 mm			
6¼"	—	160 mm	35"	—	890 mm			
6½"	—	165 mm	36"	—	915 mm			
6¾"	—	170 mm	37"	—	940 mm			
7" Fibre discs only		178 mm	38"	—	965 mm			
7"	—	180 mm	39"	—	990 mm			

To obtain the metric size for dimensions under 60", not shown in the above table, multiply the Imperial size in inches by 25·4 and round to the nearest millimetre taking **0·5 mm** upwards.

e.g. 9⅛" × 25·4 = 231·8
= **232 mm**

To obtain the metric size for dimensions over 60" multiply the Imperial size in inches by 25·4 and round to the nearest **10 mm taking 5 mm** upwards.

e.g. 67" × 25·4 = 1701·8
= **1700 mm**

THE CORRECT TIP FOR THE SCREW

mm	METRIC mm	GAUGE No.
2.5	1.6	1
3.0	1.6	1
3.5	2.0	2
4.0	2.5	4
5.0	3.0	6
5.5	3.5	6
6.5	4.5	8
8.0	5.5	10
8.0	5.5	12
10.0	6.0	14 & 16
12.0	7.0	18 & 20

Correct tip for the screw

This table gives the size of drill needed to make clearance and pilot holes for each screw gauge. The sizes are given as mm/inches.

Screw	Hardwood		Softwood	
	Clear hole	Pilot hole	Clear hole	Pilot hole
1	$2/^5/_{64}$	$1.2/^3/_{64}$		
2	$2.5/^3/_{32}$	$1.6/^1/_{16}$		
3	$3/^7/_{64}$	$1.6/^1/_{16}$	USE	
4	$3.5/^1/_8$	$2/^5/_{64}$	BRADAWL	
5	$3.5/^1/_8$	$2/^5/_{64}$		
6	$4/^5/_{32}$	$2/^5/_{64}$		
7	$4/^5/_{32}$	$2.5/^3/_{32}$	$2.5/^3/_{32}$	$1.6/^1/_{16}$
8	$5/^3/_{16}$	$2.5/^3/_{32}$	$2.5/^3/_{32}$	$1.6/^1/_{16}$
9	$5/^3/_{16}$	$3.5/^1/_8$	$4/^5/_{32}$	$2/^5/_{64}$
10	$5.75/^7/_{32}$	$3.5/^1/_8$	$4/^5/_{32}$	$2/^5/_{64}$
12	$6.5/^1/_4$	$3.5/^1/_8$	$4/^5/_{32}$	$2/^5/_{64}$
14	$6.5/^1/_4$	$4/^5/_{32}$	$5.75/^7/_{32}$	$3/^7/_{64}$
16	$7.25/^9/_{32}$	$5/^3/_{16}$	$5.75/^7/_{32}$	$3/^7/_{64}$
18	$8.25/^5/_{16}$	$5/^3/_{16}$	$5.75/^7/_{32}$	$3/^7/_{64}$
20	$9/^{11}/_{32}$	$5.75/^7/_{32}$	$5.75/^7/_{32}$	$3/^7/_{64}$

Drill sizes for screws

BOOKS BY JOHN SAINSBURY

The Craft of Woodturning (McGraw Hill, 1980)
Woodturning Projects for Dining (Sterling, 1981)
Woodworking Projects with Power Tools (Sterling, 1983)
Planecraft (Sterling, 1984)
Sharpening and Maintenance of Woodworking Tools (GMC Pubs Ltd, 1984)
Craft of Woodturning (Sterling, 1984)
John Sainsbury's Router Workshop (David & Charles, 1988)

Turning Miniatures in Wood (GMC Pubs Ltd, 1989)
John Sainsbury's Guide to Woodworking Tools and Equipment (David & Charles, 1989)

Also, jointly with Garry Chinn:
Garrett Wade Book of Woodworking Tools (Crowell, 1980)
Carpenters' Companion (Marshall Cavendish, 1980)

ACKNOWLEDGEMENTS

A great deal of help has been given by people in many parts of the world, for which I must acknowledge my gratitude and trust that there are no omissions.

Thanks to Peter Peck of Record Marples, Meadow Street, Sheffield for artwork and bench equipment; Black and Decker and Elu at Slough; Nick Davidson at Craft Supplies, Millersdale in Derbyshire; John Bland of Myford Ltd, at Beeston, Nottingham; Mike Draper of Startrite Tools, Gads Hill, Gillingham, Kent; John Gibson of Titman Tip Tools, Kennedy Way, Valley Road, Clacton on Sea, Essex; Geoff Brown of Brimarc Associates, Unit 8, Ladbrook Park, Millers Road, Warwick; Sjoberg Benches; Tue Lervad, Lervad (UK) Ltd, Denham Parade, Oxford Road, Denham, Middlesex; Neil Webb of Wolfcraft UK, Griffin Industrial Park, Totton, Hampshire for tools and artwork; Woodfit at Chorley, Lancs for artwork; Paul Merry of Arbortech M&M Distributors, PO Box 128, Bexhill-on-Sea, Sussex; Christopher Taylor of Taylor Design, Courtdale, Dallas, Texas for the Incra Jig; Rick Newcombe of Leigh Industries, Port Coquitlam, BC Canada; Chris Thomas, Jet Clamps, TMT Design, Queensway Trading Estate, Leamington Spa; Tony Walker of Robert Sorby Ltd, Sheffield.

Also to Gary Workman and Bronte Edwards of Woodfast Machine Tools, Woodville, South Australia; Stephen Brandrick of Panasonic, Willoughby Road, Bracknell, Berks; Kerry Crotty of Festo Ltd, High Street, Teddington, Middlesex; Sheree Dubock of Robert Bosch Ltd, Power Tools Division, Broadwater Park, Denham, Middlesex; Kim Cave of Stanley Tools, Woodside, Sheffield for the use of photographs and permission to use the Stanley illustrations.

My thanks also to Sheila Kew for her care in reading the proofs, and my wife for suffering me and the book.

INDEX